The Parks of Colorado Springs

Building Community, Preserving a Legacy

Nancy Lewis
with Deborah Odell

Research Assistance from Judith Rice-Jones

Brown Books Publishing Group
Dallas, Texas

The Parks of Colorado Springs: Building Community, Preserving a Legacy

Cover and text designed by Nancy Stannard Graphic Design, 2011.

Proceeds from the sale of this work will support the preservation of the Garden of the Gods Park.

Includes bibliography, appendices, and index.
Parks—Colorado—Colorado Springs—History. I. Odell, Deborah. II. Rice-Jones, Judith

Brown Books Publishing Group
16250 Knoll Trail Drive, Suite 205
Dallas, Texas 75248
www.BrownBooks.com
(972) 381-0009

A New Era in Publishing™

Hardcover ISBN 978-1-61254-029-0
Paperback ISBN 978-1-61254-050-4

Library of Congress Control Number 2011935890

Printing in the United States
10 9 8 7 6 5 4 3 2 1

For more information, please visit: www.TheParksOfColoradoSprings.com

Dedicated to
All those who have cared for
The parks of Colorado Springs,
Whose story this is.

ACKNOWLEDGMENTS

"I just want to tell a story . . ."

When work began on this project, we simply wanted to tell the story of the parks of Colorado Springs and the people who have made them possible, before the story was lost. And one story led to another. In the process of weaving together so many threads, so many details of who did what, and why, and when, and how, we found ourselves in a maze of ideas, thoughts, and information. It is only with the help of others that we have found our way through.

Since the early days of 1878, when the *Colorado Springs Gazette Telegraph* was first published, local journalists have recorded and documented the history of Colorado Springs on a weekly and daily basis. To them—some never named and others acknowledged—we owe an inestimable debt. Through them, we were able to find and re-tell the real-life stories of the people who lived here and played, socialized, laughed, and grew in our local parks. Without these attentive and interested writers, no one would know what people were doing and saying, what their ideas and motives were. Without these journalists, we would have lost our history.

In our search for these stories and the photos that illustrate them, the staff at the Pikes Peak Library District, and in particular Katie Rudolph and Jody Jones, happily and tirelessly assisted. Likewise, Leah Witherow and her assistants at the Colorado Springs Pioneers Museum offered valuable support over the many days we made our way through boxes of images from the Parks and Recreation Department and Pioneers Museum photographs. Colorado College Tutt Library librarians graciously provided assistance when we called upon them.

Other park-lovers contributed wonderful imagery and enthusiastic encouragement. Our thanks to Don Kallaus, who generously, and without hesitation, shared his amazing collection of Glenn Murray's photographs of Colorado Springs from the 1920s to the 1960s. We are privileged to include these never-before-published images in this book, and appreciate Don's faith in our work. Carey Harrington cheerfully offered her photos of Colorado Springs' xeriscape gardens and open space activities, while Andy Morris and Ron Wright gathered beautiful photographs capturing idyllic activities at the historic Rock Ledge Ranch. Lyda Hill filled in important gaps with her insightful perspective, providing unique photos of open space and outlying areas. And we are grateful to include the professional work of photographers Cynthia Holling-Morris, Tom Kimmell, Wendy Pearce Nelson, and Brett Tennis, whose images so accurately convey the quality of our parks.

Many beautiful photographs came from the wonderful staff at the Garden of the Gods Visitor and Nature Center, who provided their usual extraordinary support. Linda Carter, Bonnie Frum, and Penny Whalen never cease to amaze with their instantaneous response, upbeat outlook, knowledgeable insight, and can-do attitude. We thank them for sharing their genuine excitement for the project, professional abilities, steady encouragement, and the friendship that carried us over many rough spots.

Early readers Eric Odell, Meegan Flenniken, Fred Mais, Sharon Hare, and Carla Hartsell kindly offered thoughtful comments and interesting questions that helped us explain details and advance the story. Paul Butcher, Kim King, and Kurt Schroeder checked our facts and supplied missing information. Forum participants Paul Butcher, Bill Ruskin, Mike Anderson, and Jim Colvin sparked more conversation and ideas that brought important considerations into focus.

Our core team, without whom we would never have come to an end, has been irreplaceable. Mary Mais, stalwart, steady and generous, readily gave innumerable hours to help us get the story right. Her consistent and quiet perspective held us to a high standard. Judith Rice-Jones, wonderful former Parks Board Chair who gives true meaning to the term "a lifetime love of parks," provided marvelous details, a wealth of knowledge, and a rigorous ecological awareness that infuse the book. Nancy Stannard, professional designer extraordinaire, has made this story visually real. We are grateful for her intuitive design, creative expertise, professional work ethic, and remarkable flexibility that have brought this project to life. To all, we thank you for the laughter, commitment, caring and effort.

In telling this story of the parks of Colorado Springs, we found many stories, more than we could possibly tell in one book. We have tried to select and arrange those details that describe and explain what we believe is the essential importance of our parks and the legacy that we have inherited. No doubt we have inadvertently left out some significant tales. That fault is ours alone, and we ask your understanding.

Most importantly, no matter what stories we may have overlooked, we acknowledge our deep appreciation and gratitude to all of the staff of the Colorado Springs Parks and Recreation Department. They are the unsung heroes of our environment, of our quality of life. They are the ones who show up daily and do the tasks that need to be done. Without their quiet efforts, we would have no parks. Our heartfelt thanks to them for all that they do.

—Nancy Lewis with Deborah Odell

Contents

Parks have been a source of pleasure and enjoyment to me for as long as I can remember. From the marvelous Miller Park in Omaha, where I spent much of my childhood, to the wonderful Monument Valley Park in Colorado Springs, where I found that same spacious beauty and comfort in my new hometown, I treasured the wonder of the out-of-doors and the peace it offers.

When I came to Colorado Springs in 1958, I little knew that my professional life would encompass a gratifying career with the Colorado Springs parks system, but it has. And what a wonderful journey it has been. I have now spent forty-two years working with the parks and their people—twenty-seven with the parks system, the last six as director, and since then fifteen more as president of the Garden of the Gods Foundation. Over all these years, I have grown to respect the parks and the people of Colorado Springs more and more.

But this is not my story. This is the story of a wonderful park system that is grounded in a belief in the value of the public good, the beauty of the land, and the rewards of a vibrant community. It is the story of as fine and dedicated a parks staff as can be found anywhere in the nation. It is a story that takes place among people, those for whom the parks are held in trust and those who care for them. This story is about all those who have given their energy and their hearts to the parks of Colorado Springs, for the benefit of all who live here.

I believe if you are going to live in a community, you have to be a part of it. Giving back is the balance to taking. Our park system is a treasure that we were given, that we enjoyed, that we grew, that we now see passing into the future. We are responsible for seeing that done well.

How do we sustain a system as people come and go? How do we help it transcend time? How do we adapt to changing needs and preserve what is best and most precious?

We begin by knowing the story. When we understand what we have, where it came from, and why we have it, the best can endure. I hope the story of the parks of Colorado Springs will inspire you as it has inspired me to take pride in my home and to do my best to be helpful.

Nancy Lewis
January 2011

Monument Valley Park, early 1900s.

A City of Jewels

1871–1910: The Beginning—Palmer and His Parks

"This generous present from General Palmer to the people of Colorado Springs opens up a wonderful future for the City. . . . It constitutes a legacy which we must cherish and enlarge for those who shall occupy the land after us."

—Report of the Park Commission, 1908

THE DREAM

When General William Jackson Palmer founded Colorado Springs in 1871, he envisioned a grand and gracious park system ringing the community, connecting all its residents to the discovery, pleasures and peace that nature provides.

A man of both poetic sensibilities and corporate acumen, Palmer first traveled to the Pikes Peak region in 1867, at age thirty-one. He was manager in charge of construction for the Kansas Pacific Railroad, journeying from Kansas to California and back on a 4,000–mile surveying trip. Like the adventurers before him, he found the rock sentinels, rolling foothills, canyons, streams, valleys, and red rock spires approaching Pikes Peak to be wild and inspiring. Unlike the others, he determined to make this splendid place his home.

Not only soldier, explorer, surveyor, and railroad man, General Palmer was a thoughtful and imaginative entrepreneur; he recognized a value in the area that few before him had conceived. Palmer believed that the foothills of the Rockies offered the potential for a resort area as magnificent as those developing in the east—new communities then emerging in response to the affluence and leisure resulting from Civil War profits. He knew, also, that Colorado was earning a reputation as a health center for curing consumptives and asthmatics, and he saw a future for healing and growth in these western foothills.

Moreover, he had a romantic dream to fulfill. He had fallen deeply in love with Mary Lincoln "Queen" Mellen, a young woman from Flushing, Long Island. He believed this breathtaking place offered a wild and magnificent home where they could build a community of culture, sensibility, and comfort. He fixed upon a glade at the north end of the Garden of the Gods to be their home site, naming it "Queen's Canyon." His almost daily letters to his beloved relayed to her the delights he had found at the foot of Pikes Peak, describing his dream:

Glen Eyrie, built by General Palmer for his wife, Queen, in Queen's Canyon.

> *. . . how the Castle should be on one of the bold, pine-topped hills near the mountain foot, and the farm-houses in the smooth, rounded valleys; how there should be fountains and lakes, and lovely drives and horse-back trails through groves—all planned and planted by ourselves . . . here, where the air is fraught with health and vigor, and where life would be poetry—an idyll of blue sky, clear, intense atmosphere, fantastic rock, dancing water, green meadow, high mountain, rugged canyon, and distant view of the kind that gives wing to the imagination and allows no foothold for it to halt upon, short of infinity.*[1]

A COMMUNITY BEGUN

Palmer was a Philadelphian Quaker turned westerner, a gentle man, disciplined, tidy, reflective, and transfixed by the grandeur of the land to which he had traveled. Brave, quiet, and devoted, he had served with distinction as leader of the Fifteenth Pennsylvania Volunteer Cavalry through the Civil War, retiring as Brigadier General by war's end. After becoming a director for the Kansas Pacific Railroad, he determined to develop a north-south railroad from Denver through New Mexico to Texas and Mexico. In this conception he was totally western, envisioning the economic development of the area over searching for ways to connect the east and west coasts.

In October 1870, he founded the Denver and Rio Grande Railroad, and began building his railroad south from Denver on July 28, 1871. At the same time, in the spring of 1871, he created the Colorado Springs Company, a firm to establish the town of Colorado Springs. The company was to handle sales of town site property to the members of the Fountain Colony, consisting of Palmer and his colleagues, who would then plat and develop the community.

Top left: General Palmer, in the center of the photograph, and two associates survey the treeless plain to locate the site of Colorado Springs, 1871.

Bottom left: Palmer Hall, the first building of Colorado College, with Pikes Peak behind, 1880.

Top: The young General William Jackson Palmer.

On July 31, 1871, a stake was driven at the plow furrow junction marking the corners of Pikes Peak Avenue and Cascade Avenue, and Palmer's dream was begun. As he wrote to Queen Mellen at the time, "My theory for this place is that it should be made the most attractive place in the West for homes—a place for schools, colleges, literature, science, first-class newspapers and everything the above imply."[2] Central to Palmer's vision was the establishment of an inter-connected park system, inspired by those grand parks he himself had experienced and treasured on his own youthful trips to such remarkable places as Versailles, Fontainebleu, and Central Park.

Not everyone shared the vision that Palmer imagined. The early town was bleak and bare. The burning sun, thin air, raw wind, and dry soil were daunting. Indeed, in 1873, upon arriving on a journey west, novelist and Native American advocate Helen Hunt Jackson[3] wrote:

> *I shall never forget my sudden sense of hopeless disappointment at the moment when I first looked on the town. It was a gray day in*

Colorado Springs Huerfano Street Bridge, looking west, circa 1900.

> *November. . . . There stretched before me, to the east, a bleak, bare, unrelieved, desolate plain. There rose behind me, to the west, a dark range of mountains, snow-topped, rocky-walled, stern, cruel, relentless. Between lay the town—small, straight, new, treeless.*[4]

And yet Helen Hunt Jackson, as well as thousands of others, would grow to love the city and its surrounds with the same enthusiasm and devotion as its founder, who had every intention of making his dream a reality.

In the development of Colorado Springs, General Palmer and his company were thoughtful in their plan's details, imaginative in their design, and always responsive to their environment. Palmer set Pikes Peak Avenue—telling his Vice President of the Fountain Colony, Robert A. Cameron, "Take your center line from here to the summit, reverse your instrument, and you have Pikes Peak Avenue."[5] From there Cameron platted one thousand acres of lots and wide streets, running a half mile east from Monument Creek and nearly two miles north to south. It was Cameron who developed the unusually wide streets of early Colorado Springs, leaving space for sidewalks and center parkways, though Palmer often is credited with the idea. These "parked"—i.e., planted with blooming flowers, trees, and shrubs—medians were thus a feature of Colorado Springs from its inception. In 1901, in his letter for the Century Chest, Edgar Ensign reported on the Public Parks and Parkways:

At this time, Nevada Avenue is 'parked' (rows of trees and a strip of grass) along its center through nearly its entire length. Wood Avenue has a similar parking for about two blocks, and steps have been taken to park (more elaborately) six blocks on Cascade Avenue, extending from the college reservation northward. It was undoubtedly the expectation of the founders of the town that in due course of time all the resident portions of the avenues and wider streets should be parked. We have faith to believe that this good work, fairly begun by ourselves, will be fully carried out and improved upon by our successors. Not only would the 'dust nuisance' be much abated thereby, but the streets would be greatly improved and beautified.[6]

The original town site plat provided a city block for a park, Acacia (or North) Park, located centrally in town. Additionally, Antlers Park was given to the city by the Colorado Springs Company on November 9, 1882,[7] and Alamo Park (South Park) on April 7, 1899. Of these, Edward Ensign reported in 1901:

The most useful pieces of public ground we have at the present are Acacia Park and Alamo Square, both of which are in the heart of town. They are each of the size of an ordinary city block, are shaded by cottonwood trees (a few of other kinds just started), have walks extended through them, and drinking fountains in the center. Upon their grassy surfaces and beneath the shade of trees are placed seats for the accommodation of those who wish to use them. On summer evenings bands of music entertain the people here. They are much frequented by both residents and tourists. The new County Courthouse is being erected in Alamo Square. This building will occupy a portion of its space, but is not likely to greatly curtail its usefulness as a park. . . . The Antlers Park is quite good of its kind. It has considerable shade, grass, walks, trees, some flowers, and benches (or settees). The city owns seven acres of this ground and the hotel company two acres.[8]

Acacia Park's tree-lined walkway.

The famous landscape architect John Blair, a Scottish emigrant well known for his work in Chicago, designed the city parks. But these were only small city retreats. General Palmer had larger plans for the city of Colorado Springs. An extensive park system to lift the spirits and stimulate health and heartiness was in Palmer's mind from the beginning of his endeavors. Palmer had traveled widely and his impressions of the grand cultivated gardens of New York, Paris, and London (among others) influenced his desire to cultivate a community of similar beauty.

INSPIRATIONS, ASPIRATIONS, AND ACCOMPLISHMENTS

As a young railroad man, Palmer had been to England and Wales to study the operation of the railroads in 1855-56, particularly how they used coal as a fuel. Not from a wealthy family, he paid in part for his travels by writing articles on coal mining and mining methods for the Pottsville (Pennsylvania) *Miner's Journal.* He saw much of the countryside and its famous English gardens and landscape as he traveled, and made copious notes regarding birds, plants, and designs. In the fall of 1855, he visited France, witnessing firsthand the renovation of Paris, experiencing the magnificence of Fontainebleu, and relishing the delights of Versailles, which he called "the finest park I ever saw."[9] He also made numerous visits to New York City, and was in New York when Frederick Law Olmsted and Calvert Vaux were building Central Park.[10] Furthermore, his travels by train across the American continent in the late 1800s took him through many cities that were developing large park systems, one of the finest being that designed by H.W. S. Cleveland in Omaha, Nebraska. This was the great American park-building period, and Palmer was deeply attuned to it.

Skaters on Prospect Lake, 1900.

Consequently, a comprehensive park system was central to Palmer's plan for his city of Colorado Springs. First, they needed water. By 1872, the El Paso Canal had been designed, dug, and put into operation. The canal spanned from Thirty-Third Street in Old Colorado City, over the bluffs, and crossed Monument Creek at Roswell via sluices to what would be Monument Valley Park. Two large storage areas at what today are Boddington Field (in Monument Valley Park) and Boulder Park (adjacent to the present-day Memorial Hospital) provided reservoirs. The nineteen-mile canal ended in Prospect Lake (added in 1890 to receive overflow from the canal), from which Evergreen Cemetery was eventually watered.

By 1873, E.S. Nettleton, Chief Engineer for the Colorado Springs Company, had completed a second long irrigation canal, and Director McAllister had arranged for five thousand cottonwoods to be planted along the ditches lining the main streets.[11] These were the round-leafed cottonwoods, which provide greater shade, but which generally do not live beyond fifty years. Gradually, they would be replaced with maple, ash and elm trees.

On March 26, 1903, the *Gazette* noted the arrival of six thousand new trees (elms, catalpa, arbor vitae, and soft maple) and shrubs (snow-balls, almond, and honeysuckle) to be planted by Paul Borke, "an expert landscape gardener," in John Coughlin's Zoological Park on Cheyenne Road. Later, in Monument Valley Park, General Palmer would have every tree and shrub species found in Colorado included. To this end, Palmer employed a large crew of workers to maintain the city's parks and trees, and by 1910 the City Council had created a Department of Forestry, a tree ordinance, and a city forester position.

Cascade Avenue, with irrigation ditch. Houses on left owned by Judson Bemis and James J. Hagerman, 1886.

The city had begun to flourish under the thoughtful care of its founder and his colleagues. Writing his personal letter for the Century Chest project, General Palmer addressed the development of the park system in 1901 as follows:

> *Although there were two open spaces laid out and planted at the original plotting of the town on Tejon Street and the Experimental Garden in front of where the Antlers Hotel now is, the real development of the parks of Colorado Springs may be said to have begun with the present year. The Antlers Park was graded and grassed and partially planted during the present spring. Also the College Park and the Mesa Road Park at the crossing of Monument Creek on the way from the town to Glen Eyrie. The writer [Palmer] has also just bought Austin Bluffs, some 4 miles northeast of the Antler's Hotel and has advised the Mayor of his intention to give the surface, some 700 acres, to the city as a park.*[12]

As Palmer intended, Palmer Park—originally named Henry Austin's Bluffs for Henry W. Austin, a Chicago hardware merchant who bought the land in 1873 to raise sheep—was opened in 1902 with roads, trails, and paths for "out of door life and happiness." About five miles east of the city and five hundred feet above it, Palmer Park provided magnificent views of the whole Pikes Peak region, offering an inspiration point for city residents. Being at the convergence of the plains and the foothills, the park featured

View of the Paseo from Palmer Park, with Pikes Peak in the distance, 1908.

many interesting geological examples as well as a wide range of plants found in both zones. As explained in the 1908 Park Commissioners' Report, Palmer required that "[t]his land should be kept and maintained as a park so far as possible in the condition in which nature has fashioned it. . . . [N]othing should be done to detract from the natural beauty of the land, or its fitness for the superior and controlling purpose of the out-of-door recreation of the people."[13]

The North Cheyenne Cañon acquisitions also exemplified Palmer's belief in the value of the natural wilderness landscape, a growing focus of Americans in the late nineteenth century that was evidenced by the establishment of Yellowstone National Park, amongst others. Filled with pines, fir and cedar, deciduous aspen and scrub oak, rushing waterfalls, rapids, and the boiling Cheyenne Creek, Cheyenne Cañon had been a retreat for Colorado Springs' early settlers and visitors, as well as the native Utes and Cheyennes before them. By the 1880s, it was a highly popular area for local residents, who prized its cooling shade and bubbling waters. In 1885, the city purchased 640 acres that formed the core of the canyon from the College Land Company, with the intent to set aside and preserve its natural beauty as a wilderness area.[14]

More than a decade earlier, Palmer also had purchased for the Colorado Springs Company 160 acres along North Cheyenne Creek, including the falls later known as Helen Hunt Falls, and he acquired the site of the Bruin Inn, a substantial log house near the junction of High Drive and Gold Camp Road. While holding these properties, Palmer established a carriage road through the upper canyon and over the High Drive and developed many hiking trails. He intended from the beginning to preserve this property for its scenic beauty, and in 1907 he donated his 480 acres to the city of Colorado Springs.

Left: North Cheyenne Cañon, circa 1915.

Top: Helen Hunt Falls in North Cheyenne Cañon, 1908.

Monument Valley Park, 1915.

But it was Monument Valley Park that ultimately met the General's aspirations to provide city residents with the beauty and serenity of a parkland retreat. As Palmer explained in his 1901 Century Chest Letter:

> *Before the year is over, I hope to put into effect my original plan of setting aside the ground for a frontal park along the immediate Monument Valley, from near the Antler's Hotel northward to the upper confines of the town some two miles or more. When undisturbed, shrubbery and wildflowers grow naturally in these creek bottoms without irrigation—making it easier to carry out the purpose of affording an open and verdurous space removed from the dust and noise of the streets and roads, yet readily accessible from all parts of the town—where the citizen can come to walk (not ride or drive as that means dust) and his children to play—and all be refreshed by a little taste of country, without going too far afield.*[15]

Monument Valley Park—an artfully cultivated contrast to the wilderness of Cheyenne Cañon—became the final jewel in the crown of the early Colorado Springs park system. The area began as a worn-out strip of 165 acres on both sides of Monument Creek, through which arriving trains passed. Here railroad passengers were greeted by discarded cans, sarsaparilla bottles, trash, worn-out furniture pieces, and such broken-down and ugly remnants as are coughed up by a young sapling frontier town. Palmer began by purchasing lots to improve the view of trains coming into the community.

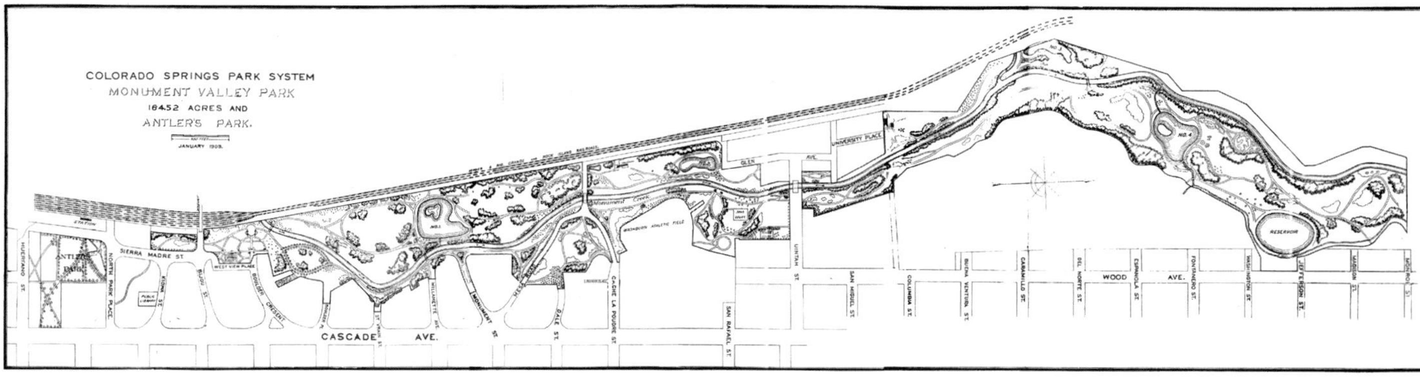

He then engaged Charles Walford Leavitt, a well-known landscape engineer, to plan the linear park.

In 1903, Leavitt presented Palmer with his grand design, and by 1907 an elaborate series of charming gardens, winding walks, bubbling cascades of water, picturesque bridges, ponds, and creeks was ready for public use. Leavitt's plan for Monument Valley Park embodied his belief that "[o]ur gardens and parks should symbolize local conditions of land and light and atmosphere and color, trees and shrubs and flowers and rocks, and they should also contrive to gain some of the human flavor and whatever background the district may possess from the passage of years."[16] The park, with all its improvements and equipment, was officially deeded to Colorado Springs on March 27, 1907—General Palmer's greatest gift to his city.

In this manner, parkland had been gradually acquired by Colorado Springs during its first decades, mostly due to the largesse of General Palmer. In addition to Acacia Park, Antlers Park, and Alamo Park—all gifts of the Colorado Springs Company—and the larger Palmer Park, North Cheyenne Cañon, and Monument Valley Park, the General secured and generously donated other public recreation grounds within the city: Thorndale Park, roads and lands around Bear Creek Canyon and North Cheyenne Cañon (High Drive), Bruin Inn, countless hiking trails to Cutler Mountain and Crystal Park, Cascade Avenue's center parking, and the right of way of today's Manitou, Palmer Park, and Paseo Boulevards. He also provided a significant sum for the improvement of Dorchester Park, a charming neighborhood recreational spot that was purchased for the city by public-spirited citizens in March 1892.[17]

Top: 1908 Park Commissioners Report: Plan for Monument Valley and Antlers Parks.

Bottom: Shaded bench in Monument Valley Park, 1908.

THE CONTRIBUTIONS OF OTHERS

While Palmer was the driving force for this careful development of the Colorado Springs park system, there were other citizens who gave to the community. Winfield Scott Stratton, a common man's carpenter who became an overnight millionaire with the success of his Cripple Creek gold mine, the Independence, built Stratton Park in 1900. For $40,000, he purchased a portion of the Dixon Ranch at the junction of North and South Cheyenne Creeks, where he provided landscaping, created ponds, built a bandstand, installed many swings for children, and provided picnic areas and iron benches. He pledged $5,000 a year for maintenance, $4,000 for Colorado Midland Band concerts in the summer, and $4,000 for dance music. And yet this park, which was opened on June 6, 1901, lasted less than a quarter century, despite Stratton's intentions to donate it to the people. In 1925, most of the land was

Top: Children swing in Stratton Park, circa 1910.

Bottom: Swimming hole in Stratton Park, circa 1910.

sold to Pierce Kampe, a real estate man, who developed it as a residential area.[18]

The citizens of Colorado Springs also displayed a growing interest in community beautification through gardening; the first Annual Show of the El Paso County Horticultural Society was held in 1898. In her 1901 letter for the Century Chest, Patty Jewett described the progress of local horticulture. Though complaining of the "lack of enterprise" among some local homeowners, she successfully grew roses "in this adobe soil with cold winters" and praised the success of Palmer's irrigation canal, noting: "the lawns here are like green velvet and are the feature of the town. The streets are all bordered with irrigation ditches and every place is flooded once a week with 6-8 inches of water."[19]

Top: The Jewett Residence at 1515 North Cascade Avenue, 1908.

Bottom: Plaque in Garden of the Gods commemorating gift of Charles Perkins' children.

Another civic-minded donor was her husband, W. K. Jewett. In 1909, the town citizens comprising the Colorado Springs Golf Club (formerly the Town and Gown Golf Club) leased 300 acres of land and a rented clubhouse north of town. In 1919, W. K. Jewett would buy the entire property and give it to the city of Colorado Springs in memory of his wife—the present-day Patty Jewett Municipal Golf Course.

But the most significant gift of parkland besides Palmer's donations came from another railroad magnate, and this was certainly the result of Palmer's influence. At Palmer's urging, Charles E. Perkins, president of the Burlington Line, had purchased 240 acres in the Garden of the Gods in 1879. Early pioneers had avoided the Garden, which, lacking water, offered poor prospects for farming and grazing. But Palmer had encouraged Perkins to purchase there, hoping to have him soon as a neighbor to Glen Eyrie. Perkins originally had plans to build his home in the Garden, actually having designs drawn, yet he kept his family in Burlington, Ohio, where his railroad operations were based.

The idea of creating a park free to all came to Perkins early on, and he later bought two additional parcels of 80 and 160 acres. By then he had acquired 480 acres total, reportedly costing him a grand total of $10,500. He left the property open to the public, and frequently discussed with General Palmer and William Bell the possibility of donating the property to the City of Colorado Springs.[20]

Garden of the Gods, early 1900s.

But when he died in November 1907, the same month that Monument Valley Park opened to the public, his children—two sons and four daughters—inherited the property. Two years later, on December 22, 1909, they deeded the 480 acres of the Garden of the Gods to Colorado Springs, "influenced by their father's wish, by his friendship with Palmer, and by the example of Palmer's multi-million dollar park system totaling 1,638 acres." The children indicated their intention that the park would remain open to the public "free of charge forever" and that "no building or structure shall be erected on the premises for purposes other than may be necessary to properly care for, protect and maintain the same as a public park."[21]

THE DREAM REALIZED

Over a period of less than forty years, General William Jackson Palmer had achieved the parkland vision he had imagined for the city that he loved. From 1871 to 1907, Palmer secured and donated extended areas in Colorado Springs for a splendid park system. Emulating the development of interconnected-boulevard-park systems that he had seen in his travels, Palmer's system included Cheyenne Cañon, Dorchester Park, Antlers Park, Acacia Park, Monument Valley Park, and Palmer Park—all connected via a parkway or park thoroughfare. Trees were planted along these streets and many were watered via the engineered canals. By 1907, he had donated over 1,500 acres, "comprising completed parks, boulevards, broad roads, driveways, trails and foot-paths, in the City itself and over the Mesas, and into adjacent mountains."[22] He had designed a system that would preserve the natural beauty of the area and provide points of inspiration for its residents.

Acacia Park, 1908.

Palmer's donation of parks was reported in the front page of the *New York Times* on May 1, 1907. The article, entitled "Gives Big Park System," describes General Palmer's gifts:

> *[A] park system embracing 1,500 acres, also the Boulevard Paseo and high drive roadways connecting them, and $45,000 for maintenance. Palmer Park embraces 800 acres, including Austin's Bluff. Palmer has already expended $750,000 on beautifying Monument Valley Park in city limits. A conservative estimate places the value of the gift at $1,500,000.*

Palmer intended for the parks to be a perpetual resource "solely for outdoor recreation enjoyment and use of the people of Colorado Springs." His deeds included very specific conditions as to the use and maintenance of the parks. There were to be no intoxicating liquors on the premises, no building upon parklands, no new roads or streets to be opened, nor any portion of the properties sold. If any conditions were broken, all rights to the parks were to revert to "the grantor and his heirs."[23]

To ensure the preservation of his gifts, General Palmer provided funds (additional to those raised by taxation) for the maintenance of the parks he had given, agreeing to pay $45,000 into the Park Tax Fund, "in descending sums, beginning with $8,000 in 1908 and ending with $1,000 in 1917."[24] As explained in the May 1909 *Gazette*:

> *Realizing that the care of the parks and drives will entail considerable expense, he [Palmer] also offers to donate $45,000 to aid in defraying this expenditure. . . . The parks now owned by the city cost between $6,000 and $7,000 to maintain each year. It is estimated that the new parks*

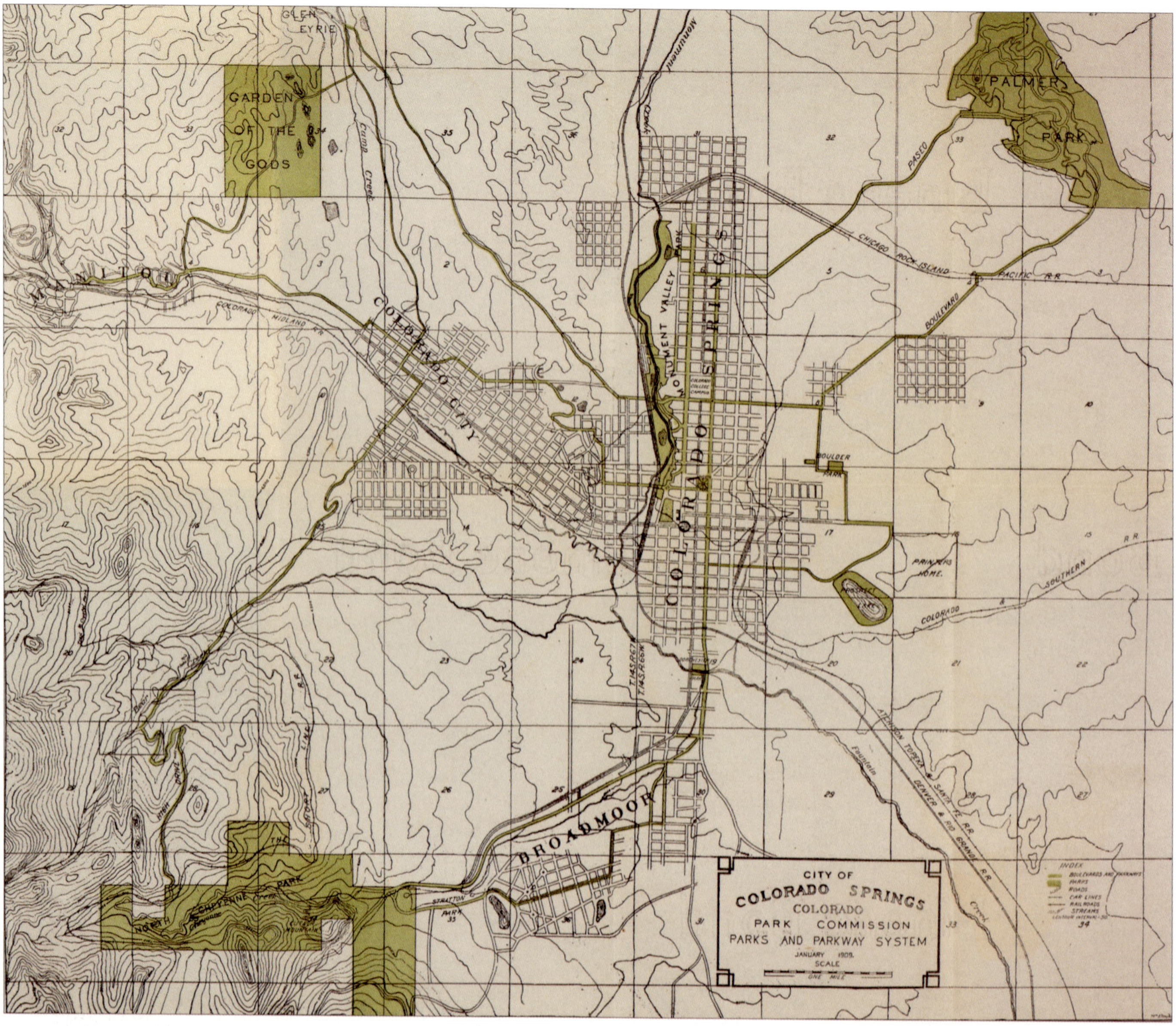

Top: 1908 Park Commissioners Report: Parks System of Colorado Springs.

Opposite: General Palmer at home in Glen Eyrie.

to be donated by General Palmer will cost about $12,000 additional per annum, although this amount will be materially decreased as the parks grow older and the grass and shrubbery become hardier. From this $12,000 will be deducted the yearly payments made by General Palmer, so that the actual additional cost to the city will be comparatively littler each year.[25]

Palmer also required that an independent entity be created to administer the park system, free from "partisan and political strife" and able to provide a broad and long-term vision of what was appropriate for the city.

The resulting Park Commission issued its first report in 1908. In a comprehensive overview of the gifts of parkland to Colorado Springs, the Park Commissioners' report of 1908 remarked:

> *General Palmer's plan for a park system was bold, far-sighted and comprehensive. He sought to make practical and effective use of every advantage which the position of the City gave it; its open air and sunshine, mountains, and plains; to surround the city with near-by parks, mountain driveways, woodland paths, and trails; to furnish places for healthful out-door exercise, and quiet, restful enjoyment; thus capitalizing for us these natural resources, otherwise practically unavailable to our people except to the most limited and crude extent.*[26]

A gentle, dignified Philadelphian who loved the adventure of the wild outdoors, a daring and brave soldier who cherished peace, a keen railroad man who believed in the healing value of nature, a city founder who envisioned a dynamic park system to stimulate growth and well-being, William Jackson Palmer was a model of generosity and sensibility. He imagined and grew the first genuine resort town west of Chicago from the wild beauty of the western frontier. Motivated by love, pride, altruism, and a strong sense of order, he provided the vision and leadership to create a system of parks that sustained then—and offers today—a unique identity and sense of place for this region. Palmer's commitment to stewardship, appreciation for natural beauty, resourcefulness in developing the land, and strong consciousness of order and aesthetics created a priceless legacy for all citizens of Colorado Springs to enjoy.

The decorative wrought-iron entryway to Patty Jewett Golf Course was designed by architect Thomas MacLaren; the Scotsman also designed City Hall, City Auditorium, Grace Episcopal Church, Cragmor Sanitarium, and many other Colorado Springs buildings before he died in 1928.

Sending Down Roots

1910–1960 : A Half-Century of Growth

"All should strive to guard what all may share;
A general good should be a general care."

—Quotation posted in park at Medicine Hat, Alberta[1]

THE COLORADO SPRINGS PARK COMMISSION

When General Palmer completed work on Monument Valley Park and deeded the parks to the city in 1907, he established an independent Park Commission to assume responsibility for these properties. As one of the Commissioners, Asa T. Jones, explained in 1916:

> *. . . he [Palmer] determined to place all these properties in the hands of a self-perpetuating body of men, who would accept his princely gifts as a sacred trust and administer them without selfish interest for the use of the public. It is in this spirit that the members of the park board enter its unpaid service. General Palmer appointed his own personal friend and attorney, Judge Lunt, as the first president . . .* [2]

The parks of Colorado Springs were to be governed by a board of six Park Commissioners, established as a municipal board under the city charter and operated under the laws of the state of Colorado. The first commission in 1907 included three individuals serving one year and three serving two.[3] At the end of each commissioner's term, the remaining members named the retiring commissioner's successor. Once seated, subsequent commissioners could retain their seats at will. Thus a self-perpetuating board was created, independent of politics and marked by the individuals' commitments to the purpose and vision of the city parks. Commissioners served without pay and had complete control of the park funds, for which the City Council was

authorized by law to levy annual property taxes; Palmer's fund provided additional moneys for the parks.

Service as a Park Commissioner was an honorable and respected position; many of the city's most outstanding citizens made that selfless commitment.

1910–1930: CIVIC PRIDE AND PLEASURE IN BEAUTIFUL PARKS

By 1910, Colorado Springs was nationally renowned as a resort destination and beneficial health retreat. Its extraordinary parks were a key element to the city's appeal. The economy of the city depended in large part on meeting visitor expectations, and much was made of the city's resources and its beauty. As noted in a 1912 *Colorado Springs Gazette* article:

> *Not many cities on the American continent can boast of a public park system that even approaches in natural beauty, in variety or in extent, the magnificent chain of parks, boulevards and trails that compose the complete and magnificent system of playgrounds which it is the good fortune of Colorado Springs to possess.*[4]

Commissioner Asa T. Jones commented in 1916 that the visiting Governor of Connecticut "could not sufficiently express his envy of a city which possessed a park like North Cheyenne Cañon."[5] Indeed, the city repeatedly prided itself on having a park system that was "unique in a country of parks," asserting in 1917 that "famous landscape gardeners have declared that [our park system] will bear comparison with those of much older municipalities."[6] The 1918 headline of the *Colorado Springs Gazette* read: "City Park System Is Spacious and Beautiful and Famous the World Over."[7] A 1921 article was titled: "Most Wonderful Park System in the World: Natural Beauty Spot Delight of Thousands."[8]

Top: Cheyenne Creek in North Cheyenne Cañon, early 1900s.

Bottom: Local residents enjoy a warm winter day in Acacia Park, 1915.

This is what Palmer's vision for his parks had been. They were to be magnificent, inspiring, and exceptional—beautiful pastoral pleasure grounds—much in line with the thinking of the great nineteenth century landscape architects and park designers. Attunement with nature was

Monument Valley Park lake, circa 1915.

believed to uplift the human spirit and alleviate the problems of daily life. Colorado Springs' original city parks—meandering, peaceful, restorative—were to provide a sense of natural order and inspiration, enhanced by active exercise and invigorating outdoor experiences.

Monument Valley Park, Palmer Park, Cheyenne Cañon, the Garden of the Gods, and the smaller parks as well—Acacia, Alamo, Antlers, and Dorchester, for example—provided opportunities for unstructured pleasures, walking especially, as well as horseback riding, bicycling, ice skating, toboggan sliding, and other such spontaneous activities for individuals, families, and groups. Places were provided where children could romp, adults walk, men and boys play, and individuals reflect. These early parks of Colorado Springs met the ideals of Charles S. Sargent, editor of *Garden and Forest*, who wrote in 1894:

From 1911-1913, Ute Indian natives returned to the Garden of the Gods for their traditional celebration, Shan Kive. Buckskin Charlie, Southern Ute chief who had been born in the Garden, led the 1912 tribal dances attended by more than 7,000 spectators.

> *No mere playground can serve the purpose of recreation in this truer, broader sense—the purpose of refreshment, of renewal of life and strength for body and soul alike. The truest value of public pleasure grounds . . . is in the rest they give to the eyes and mind, to heart and soul, through the soothing charm, the fresh and inspiring influence, the impersonal, unexciting pleasure which nothing but the works of Nature can offer to man.*[9]

General Palmer had inspired such a parkland system, one that established an order and tradition, offered respite and enjoyment, and, within park boundaries, transcended the problems of alcohol, politics, commercialism, and violence. Informal, picturesque, and rustic, these parks were sanctuary to city residents and visitors alike.

FROM PASTORAL TO PLAYGROUNDS

The Colorado Springs Park Commission followed Palmer's lead, maintaining his vision. Yet they would gradually move to a focus on providing citizens more active sources of recreation and entertainment rather than simply maintaining spaces designed for quiet reflection. In their first report, issued December 31, 1908, they described their progress, explained funding and expenditures, and established priorities and hopes for the future.

Of Monument Valley Park, they noted "[i]t is of the greatest importance that more provision be made for the amusement of young and old. It is necessary not only to maintain the park system, but to make it popular, a

source of instruction, as well as a safe and healthful resort and playground."[10] Their proposed construction included a pavilion looking out on a sunken field that would provide space for baseball, basketball, and similar sports in summer, and be flooded for skating in winter. Plans also called for tennis courts, an outdoor gymnasium and wading pool, and improved lighting facilities.

As Palmer had instructed, Commissioners stated that no automobiles or "auto cycles" would be allowed in Palmer Park; only a few drinking fountains were needed. In North Cheyenne Cañon, plans included bridle paths, a footpath distinct from the roadway, shelter on Cutler Mountain, seating along the canyon sides, and signage "so that the proper route to the High Drive and Crystal Park trail may be more readily found." In the smaller parks, more lighting, equipment, curbing, playground features, and amusement facilities were called for.[11]

The Commissioners focused on care, maintenance, and thoughtful development of the city's parks for the pleasure of Colorado Springs residents. They knew that with increased population, there would be increased need for "playgrounds, suitable shelter and refectory buildings, public comfort stations, band stands, etc."[12] Perhaps unknowingly, they were following a national trend in park usage and design: a move to define the purpose of parks as not simply to provide a restorative landscape, but to offer leisure time activities for people

Top: Ice skaters on Monument Valley Park lake, early 1900s.

Bottom: Children playing in Monument Valley Park.

A distant horse-drawn carriage on Palmer Park's dirt roads was allowed where "auto cycles" were forbidden, early 1900s.

in those spaces.[13] This layering of purpose—restoration and recreation—became evident in the Colorado Springs system as new parks were added and old parks were improved.[14]

During the ensuing two decades, the city and Park Commissioners developed and managed their parks. A full-time Park Superintendent, W. H. Dunman, was hired to oversee the system.[15] A Department of Forestry was created in 1910. In 1909, the city drained one of its two reservoirs, Boulder Reservoir, and developed the area into Boulder Park on the east side. A second water storage system, Prospect Lake, which collected water from the El Paso Canal (water used for irrigating Evergreen Cemetery), remained part of city holdings. Little improved in 1909, the lake would become a popular camping and recreation area in the next decade. Bear Creek Cañon Park came into the system in 1915, Bott Park and Thorndale Park were donated to the city when Colorado Springs annexed Old Colorado City in 1917, and the Patty Jewett Golf Course was given to the city in 1919.[16]

In 1910, however, the city lost its last opportunity to acquire South Cheyenne Canyon and Seven Falls as part of its park system. At the time, the Park Commission took an option to buy the area for $217,500, and proposed issuing $220,000 in bonds to complete the purchase. The plan was to continue charging tolls into the area until the bonds were paid off, a period of about twenty years. However, on May 24, 1910, Colorado Springs' taxpayers voted 1,011 to 236 against the bond proposal and consequently South Cheyenne Canyon would remain permanently in private ownership.

Maintenance required time, money, and attention, but it was the new public recreational activities that generated the most growth in the parks. The *Gazette* reported in 1912 that the Park Commission, though "more or less hampered by lack of money from carrying out its plans for perfecting the park system," had managed to improve roads and trails in the Garden of the Gods; plant a permanent wildflower garden there; install new water closets, steps, and bridges in North Cheyenne Cañon; maintain lakes in Monument Valley Park for skating in winter and boating in summer; and improve numerous drives and trails throughout the city. In 1913, the U.S. Forest Service planted nearly 750,000 two- to four-year-old saplings to reforest North Cheyenne Cañon, and in 1914 the first of ten stone bridges was built in the Cañon, replacing the old wooden bridges.

Two men and two women golfing at the treeless Patty Jewett Golf Course with young caddy standing by.

The Commission gave increased attention to developing the playground features of the parks—particularly Monument Valley, Prospect Lake, Dorchester, and Boulder. In 1915 a summer playground park program was created with supervised games, for which the Commission assumed direct charge in 1917. By then, Park Commissioners were adding new equipment on an equal basis to each park, with expenditures for these items often supported by public-spirited citizens' fund-raising efforts.[17]

Prospect Lake enjoyed particular popularity. A thirty-foot slide had been added to the playground, separate swimming areas were established for

Auto campers at Prospect Lake, 1924.

boys and girls, and thousands of automobile tourists were camping there annually. Because the city provided running water and sewer facilities to accommodate campers, the lake was at first under the care of the city Water Department, but by 1921 responsibility for the lake was transferred to the Park Commission.[18]

Dorchester, a small neighborhood park in the south end of Colorado Springs, between Nevada Avenue and Tejon Street, was also well used. Its playground was described in the 1917 annual edition of the *Gazette* as:

> *. . . one of the best patronized in the park system. A supervisor is on duty there during the summer months and directs the games and activities of the hundreds of little ones who spend their outdoor life within the confines of the park. Fountain Creek flows thru the center and adds to the attractiveness of the place.*[19]

The general satisfaction with the effects of newly developed park playgrounds, despite the handicap of tight funding, was clear, as the article further stated:

> *That the playgrounds have had a beneficial effect on the youth of the city is evident from the statement of the county probation officer, Harry Allward, that since the establishment of the city playgrounds, his work has been greatly lessened. The children are engaged in healthful play which improves their mental and moral makeup and keeps them out of mischief.*[20]

In many ways the parks were meeting the growing recreational needs of the Colorado Springs community. New pavilions, additional lights, and tennis courts were all welcomed improvements; special activities included doll shows, Mother's Day festivities, and Fourth of July celebrations.

BUILDING, DEVELOPMENT, AND MAINTENANCE

Monument Valley Park remained the pride of Colorado Springs. By 1917, the park offered residents not only a naturally attractive environment, but a modern concrete swimming pool—the $12,000 gift of Spencer and Julie Penrose, tennis courts donated by W. D. Quackenbush, baseball and football fields, a large band pavilion—the gift of Mrs. A. E. Carlton, and, on the largest lake, the availability of boating in the summer and ice skating in winter. Plans for building the first unit of a stadium around the athletic fields were begun. Residents enjoyed all of the park's attributes. In the spring of 1918, reportedly over ten thousand people visited Monument Valley Park in one week when the lilacs were in bloom.[21]

Top: Workers building a trail in Palmer Park, 1926.

Bottom: Monument Valley Park pool, the gift of Spencer and Julie Penrose, opened in 1916.

The Park Commission also oversaw the building of the Hidden Inn at the Garden of the Gods, more bridge construction in North Cheyenne Cañon, the maintenance of drives throughout the city, new roads in Palmer Park, and the construction of the Willamette Avenue entrance to Monument Valley Park.[22] In 1917, the Bruin Inn in North Cheyenne Cañon was expanded as a regional landmark and restaurant. A small log cabin curio shop, the Cub, was erected nearby.

Peter Pan wading pool in Monument Valley Park was donated by Mrs. William H. (Augusta B.) Evans in 1930.

Commissioners managed the work necessary to make the parks accessible during the 1920s, even as maintenance and labor costs continued to increase with new park acquisitions. In Palmer Park, roads were reconstructed to accommodate motorized traffic, a necessity unforeseen by Palmer as automobiles came to replace horse-drawn carriages. Bancroft Park in west Colorado Springs was created, and considerable riprapping and improvements to the water system in Monument Valley were done. New center parkings were installed. Roads were graded in the Garden of the Gods; culverts and bridges constructed. A new two-way road was built in North Cheyenne Cañon, replacing the original one-way track destroyed by a flood in 1921. Stone comfort stations were also added to the Cañon, and smaller improvements were performed throughout the system.[23]

NATURAL BEAUTY FOR CITY PARKS

As the Park Commissioners addressed the city's needs for neighborhood parks and playgrounds, they did not lose sight of the economic benefits of city beautification. Colorado Springs remained a center for tourists and health seekers. Planners consciously strove to maintain artistry while promoting utility in its parks. Citizens appreciated that the parks' amenities enhanced the city's economy and commercial appeal. As noted in the 1913 *Gazette* editorial: "First impressions are lasting, and the visitor who, after a drive about town, exclaims 'This is the prettiest place I ever saw,' is a great deal more likely to stay here than the one who is disgusted by unkempt street."[24]

Tree-lined North Cascade Avenue with wide center median, looking south, 1916.

Commissioners realized that "the City of Sunshine is supplied equally well with driveways, boulevards and trails as it is with park areas, and in many instances these roadways form an integral part of the park system."[25] While they prioritized beautification of the parks proper, they also oversaw planting and care of the center median parking.

The streets of Colorado Springs had been designed to be wide and spacious, and the median "parking" not only added beauty to the cityscape but also reduced dust from the wheel-worn gravel roads. Over several

Formal garden in Monument Valley Park, circa 1932.

decades, medians were developed on Wood, North Cascade, Nevada, Wahsatch, Platte, South Cascade, and Willamette Avenues and Kiowa Street. Annual plantings of flowers, shrubbery, and trees, and the maintenance thereof, were attended to by both the Parks Department and the public. Some costs were born by property owners, some shared between private owners and the city. The Park Commissioners' annual reports regularly addressed expenses associated with provision for median work.

In 1916, a Shakespearean garden was planted in Monument Valley Park, honoring the bard's tercentenary. Flowers popular in the 1600s were planted—iris, columbine, pansies, and pinks—as were cedar trees and elms.[26] Beautiful formal gardens behind the pillared Bijou Street entrance to Monument Valley included rose gardens, arbors, and trellises, and a variety of flowers and trees, requiring hand watering, hand weeding, and general hand care. The nursery located at the newly constructed Willamette Avenue entrance to the park was thoroughly overhauled and restocked in 1917. In 1918, the *Gazette* reported:

> *A movement is now on foot by the Park Commission, aided by Philip B. Stewart, to add to the long list of native evergreens all of the native trees that grow in Colorado. These will be labeled and the citizens and visitors will learn from the planting to name and distinguish all of the evergreens encountered on their trips through the mountains. Hundreds of evergreens have been planted in the park nursery to be transplanted from time to time in the different parks.*[27]

Monument Valley Park was also home to many species of birds; over one hundred were noted by ornithologist Edward Warren in 1915. In addition to robins, house wrens, juncos, and tree sparrows, he delightfully described many of the park's feathered families in a *Gazette Telegraph* article that May:

> *I have found the nests of some of the following named species—others, I am sure, nest there because they are about all summer: Kingbirds and flycatchers, Bullock's oriole, meadow lark, Brewer's blackbird, goldfinch, chipping sparrow, mountain and green-tailed towhees, black-headed grosbeak, lazuli bunting, the males of which are a bright blue above, and make one think of the tropics, with their brilliancy of their color; warbling vireo, yellow warbler, catbird, mourning dove and red-headed woodpecker. These all make their summer home there and raise their broods. A pair of sparrow hawks occupied an old flicker's hole in 1914; the flickers have it again this year.*[28]

This appreciation for nature and the thoughtful cultivation of parks were typical for Colorado Springs residents during the early 1900s. When Parks Superintendent Dunman resigned his position in 1921, the Park Commissioners retained German-born Gustav Hennenhofer, formerly head of Pueblo's parks, to become Colorado Springs' next Park Superintendent. Hennenhofer was an expert horticulturalist, with extensive knowledge of plants, shrubbery, and landscaping in the west. His many contributions to landscape architecture and rock gardening in the Pikes Peak region were commemorated in 1935 by the Colorado Springs Garden Club; in 1969, a former employee, Ted Borgars, described the mammoth job of creating the rock garden at the Bijou Street entrance to Monument Valley Park that took place in the early 1920s. Hennenhofer supervised:

> *The city used an overhauled Army truck to haul 100 loads of rock from Palmer Park to the rock garden, Borgars said. "The rocks, some of them huge, were loaded and unloaded by hand," he recalled. "Hennenhofer told us not to be particular about positioning the rock for the garden. He said to pick one up, throw it, and where it landed would be just right because it would look natural." The garden, he said, was good-looking when it was first constructed. It had hills and mounds and*

overall was irregular, and the paths and fishponds made it interesting. In it, Borgars and two other park employees planted alpine plants from Switzerland and Germany and some of the first grape hyacinths to appear in Colorado Springs. Borgars and Hennenhofer even dug up a patch of buttercups near Cheyenne School to plant in the garden.[29]

Throughout the 1920s, residents and visitors enjoyed the novelties and features of the Springs' elaborate parks. From the primeval natural landscapes of the Garden of the Gods, Palmer Park, and North Cheyenne Cañon to the serenely cultivated gardens and quiet spaces of Monument Valley, Acacia, Alamo, and the Antlers parks, as well as the elaborate plantings of roadway medians, various natural environments offered respite and inspiration. In 1921, the first Easter Sunrise Service was held at the Cathedral Spires in the Garden of the Gods. In May 1926, the Park Commission erected the shelter over the mineral spring in Monument Valley Park, Tahama Spring, as a memorial to three early pioneers: Lieutenant Zebulon Pike, the explorer; William J. Palmer, the city founder; and Tahama, a Sioux Indian, famed for refusing to fight against the white settlers and assisting Lieutenant Pike in the early 1800s. It is not surprising that, in describing the parks of Colorado Springs, a 1927 *Gazette Telegraph* article quoted the poet, William Cullen Bryant:[30]

Monument Valley Park rock garden, built in the 1920s.

"To him who in the love of nature holds
Communion with her visible forms, she speaks
A various language."

The first Easter Sunrise Service in the Garden of the Gods, 1921.

1930–1940: THE DEPRESSION, DISASTER, AND RECOVERY

By 1930, Colorado Springs residents were hopeful of developing a recreation center at Prospect Lake, the most popular swimming area of the region, and seeing the continuing growth of their parks and associated programs. A series of trails—Captain Jack's, Chutes, Columbine Springs, Helen Hunt Falls, Mount Cutler, St. Mary's, and Stratton—were all opened in North Cheyenne Cañon. City residents regularly enjoyed themselves swimming in Prospect Lake in the summer and skating on the frozen ponds in Monument Valley Park in winter. In June 1930, the *Gazette* happily announced expectations for a play-filled summer in an article titled "Glorious Playground Season Opens in City's Parks Tomorrow Afternoon," predicting "one continuous round of fun."[31] An adult "playground" was officially

opened in Antlers Park in 1931, featuring two shuffleboards and five horseshoe courts. In 1932, the city purchased another 275 acres of the Garden of the Gods, including the Balanced Rock and Steamboat Rock areas, for $25,000, making them public property forever.[32] Residents held high hopes for their parks.

But the decade of the Great Depression, of financial collapse and uncertain futures, was to take its toll on the growth and development of the Colorado Springs park system.

Top: Swimmers wading into Prospect Lake.

Bottom: Local residents enthusiastically tore down the private fence surrounding Balanced Rock upon the city's purchase of the Goerke property, 1932.

Improvements were slowing down by 1933, accomplishments becoming smaller in scope. On January 20, the *Gazette* reported that the only new improvement for 1933 would be the "beautification of the three blocks of center parking on Nevada Avenue left barren with removal of street car tracks and poles. The three blocks, from Cache la Poudre to Uintah Street, will be planted with lawn, trees and shrubbery." In January 1934, the lack of funds was of particular concern to the Park Commission:

> *[The Commission met] to frame its 1934 budget and activities. With a city appropriation that is $6,000 less than the 1933 figure, and faced with the necessity to seed and improve 18 blocks of new center parking on Wahsatch and Nevada Avenues, the Commission will be forced to drastic economies to perform necessary maintenance this year. . . . There can be no other improvements than completing the center parking.*[33]

By the mid-1930s, the nation was deep into the Great Depression. Banks in thirty-two of forty-eight states had closed, less than half the workforce was employed full time, and in over three years suicide rates had tripled. In Colorado Springs, lines of needy unemployed reached around a city block as people waited for help from the Salvation Army. The Volunteers of America operated a local relief program providing substantial meals to women and children every afternoon and baskets of food on Sunday morning, and over 320 community gardens had been planted as self-help projects for the unemployed. And an unprecedented drought was occurring all along the Front Range and eastern plains.[34]

Nonetheless, the Park Commission stayed focused on the care of the parks. Committed to a new policy for greater adult recreational facilities, they were planning tennis courts in Monument Valley, shuffleboard courts in Acacia, and the construction of a softball field in Boulder Park in May 1935, with the promise of floodlights for the following year.

Three months earlier, after Hennenhofer's death, the Parks Superintendent position had gone to T. C. Kirkwood, a prominent businessman who had already served Colorado Springs as a City Council member in the 1920s and as a Park Commissioner for twenty-eight years. His experience, influence, and enthusiasm were to help sustain the parks through the difficult times ahead. As noted in the *Gazette Telegraph*, the new Superintendent was "devoted to the ideals of General William J. Palmer, founder of Colorado Springs and donor of its 2,526 acre park system. Mr. Kirkwood is also in step with modern trends of broader public use of the parks and the development of adult recreation."[35]

Top: Curvilinear wall in Monument Valley Park, 1934.

Middle: Dog drinking from the Tahama Spring in Monument Valley Park.

Bottom: Monument Valley Park lake and building prior to the 1935 flood.

The Bijou Street bridge over Monument Creek after the 1935 flood.

THE 1935 FLOOD

Yet further disaster loomed. In 1935, on Memorial Day, while southeastern Colorado was being ravaged by sky-blackening dust storms, a massive flood occurred in Colorado Springs. It was the worst flooding in the history of Monument Creek, causing several deaths and extensive damage to the city, including General Palmer's crown jewel, Monument Valley Park. Little Dorchester Park was gutted.

As described in the *Colorado Springs Free Press*, the unexpected deluge was caused by a storm blowing in from the northeastern county of Elbert with hurricane force, falling on land already saturated by seventy-two hours of steady drizzle and intermittent showers—precipitation originally welcomed as respite from a dry, dusty winter. Repelled and held fast by the mountains, the storm clouds released a flood of rain. Monument Creek became a raging river. The resulting violent flood decimated Monument Valley Park:

> *It is said waves ten feet high were not uncommon and some eyewitnesses estimated that the crests at times reached the height of fifteen feet. Many houses along Monument Creek were severely damaged and a number were entirely washed away. Beautiful Monument Valley Park,*

Former Park Superintendent Gustav Hennenhofer's house on Uintah Street destroyed by the Memorial Day flood, 1935.

the pride of Colorado Springs, was buried under hundreds of thousands of tons of gravel and debris. The lakes and ponds were basins of mud. While the Penrose Pavilion (still at the swimming pool) withstood the onslaught, the pool itself was filled with gravel and mud and the equipment destroyed.[36]

Six deaths were attributed to the disaster. The damage in Colorado Springs was a reported $1,769,000. Besides the damage to Monument Valley and Dorchester parks, hundreds of homes and businesses were destroyed and railroad lines were inundated. All the bridges, except the Bijou viaduct, were washed away. The electric plant stood in water twelve feet deep.[37]

THE PUBLIC WORKS PROGRAM AND CIVILIAN CONSERVATION CORPS AID RECOVERY

The federal programs that had been developed to counteract the devastation of the collapsing economy proved permanently beneficial to the Colorado Springs parks system, particularly in the aftermath of the flood. In 1934 the Civilian Conservation Corps (CCC) had set up local camps to combat erosion, build roads, and improve structures in Palmer Park. Workers completed erosion control and dam and bridgework, constructed new roads, and widened and improved old ones. They also built stonewalls, fireplaces for picnickers, and stone comfort stations. They improved landscaping. The success of these programs determined plans for further reconstruction in the Garden of the Gods and North Cheyenne Cañon.

Top: Tahama Spring in Monument Valley Park damaged by the 1935 flood.

Bottom: Civilian Conservation Corps workers pitched tents in local parks during the 1930s.

In 1935, Works Progress Administration (WPA) and CCC resources were called upon to help recover what had been lost to the flood, and by April 1936 more than five hundred men were at work on the reconstruction project. The workers completed major re-channeling and riprapping of Monument Creek; however, the reconstruction left only ninety-nine acres of the park's original 164 acres beyond the channel. The widened channel could safely carry fifty thousand cubic feet of water per second—the 1935 flood was probably around thirty thousand feet—but the parkland lost to the widened channel, which became largely a wild area, was inaccessible to pedestrians

Restoration in Monument Valley Park widened the channel for Monument Creek. Tahama Spring Pavilion stands above the creek bed, 1935.

due to the channel's steep sides. WPA workers also rebuilt retaining walls, creek channel walls, stairs, benches, and entry points to the park, and a grandstand for one of the baseball fields. The rockwork wall lining Monument Creek was built in stages, reaching completion in 1941. Material for reconstruction came from the last major quarrying in Red Rock Canyon.

The benefits of federal relief were acknowledged locally. The 1936 Tourist Edition of the *Sunday Gazette Telegraph* reported that "While the flood wrought damage to the beautiful lawns and flowerbeds in Monument Valley Park, the Depression projects, besides providing employment for many of the men in the city, have changed the map of roads, trails and walks."[38] The article gratefully acknowledged the benefits of the public relief projects, noting that workers provided overall improvements "a step ahead in what would have been many years of normal city improvement work."[39]

Restoration took time. By 1936, lilacs, evergreens, and Norway maples were transplanted to Boulder Park to replace dying cottonwoods. Other trees (salvaged from the widened channel of Monument Creek) were transplanted to Bott Park, and improvements around Prospect Lake included the planting of more lilacs and trees.

Park administrators continued to plan for the future, including maintenance and improvements in the parks, the rehabilitation of Dorchester Park, and the establishment of more children's playgrounds. In particular, plans were in the making to develop the city-owned land just north of Prospect Lake, and in 1936-37 a modern bathhouse at the lake was built for $26,000 as a work relief project, along with a sandy beach for swimmers. A shaded area for picnickers and a playground with swings and teeter-totters for children were included.

Park priorities were clear: restore damage, provide recreation, maintain beauty, meet community need, budget carefully. And a new emphasis on providing neighborhoods with parks was becoming apparent. Parks Superintendent T. C. Kirkwood asserted that improvements to smaller neighborhood parks—Boulder, Bott, and Thorndale—were particularly important, explaining:

It is my idea that we should develop these outlying parks as well as the more central spots. . . . The parks are situated in residential areas, within a few strides of everyone in the neighborhood. And in many cases the people who most need to use parks are least apt to have transportation facilities. Thus by developing these smaller parks we do, in a sense, take the parks to the people instead of making the people come to the parks.[40]

Top: The Prospect Lake bathhouse, a Works Progress Administration project completed in 1937.

Bottom: Bancroft Park.

By 1937, the *Colorado Springs Gazette* reported that Acacia Park was crowded daily with people playing cards, horseshoes, and shuffleboard, and listening to summer band concerts; Antlers Park offered shuffleboard courts and a baseball diamond; Boulder, Bott, and Thorndale provided children playgrounds; and Prospect Park, at Prospect Lake, with its new beautiful bathhouse and sand beach, had become a particularly popular destination for residents. Many continued to enjoy the scenic beauty and picnic spots of the Garden of the Gods, Palmer Park, and North Cheyenne Cañon. In 1937 the city received title to an additional 200 acres in North Cheyenne Cañon—160 acres donated by Fred Chamberlain and the other 40 an anonymous gift. People were happily using the playgrounds, tennis courts, swimming pool, and baseball fields of Monument Valley Park, and "appreciated the renovated gardens."[41]

Much had been done that year to enhance the city's center parkings, which featured gorgeous flower gardens. Over thirty thousand annuals had been set out, in addition to the shrubs and perennials planted throughout. Wahsatch and Willamette Avenue medians were added in 1937, featuring dwarf junipers and pines, elm, barberry, and spirea. The *Gazette Telegraph* proudly described the projects:

Probably overlooked by many as a park responsibility, these center parkings require a tremendous amount of work—and the result of this work is the praise and acclaim which people give Cascade Avenue, Willamette Avenue, Platte Avenue and the rest of the center-parked streets. . . . Like the gardens of a vast estate, the city's parks are ready for the use of the thousands of persons who will be Colorado Springs' guests this summer.[42]

Restoration was well in hand. The contribution to the Colorado Springs park system by the federal relief programs of the 1930s—particularly the CCC and the WPA—cannot be overstated. CCC crews, working by hand and with graders and a dozen trucks, eliminated an eroded and haphazard system of roads in the Garden of the Gods and replaced it with three widened, graded, and oiled drives. They restored the grounds to their natural beauty by planting thousands of juniper saplings and vegetation. They dug trenches for water lines to hook onto the six-inch main line on

Columbia Road, providing water for irrigation, comfort stations, and the Hidden Inn. They transitioned the Garden from its man-made, over-run scarring to its natural origins, while making it more accessible to appreciative tourists and residents.

They had also transformed scenic Palmer Park into a well-developed, popular, accessible picnic and outing site, and by 1937 had begun to bring Monument Valley Park into its own again. Other improvements included repairs and remodeling to the Bruin Inn in North Cheyenne Cañon, grading the High Drive, and planting extensive flowers in the parks and center parkings. WPA workers also helped build a new greenhouse and potting room beside the old one on Mesa Road, and these, with the existing cold frame, were useful in accommodating the more than thirteen thousand perennials that were transplanted to parks and medians.

Top: From the High Drive in North Cheyenne Cañon, travelers viewed rocky cliffs, trees, train cars, and a vista of the eastern plains.

Bottom: The Bruin Inn by Helen Hunt Falls in North Cheyenne Cañon was built around 1883 by Colorado College students. It remained a tourist attraction until it burned down in 1957.

The Park Commissioners and the Parks Department had worked closely with those providing these programs. Despite the devastations of natural disasters and the hardships caused by the Great Depression, park administrators and city residents had held steadily to the vision of a beautiful park system for the benefit of all the people of Colorado Springs.

1940–1960: WAR, HOMECOMING, AND CHANGE

Most park development across the nation was delayed during the 1940s by the economic, material, and personnel demands from U.S. entry into the Second World War in 1941. Colorado Springs was no exception. While the desire for more recreational facilities was powerful, resources were unavailable. New development—and even long-term maintenance—would only begin to boom again after the war had ended.

Nonetheless, during World War II, the Colorado Springs park system helped provide entertainment and recreation to both military and civilian personnel in the region, many of whom were stationed at Camp Carson.[43] Prospect Lake and the swimming pool at Monument Valley were especially popular, as were North Cheyenne Cañon and Garden of the Gods. In 1946, the first public rock-climbing exhibition by Camp Carson soldiers was held at the North Cheyenne Cañon amphitheatre.[44] On more than one occasion, several hundred soldiers gathered in Garden of the Gods, with a full field kitchen set up to prepare the meal, for their rest and recreation. The number of hometown users of parks increased due to mileage rationing, and picnic areas were crowded through the summer of 1943.

Colorado College students planted community gardens during the 1940s.

Despite manpower shortages, the lack of equipment, and budgetary restrictions brought on by the war, the Colorado Springs Parks Department continued to maintain holdings and to grow and put out plants for the beautification of the city. In 1943, the city had planted 61,148 plants and set out more than 250 trees. In 1944, more than 50,000 plants were growing in city-owned greenhouses. Local citizens also turned their efforts toward cultivation, converting much parkland to "Victory Gardens" to increase needed food production, a carry-over from World War I and the Depression years.

Even the demands of war had not diminished the city's dedication to beauty and recreation; indeed perhaps the wartime experience had heightened appreciation for what the parks offered. Returning soldiers had seen extraordinary destruction, such that they were more determined than ever to make their hometown a peaceful and beautiful place to live and raise their families.

PLANS FOR BEAUTIFICATION AND RECREATION

In 1945, the Colorado Springs Park Commission announced an ambitious long-range program for further beautification of the parks and improvement of the sports and recreational facilities. Major projects included landscaping of Cascade and Wahsatch Avenue parkways, improvements and landscaping at Boulder Park, and further improvements to Monument Valley Park. Landscaping plants and trees intended for the parkways included French and Persian lilacs, varied hued roses, flowering crabapple, white maple, birch, red oaks, golden willows, hopa crabs, chrysanthemums, golden rain trees, European mountain ash, and Oregon grape shrubs.[45] Boulder Park projects featured tennis courts, a basketball court, a baseball diamond, a children's playground, and picnic area.

In Monument Valley, work was still being done to restore areas damaged by the 1935 flood; plans called for a rock garden, bowling greens, lawns, and pathways. Pedestrian trails and bicycle paths were to be developed, as were coasting lanes—for wagons in summer and sleds in winter. Additionally, improvements were planned to the existing baseball diamond and the grandstand, while a softball diamond, handball courts, and a horseshoe court were added. The proposed projects were extensive—including a bird sanctuary, deer preserve, fire rings for Girl Scouts and Boy Scouts, and further development of the pinetum north of Colorado College. All four project plans had been drawn by S.R. DeBoer, well-known Denver landscape architect.

Players pitch horseshoes in Monument Valley Park.

Recreational activities included such programs as the city baseball league, where competition was fierce and spectators enthusiastic. The winning of the city championship in 1949 and 1950 by the Brown Bombers, the only all-black baseball team in the league, were memorable victories recalled sixty years later by two of six surviving players, Jesse Vaughan and Joe Morgan.

The Brown Bombers, 1949.

Interviewed in 2009 by Ryan Warner on the KCFR program *Colorado Matters*, Vaughan and Morgan recalled how they "were sort of excluded from playing on the white teams." So they just formed their own team. They relished the joy of the game, and they achieved inspiring victories. As Jesse Vaughan described:

> *We just played because we loved the game. . . . We were so close together, I might say this, that whenever we took the field, we already felt like the game was ours. They had to beat us. We didn't have to beat them because we had already won. That was our attitude. And then we played that way and the folks saw that. And on Sundays and holidays when we played baseball at Monument Valley Park, you couldn't hardly get in there it was so crowded. We played teams from Fort Carson, [they] had a couple of teams, and Peterson Field had a couple of teams, and they had professional ball players on their teams, and we beat 'em. And when we beat those teams with those professionals, they said 'these guys must be good.' No ain't no must be. We are good.* [46]

Parks offered an outlet to all members of the Colorado Springs community. Segregation and its associated prejudices were a fact in Colorado Springs in the 1940s and 1950s, and no doubt its effects had surfaced within the parks. Blacks were not allowed to swim with whites in the Monument Valley pool, nor to be on the same Prospect Lake beaches, nor to sit in the same cafes and ice cream parlors. And yet, the Brown Bombers were credited with keeping baseball alive in Colorado Springs until the Sky Sox arrived in 1950. As player Joe Morgan said, "You didn't think about that type of thing too much, we were just wanting to play baseball." And all—black and white—enjoyed the thrill of the games. They packed the park to watch the sport play out. Teammate Jesse Vaughan described the racial mixture of spectators:

> *When you looked up into the stands, they were all over, everybody. Those who couldn't sit in the stands were standing along the sidelines, and they were under the trees even out in the outfield, they were all over the place, you might say the crowds were 50-50, black and white . . .* [47]

The Brown Bombers, while a direct result of the commonplace racism and resulting segregation of the times, nonetheless exemplified the sentiments expressed by Robert Moses, New York City's Park Commissioner in the 1930s, who remarked: "Parks are the outward visible symbols of democracy. That in my book is what they are for."[48]

THE PARK COMMISSION DE-COMMISSIONED

Rumblings of discontent with the Colorado Springs Park Commission established in 1907 had begun after the war. Independent and self-perpetuating, the board exclusively controlled park maintenance money that was budgeted by the City Council. But in 1946, within a year after the Park Commission had announced its long-range plans for the park system, another local organization was beginning to assert its influence. The Recreation Planning Committee, associated with the Chamber of Commerce, assumed authority to confer with City Council on the development of a memorial park in the Prospect Lake area—a responsibility that would ordinarily belong to the Park Commission. Fred Blick, chairman of the committee, was also authorized by the Chamber to spearhead planning for a long-range recreation program. By 1947, this committee, renamed the Pikes Peak Recreation Planning and Development Council, was urging that a new Parks Department be created to replace the established Park Commission. This would give City Council centralized control over all parks, parkways and recreational facilities.

In support of this political movement, a 1947 *Colorado Springs Free Press* article decried the "antiquated park [commission] clause," claiming the "citizenry of Colorado Springs . . . is aroused to the point where they want something done about extending and improving the recreation facilities for the young and old of the region." Arguing that City Council was handicapped by the Park Commission, that work begun in Boulder Park the previous year had been abandoned, and that City Council should be able to provide in the city's budget for this worthy project, the *Free Press* urged citizens to transfer power over the parks from the Commission to the Council.[49]

The appeal of this argument was also reflected in the published statement of a 1947 City Council candidate, Elmer Allen, who claimed "I am for a Charter Amendment creating a Department of Parks and Recreation. And further believe the Park Department should take steps to make a real park out of the Prospect Lake Section and improve the Baseball Park there and make it a real recreation park."[50]

Enough people were convinced to vote out the Park Commission. The change occurred April 1, 1947, when Colorado Springs voters approved—5,215 to 2,104—the repeal of the City Charter section authorizing the Park Commission and the creation of a city Department of Parks and Recreation. The new department would function directly under the supervision of City Council, on the same basis as all other city departments.[51]

Boaters enjoy Prospect Lake, 1930s.

A CITY PARKS DEPARTMENT

The Park Commission was abolished. Existing separate advisory boards for the Pioneers Museum and the Patty Jewett Golf Course were eliminated. By July of that year, City Council had adopted a general plan to appoint an advisory park and recreation commission, to establish the new Parks Department as a regular city department, and to establish a reporting hierarchy whereby the Parks Department head was answerable to the City Manager, who in turn reported to City Council.[52] In 1948, Willard J. Russell was appointed as Director of the new Parks and Recreation Department. A landscape architect with a degree in forestry, Russell would hold the position until 1955.[53]

The Colorado Springs Courthouse, which would later be home to the Colorado Springs Pioneers Museum, circa 1948.

Two units—one parks and one recreation—were included in the department; the ordinance itself provided for a Superintendent of Parks and a Superintendent of Recreation. All parks, parkways and recreation facilities of the city were under the direction of the department. The band concert program, management of City Auditorium, the Pioneers Museum, the forestry section, and Patty Jewett Golf Club were transferred to the new department. The Council further directed the City Manager to hire an outside expert to survey local needs to determine the appropriate direction for the parks.

These changes in governance marked a shift in attitudes toward park management that was occurring nationwide. Language had changed. Definitions had changed. Organization had changed. As Galen Cranz explains in *The Politics of Park Design*, during the 1940s and 1950s, across the country park departments became recreation commissions, and parks redefined as recreational facilities. A new leisure class, one that anticipated increased prosperity and happiness, simply wanted more recreational opportunities. As elsewhere, parks in Colorado Springs had become an expected feature of urban life. Their programs needed no particular justification, and citizens simply wanted their expectations fulfilled. They apparently believed a Parks Department directly accountable to City Council would be more responsive to their interests and needs than they felt the existing Park Commission had been.[54]

But with the loss of the Park Commissioners, those supervising Colorado Springs parks moved from a unique position of independent tradition, a visionary legacy, and articulated value to a position of competition with other city departments and programs for budget allocations, political attention, and civic support. The move would result in simplified procedures and streamlined services, an increased emphasis on efficiency, and eventually systems thinking and bureaucratization, especially as the Colorado Springs population and parks exploded in the last half of the twentieth century.

Ultimately, there was an attendant loss of idealism, authority and prestige as a conscious awareness of the historical legacy of the parks waned. The traditional Park Commissioners, due to their long and dedicated personal service, had preserved and inspired an appreciation for the parks and an understanding of the parks' role in the identity of Colorado Springs. With the elimination of the Commission came a loss of this public consciousness, and the civic generosity and communal support for the parks that had marked earlier decades were diminished.

MEMORIAL PARK CREATED

Interest in the popular Prospect Lake area continued to grow in the 1940s, as did hopes for developing it into a major city park. The new Parks Department and City Council moved forward to turn these hopes into

The field at Memorial Park designated for a new ballpark, 1948.

reality, but not without controversy, conflict, and delays.[55] Finally, in May 1948, City Council designated the name "Memorial Park" for the new recreation area, a response to the urgings of the American Legion and the Pikes Peak Recreation Planning and Development Council. At war's end, these organizations wished to dedicate the area as a memorial to veterans, both living and dead.

By September 1948, City Council enthusiastically reviewed the consolidated architectural and landscaping plan for Memorial Park. The proposed development included architectural designs by Thomas and Sweet, local architects, and a landscape design developed by S. R. DeBoer and Company, the Denver firm, whose scheme took into account natural vegetation, the prevailing landscape, and preservation of the magnificent view of Pikes Peak from the grounds. But not all proceeded smoothly. Conflict over whose plan—Thomas' or DeBoer's—was to prevail, and who was responsible for coordinating and communicating about Memorial Park development, erupted during City Council meetings regularly from 1946 to 1949. Original development plans called for everything from tennis and shuffleboard courts to a sled run and a football field. City Council eventually determined to await a cost study for the proposed development before deciding whether to proceed with various elements piecemeal or to submit a bond issue to the people, but all present agreed the park would be "the showplace of the west."[56]

Construction of the ballpark at Memorial Park, 1949.

Progress ended up being piecemeal. First came the ball fields. A $175,000 bond issue program was approved by the voters in the 1949 municipal election, a portion of which was spent developing Memorial Field, where the Colorado Springs Sky Sox would host western league teams beginning in 1950. A softball field, clubhouse, concession area, grandstands, and a parking area were also completed in the park for the benefit of baseball fans. But despite adopting the master plan, Council implemented no comprehensive development of Memorial Park. Instead, City Council discussed and disputed possibilities, and little by little Memorial Park evolved.

In 1953, the city amended the contract it had awarded local architects Thomas and Sweet. They determined to exclude the purchase of an adjacent trailer court and to provide for drainage for Prospect Lake rather than sealing it off. In November of that year, the city eliminated the originally planned stadium while retaining the planned-for war memorial. In bits and pieces, fits and starts, Memorial Park was being developed by committee.

Memorial Park exemplified how the process for development and maintenance of all the city parks had changed under the new governance system. Now the appointed Parks and Recreation Advisory Board developed capital improvement plans and submitted their estimate of needs to the City Planning Commission. The Commission would then incorporate reports from all departments and suggest year-to-year improvements to City Council. City Council would decide fund allocations. In its 1954 six-year improvement plan, the Parks Advisory Board—the group that had nominally assumed the function of the Park Commissioners—offered comprehensive recommendations for walks, bleachers, dugouts, a bath house, parking lots, and a field house at Memorial Park, as well as improvements to other parks. But implementation was out of their hands.

By 1962, fourteen years after Memorial Park was named, a new five-year development plan for the park was proposed and approved. The long-range program announced by City Council included a swimming center, circular memorial, a planned garden center and arboretum. A divided entrance with fountain would lead to the winding drive through the area. Plans also included an artificial lake, outdoor amphitheatre, eight tennis courts and handball courts beyond the baseball park. New boating facilities for Prospect Lake and a move of the fishing area, as well as landscaping and new trees, were included in the estimated costs of $500,000 to $700,000. While the plan met with approval, implementation was uncertain. In twenty years' time, a clear agreement on the purpose, development, and commitment to Memorial Park remained at bay.

CITY DEVELOPMENT AND MAINTENANCE OF PARKS

Meanwhile, little Dorchester Park was being rescued from disregard and neglect. In 1947, the park area had been used as a "dumping ground" for dirt taken during excavation for the South Nevada Avenue underpass; the *Gazette* reported that Dorchester "currently bears no resemblance to a park, living or dead."[57] In 1948, City Council gave first approval to a commercial rezoning for contiguous lots (some of which extended into the park proper) for a tourist court, despite attorneys' caution that the property had been deeded to the city to develop into a park. The following year, L. C. Dorr, one of the property heirs, notified the city he would take legal action to enforce the covenants or reclaim the property.

The local Naval Reserve (Company 9-30 of the Ninth Naval district) bailed out the city by proposing to use restoration of the area as a training program. They offered to level the entire area, construct a levee along the creek bank, and re-condition water lines, with the city installing non-return valves for drainage through the levee. By June, they had built restrooms, repaired and painted the old pavilion, installed an underground sprinkling system and drinking fountain, and built a large graveled parking area. Upon completion, the entire area was reseeded for park purposes. By 1951, the Parks Department had transplanted thirteen evergreen trees, bushes, and shrubbery in the park, had added a decorative log rail fence, and was planning picnic tables, fireplaces, and a softball field. Dorchester was restored to the neighborhood.

The city continued work to develop and improve park resources. In his 1950 report, the Park's Director of Recreation, Jay Ver Lee, outlined the progress made in recreational facilities. In addition to construction at Memorial Park, he described improvements to Patty Jewett Golf Course, swimming and tennis at Monument Valley, several new playgrounds—including baseball and softball diamonds at the newly developed Bonnyville Park—tennis, basketball, and softball at Boulder Park, and many other similar efforts.

Administrators, residents, and visitors now emphasized—and expected—an extensive variety of recreational programs: hockey, baseball, swimming, football, basketball, soccer, touchball, speedball, volleyball, kick ball, dodge ball, golf, tennis, boating, fishing, track, darts, tumbling, horseshoes, croquet, and even kite flying. The report specified thirty-three separate sports, as well as handicraft projects, drama, music and entertainment, and social activities. All were justified by the growing number of happy participants and spectators.[58]

Serpent play sculpture in Conejos Park, 1958.

In 1952, members from several civic organizations met with Park Superintendent Russell to discuss the development of Conejos Park, ten acres just west of the city steam plant, that would replace the inadequate facilities in that neighborhood. City officials had agreed the idea was a good one, but questioned where to find the $10,000 needed to develop a ball field, playground, and picnic facilities. Funds for Conejos were ultimately provided by the Colorado Springs Junior League. Other parks and open space were to follow: Winfield Scott, Jefferson, Pike, Audubon, Westmoor, Douglas Creek, and Twain—precursors to the explosion of new parks to be developed in the next fifty years.

Children on Boulder Crescent Park play sculpture, 1957.

One of the memorable developments in the neighborhood parks of the 1950s was the creation and installation of imaginative play sculptures designed by Fred Schumm and others. First employed as a tree trimmer for the Parks Department in the early 1950s, Schumm was approached in 1957 by James Taylor, then Director of Parks, to design new playgrounds for the parks. Schumm completed his first play area in 1957 at Boulder Crescent Park in downtown Colorado Springs. Constructed of steel, resin, plastics, concrete, and wax—the result was a bright modernistic hollow igloo with a slide for children. He also designed the serpent play sculpture in Conejos Park, inspired by trips to Mexico and Mayan art. Designated Quetzalcoatl, the Mexican serpent slide was installed in 1959. The creative designs—long since removed or replaced by more standardized playground equipment—are still fondly remembered by longtime residents of the city.[59]

CITY GOVERNANCE AND PARK ADMINISTRATION

Governance of the park system continued to be based on recommendations of the Park and Recreation Advisory Board, planning by Park Department administrators, proposals of the City Planning Commission, and budgeting and final approval from City Council. Advisory Board members still asserted an active role in park planning, but their influence was uncertain as final authority clearly rested with City Council. In 1951, the Parks Advisory Board and park administrators sought City Council adherence to a comprehensive set of principles; these included land set aside for parks and schools by private developers, a walkable distance of less than one-half mile to local neighborhood parks, development of "playfields" for larger groups within a mile's distance, desirable features for general city parks and specialized parks and facilities, "tot lots" for local neighborhoods, and maintenance of features in outlying parks—bridle paths, fishing, hiking, and scenic drives.

In 1953, the Parks Advisory Board put forth a six-year capital improvement program that called for an expenditure of $1,582,700. When the City Manager reduced the request for operating funds for the Parks Department that year, the Advisory Board requested an additional $30,000 in funds from City Council, arguing the Parks Department had been overlooked in

Kissing Camels in the Garden of the Gods.

the past and a one-million dollar tax increase was in order. Eight new parks had been added over five years, while the number of picnickers had quadrupled. New playgrounds, fireplaces, and picnic tables required maintenance, as did the twenty-nine new ball fields.[60] But disagreements between city administrators and park representatives over how to allocate funds remained unresolved.

By 1958, park administrators, the Advisory Board and the City Manager all recognized the need for additional funds to bring the parks "up to snuff," noting that over $2,778,000 was needed beyond standard operating funds. Some argued for a bond issue. But City Manager John Biery was emphatic that the creation of a special metropolitan recreational district was preferable to the current structure and process. He argued the improvements were needed, but community support should be widespread:

> *"It is my duty to protect the citizens of Colorado Springs and I will do this until somebody wakes up and does something about this overall park system," [City Manager John] Biery told those gathered for the fourth open meeting to discuss the 1959 city budget. . . . The city manager said it would not be fair to saddle a huge bond issue on the 80,000 people living within the city limits when it would equally benefit the additional 45,000 residents in the metropolitan area. "Cities just can't continue to tax their citizens to serve everybody," Biery said.*[61]

But a special district for parks never came to be in the 1950s, and city leaders continued to balance competing needs with limited funds.

Organizationally, the separate parks and recreation functions of the department were combined under one director in 1956, when James Taylor, who proved to be an ardent spokesperson for the parks, became Director of Parks and Recreation.[62] He worked closely with the City Manager, the Parks Advisory Board, and city leaders to balance competing needs and expectations. Under his administration, from 1956 to 1963, the parks, recreation, forestry, and cemetery departments were consolidated into a single Parks and Recreation Department; a separate division for center parkings and administrative and general services was added; and the Department moved its offices from downtown Colorado Springs to Glen Avenue, adjacent to Monument Valley Park—all moves that Taylor asserted would advance efficiency and development.[63] He also urged development of a park master plan to conserve what was held and to expand "usage, aesthetic and general desirability of open spaces," but the first master plan for the city parks would not materialize until 1976.

In 1963, when Taylor announced his resignation to move to New Jersey, City Manager John Biery praised him for all he had done to develop the system and generate public enthusiasm, while Taylor himself praised the close working relationship the Parks Department had with the Parks Advisory Board.[64] He encouraged the acquisition of additional land—particularly in the north and east sections of the city and adjacent to the Garden of the Gods, further development of Memorial Park, and the installation of both local and national sculpted artwork. His parting words were meant as inspiration:

> *I see an opportunity for a golden era of parks in Colorado Springs. . . . The city is growing. It has a wide diversity of people and interests. The area has the natural resources. The goal should be for the enjoyment of today's residents and visitors, and also for succeeding generations.* [65]

The city was at a crossroads. Hopes for the "golden era of parks" were shared by many, most of whom were unaware that Colorado Springs was about to enter a new phase of unparalleled growth. Since the death of General Palmer, the originally established Park Commission had carefully attended to the development, maintenance, and improvement of the city's park system. Citizens had enjoyed and appreciated its many benefits, offering widespread support for their parks and taking pride in the loveliness of their hometown. But city residents had decided to turn to a new governing system. When the city parks program transitioned into a city department, many looked forward to an elegant, exciting, and responsive parks and recreation system, one that would meet and exceed citizens' expectations and benefit the city in every way. But cracks were appearing. Whether those responsible for the parks had all that was needed—the vision, resources, support, political capital, and creativity—to meet these expectations would be the challenge of the next fifty years.

Trees cut down immediately west of Monument Valley Park marked the beginning of construction of the Monument Valley Freeway in 1957, separating the park from its western neighbors. The twelve-mile long, $12,200,000 freeway officially opened to the public on July 1, 1960—the beginning of a new era in the Springs.

Sign at pond in Monument Valley Park, 1972.

Growing Pains

1960–1980 : An Explosion of People, Parks, and Purposes

"The ultimate measure of a community is not its setting or its climate, but instead how well it provides for the needs of its citizens."

—1976 Colorado Springs Open Space, Park and Recreation Plan

UNIMAGINED GROWTH

Colorado Springs experienced a period of dramatic growth in the 1960s and 1970s, from 70,194 residents in 1960 to 130,660 by 1970; by 1980 the city's population had almost doubled again, reaching 232,000. By the year 2000, there were over 324,000 residents. The area of the city and the need for parks increased in similar proportions. Eventually, Colorado Springs would encompass a geographical area of almost two hundred square miles—larger than Pittsburgh, St. Louis, or Denver.[1] City leaders, park administrators, and citizens were faced with the complex challenges of unfettered community growth, increasing costs, and conflicting needs and expectations.

Those dedicated to keeping Palmer's legacy alive had to be flexible, open-minded, diplomatic, imaginative, resourceful, and responsive to the changing demands of a diverse community. As land, programs, services, and resources that Palmer could never have even imagined were being added to the city park system, park leaders and administrators were tasked more and more with making city parks be all things to all people. The road would be rocky.

EXPECTATIONS FOR RECREATION

Having established in the 1947 vote that the Parks Department was officially responsible for providing the community with recreational opportunities, citizens enjoyed summer day camps, winter ice-skating, and playgrounds during the next decade.[2] But while these activities were considered desirable, they were still seen as only a fringe of what parks naturally provided—a scenic and serene environment for refreshment and rejuvenation. However, the scope of parks would broaden in the next decades, both on the national level and locally in Colorado Springs.[3] The emphasis on providing a wider array of recreational resources grew dramatically. As noted in the April 1964 issue of the *Colorado Springs Free Press,* "[o]nly in recent years has Park and Recreation become a necessity to Mr. and Mrs. America—it was once a luxury."[4]

Children play on slide in Boulder Crescent Park in downtown Colorado Springs.

The five-year Memorial Park Master Plan that City Council finally approved in 1962 reflected the importance recreation had taken on. Including ball diamonds, tennis courts, picnic areas, swimming facilities, play fields, boating, fishing, water skiing, and playground developments, Memorial's plan also featured a swimming center, garden center, arboretum, and landscaped amphitheatre. While development would continue well beyond the next five years, the city's central park would eventually add many of these features, as well as an ice rink, velodrome, skateboard park, and other recreational resources for local citizens.[5]

FUNDING UNCERTAINTIES MAKE FOR HAPHAZARD DEVELOPMENT

In 1963, when Colorado Springs Parks and Recreation Director James Taylor resigned, Stu Richter was appointed the next director. He and his staff were absorbed with the need to acquire land for future city parks, generate recreational opportunities to satisfy local expectations, and secure the funding to develop and maintain both the physical amenities of the parks and the programs to subsequently take place there. This was a hefty task in the face of such rapid growth. From 1960 to 1970, they were able to add sixteen new park properties, yet much of this "parkland" sat vacant and undeveloped for several years for lack of funds.[6] The delays were to be a source of contention and political divisiveness on City Council, as well as irritation and disappointment to local residents.

James Taylor had forecast these kinds of problems prior to his departure, particularly warning about the lack of funding and planning for park areas in new developments:

> *I wish there were a district, an individual, an organization to buy, set aside and preserve spaces for a future recreational program in the periphery of our city. . . . With the exception of the northeast area, there is no plan to set aside any land for recreational purposes of the future.* [7]

Colorado Springs sudden suburban growth shows in this 1963 photo of the intersection of Palmer Park Boulevard and North Circle Drive.

Taylor had noted that while the department operated on a 1963 budget of a little over $500,000, it would take $3 million to fully develop a park and recreation program. Perhaps, he suggested, a metropolitan district for parks might be a solution to the problem.[8] Taylor further described problems with the existing requirement of the allocation of 4 percent of land or money from developers of new residential areas.[9] The city received no further financial support from developers for upkeep of the new parks once the land had been designated, and the 1951 requirement still awaited court determination of its legality.

The legal challenge to the city's 1951 requirement of developers to dedicate 4 percent of the developed area to parks—or to give the city cash of an equivalent value to the raw land—stalled parkland development. Not knowing if the policy was allowed, city leaders could not use what funds they had collected. They remained uncertain of how to otherwise finance the necessary development—whether through bonds, direct taxing, or financing through private organizations. Bond proposals failed to gain voter approval, taxing was insufficient, and donations inconsistent.

Budgets were continually subject to cuts and reallocations. When the 1965 budget was reduced due to City Council's withdrawal of a proposed 2 percent sales tax increase, Director Richter pleaded for community assistance. He particularly noted people's impatience with Memorial Park development—plans had been refined and approved but not funded—and he emphasized, "we do ask [local] groups to offer their assistance."[10]

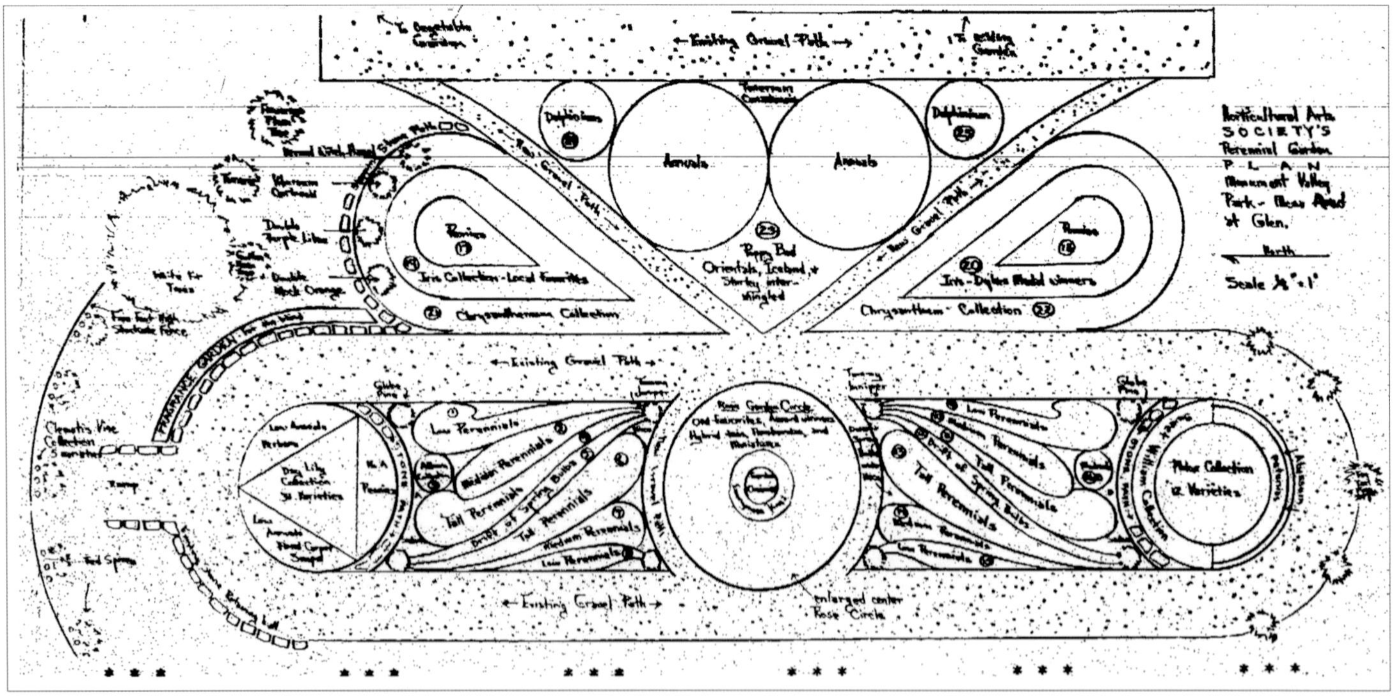

The Horticultural Arts Society's elaborate 1965 plan to restore the demonstration garden at Monument Valley Park was published in a Gazette *article.*

One group to volunteer was the Horticultural Arts Society. They announced plans in October 1965 to expand the demonstration garden in Monument Valley Park, with many local gardeners assisting in the planning, planting, and upkeep of the area: the new areas would include collection displays of roses, peonies, poppies, allium, daylilies, phlox, and iris, plus flowering shrubs, trees, and vine displays. The garden was intricately planned to blossom spanning the months of March to October, and included a fragrance garden for the blind. "Controversial" plantings included rhubarb and goldenrod.[11] The garden has flourished into the present, tended by dedicated volunteers to show newcomers what grows best in the high and dry climate.

Volunteerism notwithstanding, the Parks and Recreation Department simply lacked the money it needed. Up to 1966, it received no funding from the city beyond maintenance for capital improvements. In 1966, City Council budgeted $150,000 for capital improvements; in 1967, $75,000; in 1968, as a result of an increase in the sales tax, $274,500. An additional $300,000 gift from El Pomar and the Alice Bemis Taylor Foundation in 1968 provided for the acquisition of the historic forty-two-acre White House Ranch next to the Garden of the Gods.[12] Funding improved somewhat by the end of the 1960s—in 1968 the Parks Department received $439,000 for capital improvements and $856,890 in 1969—but no large investments were made in the parks system.

The Alamo Hotel Senior Center had opened in 1967, and Acacia, Monument Valley, Cheyenne Cañon, Memorial, and Palmer parks continued to provide residents with scenic resources and recreational outlets. But when local citizens complained in October 1970 about insufficient youth recreational programs, a lack of opportunities for girls, as well as insufficient "green" parks in new neighborhoods, park administrators admitted they were still struggling to meet existing needs and unable to plan adequately for the future.

That month, Director Richter was quoted as saying "the city has been playing a 'catch-up' game with its park development," adding that Colorado Springs would need to spend $450,000 per year until it completed its plans for park capital development. In defense of their operations, park administrators argued that the recreation program included as many activities as their budget could handle, adding there always had been limited opportunities for women in the area.[13] Richter further argued, "People see a piece of rough ground and they don't think it is a park. . . . [But] it is illogical to develop a 'green' park until the population develops in the subdivision."[14]

Park administrators further defended their programs, pointing out that softball, volleyball, tennis classes, playground programs, and actual tennis competition had been organized for girls, and more programs were in the works. Additionally, the department had organized after-school programs for about thirty schools, including bowling and roller-skating. Park administrators were trying to satisfy as many citizens as possible. But without having a clear plan or reliable source of funds, they were unable to get ahead of demand.

The Orchard House, later referred to as the White House, was built in 1907. The White House Ranch property was acquired by the city in 1968 and renamed Rock Ledge Ranch in 1995.

In November 1971, City Council voted to double the sales tax from 1 to 2 percent; the move was immediately challenged by a local tax repeal committee headed by Luke Zell. The following January, the city began collecting the additional one-cent sales tax; the funds were intended for a huge list of capital improvements, including projects in parkland acquisition as well as airport expansion, drainage, and mass transportation. But the tax repeal committee gathered over 8,000 certified protest signatures, forcing a special election to let voters decide the question in June.

Presenting to City Council that April, Director Richter argued emphatically for the need for the funds, noting: "the community is [still] about 5-10 years behind the national average in park development . . . [because] the city did virtually nothing for 40 years." He again acknowledged ongoing community dissatisfaction, noting park locations in Vista Grande and Village Seven lacked facilities:

Children enjoy neighborhood parks in the 1970s.

> *"The people are there and they want and need the parks now but we have no money to do anything to them, not even plant grass," Richter said. "It's a question of how long the public wants to wait for these park facilities. If the sales tax measure fails we will just have to wait another five years or so before we can do anything on the undeveloped ones."*[15]

So although the Parks and Recreation Department was committed to the ideal that all neighborhoods should have a maintained local park within a half-mile walking distance, many people had a longer distance to travel; more than fifteen local "parks" still awaited development. The city was deficient in public tennis courts (according to national standards) and had only three hundred acres of "flat land, recreational type" parks, despite its more than three thousand acres of mountain park property.

Meanwhile, city leaders hoped to spend $350,000 on acquisition of land around entrances to the Garden of the Gods, $360,000 for a new golf course to ease the demand at Patty Jewett, and $600,000 on a recreation center at Memorial Park—as well as fund developments of smaller projects throughout the system. All depended on the controversial 1972 sales tax passing when it came to vote in June. It did—by a very slim margin: 10,061 citizens voted for the tax; 9,416 voted against. City leaders claimed it as a "vote of confidence" and immediately moved forward with parkland projects.

Some funding issues had been resolved, but financial challenges would remain a concern. Two months later, Parks Director Stu Richter announced his plans to retire in December, after twenty years of service to the city, nine of those as director.

A SOLUTION: THE PARKLAND DEDICATION ORDINANCE

In 1973, the city attempted to solve its park funding problems by legislating the Parkland Dedication Ordinance, a requirement that developers themselves provide land for parks and schools with each new development, an ordinance that many developers considered inequitably burdensome.[16] This proposal established new regulations for the dedication of land. Written by the Subdivision Ordinance Committee, and approved by the Colorado Springs Planning Commission in July and by the City Council in August, the ordinance ensured acquisition of new parkland with each new residential development. It required the following:

> *[The assessment of] residential developments for 7.5 acres of parkland per 1000 persons living in the area. Of that acreage, 1 acre would serve as a neighborhood park, 1.5 acres as a play field, 2 acres as a community park, and 3 acres as a metro park . . . the acreage rising proportionately with the population.*[17]

Top: Coaches help football players at Memorial Park field.

Bottom: Youth enjoy park and recreation programs in Memorial Park.

The ordinance was supported by most local citizens who appeared at meetings, the Parks Advisory Board, the League of Women Voters, and the Springs Area Beautiful Association. Nonetheless, it remained controversial. Several amendments to protect developers and refine the ordinance were voted down by City Council in its August 1973 meeting, due to the "urgent nature" of the passage of the measure. The basic proposal included a provision that fees collected should be used generally in the district in which they were collected, that the small developer would be protected by a maximum fee (in lieu of land) allowed, and that land already platted could not be assessed. Further possible amendments were referred to the reactivated Subdivision Committee.[18]

The ordinance had both an immediate and long-term effect on Colorado Springs. It resolved some of the immediate funding problems, and it guaranteed the addition of parkland with each new residential development. Consequently, Colorado Springs acquired and became responsible for a remarkably large amount of park acreage as the city grew in geographic leaps and bounds. Up until the 1950s, new park acreage had been primarily a result of generous land donations from wealthy benefactors. From the 1970s on, park acquisition—particularly land designated for neighborhood and community parks—was largely the result of this ordinance, with other land acquisitions funded by the city's general fund, grants, lottery receipts, open space sales taxes, and occasional donations.[19]

In 1983, the Parkland Dedication Ordinance actually exceeded its objectives; that year the city acquired 7.778 acres of new parkland for every

Shooks Run Park.

1,000 new city residents. Parks spokesman George Dushan remarked, "That's the largest amount acquired in a single year since General Palmer's parkland gifts in 1907."[20] This was the first time since 1960 (when the city owned 41.86 acres of parkland per 1,000 residents) that the city exceeded 25 acres of parks per 1,000 residents.[21]

The Parkland Dedication Ordinance remains in effect to this day. While many Front Range cities employ a similar strategy, it was sufficiently notable to be remarked upon in the 2009 CBS News video on Colorado Springs, which explained: "Any new development in this town of 400,000 must contain a park—by law."[22] By that year, Colorado Springs had acquired 124 parks to manage and maintain.

NEW PROGRAMS OFFER NEW OPPORTUNITIES

In spite of the growth-related pressures and funding problems of the 1970s, the Parks and Recreation Department made considerable progress serving residents and visitors alike. Innovative programs were initiated, parks were maintained, capital improvements occurred, and thirty-five new parks were created during that decade.[23] True to Palmer's legacy, the Parks and Recreation Department remained focused on people and how to meet their needs. When Richard Buerkle replaced Stu Richter as Director of Parks and Recreation in 1973, he was optimistic about the future.

The new director reflected many of the priorities and concerns of Colorado Springs residents. He articulated a special need for more community centers, "where people can gather to get to know one another, to enjoy good recreation programs, and instill community pride." He also echoed Richter's concern for more open space, both as buffer zones and "green areas," and for more recreational facilities and programs. While he, too, bemoaned the lack of development of dormant parks, he positively described the existing budget for maintaining and improving the parks, and foresaw opportunities for expanding leisure time activities.[24]

To the delight of the Colorado Springs community, recreational opportunities continued to grow. In 1973, a new $625,000 municipal pool opened at Memorial Park. The aquatic activities at the Municipool, Prospect Lake, and the Monument Valley Pool included a range of new instructional and recreational opportunities.[25] In 1974, 114 youth activities were offered, and recreational programs for the handicapped were provided throughout the year. Special Olympics in track and field and swimming provided athletic competition for handicapped and disabled individuals, and after-school and summer programs were organized for both boys and girls at both the junior and senior high school level. A robust sports program that offered competitive opportunities in volleyball, tennis, soccer, golf, wrestling, gymnastics, football, basketball, hockey, softball, baseball, and track and field served virtually every age group in the community.

The spectacular all-day Fourth of July celebration—complete with fireworks, the Colorado Springs Symphony, and a live cannon salute provided by Fort Carson soldiers—first took place in 1974. A recreational program for children—Tot Lots—was introduced that summer; 7,497 three- to five-year-olds attended that first year. In 1975, a Summer Arts Fair in Monument Valley Park was hosted jointly by the Parks and Recreation Department, the Colorado Springs Symphony, and the Fine Arts Center. Another 34,000 older children, six to thirteen years of age, played in summer playgrounds. The new Second Horizon senior citizen program offered social, recreational and cultural opportunities for those over age fifty-five, and satellite programs for the elderly were provided through a multi-purpose center and the Colorado Springs Housing Authority residences, Community Action Centers, and Edison School.

This was also the decade of "school-park" plans nationwide.[26] Colorado Springs administrators followed this trend, working with local school districts to share facilities and programs. On December 12, 1973, the Colorado Springs City Council and Colorado Springs School District 11 and Harrison School District 2 agreed to provide a variety of activities and opportunities through occasional use of Doherty and Harrison High Schools. They also agreed to cooperate in the construction, maintenance, and use of tennis courts, with responsibilities split 50-50 between the two entities. Neighborhood parks were planned as joint projects between school districts and the Parks and Recreation Department.

This school-park cooperation delivered many successful programs during the 1970s and into the 1980s, but gradually opportunities dwindled. School districts were faced with budget restrictions, curriculum revisions and closures due to population shifts. These changes necessitated a corresponding change in facility availability, and eventually the school-park cooperative ventures were discontinued.

Top: Parachute play in local neighborhood park.

Middle: Large crowds enjoyed evening Summer Symphony concerts below the Fine Arts Center.

Bottom: The Second Horizon Senior Center offered social, recreational and cultural opportunities.

OPEN SPACE BEGINNINGS

New priorities were beginning to surface as people became sensitive to the impact of the city's remarkable growth. New housing developments seemed to be springing up overnight, traffic congestion was increasing, and cherished mountain views and wilderness access were being threatened. Widespread support for the development of open space within the city existed on City Council, the Parks Advisory Board, and with local citizenry. The Pikes Peak Area Council of Governments (PPACG) published a series of three reports from 1970-1971, recommending an extensive network of trails to connect city parks. In 1974, THK Associates prepared a report on "Open Space Concepts for the City of Colorado Springs," focusing on open space and recreational opportunities, specifically with regard to landforms, drainage ways, streets, and parks.[27]

Corral Bluffs pictured in 1950. The property would become Colorado Springs open space in the next century.

In January 1975, the Parks Advisory Board appointed its first nine-member Open Space Advisory Committee.[28] The Committee was charged with recommending specific purchases, establishing priorities for acquisition, and evaluating land offers. It was also asked to research alternative means of preserving open space and generating funding mechanisms.[29] The creation of the group marked the official beginning of Colorado Springs' commitment to preserving open space within city limits, but while ideas were plentiful, funding for large acquisition was not. It would take another twenty years before the city would have the financial resources to start realizing its open space goals.

PHYSICAL RESOURCES: ACQUIRING, BUILDING, MAINTAINING

Attention was directed toward immediate parkland needs. With the 1973 Parkland Dedication Ordinance providing more resources to the department, the Parks Advisory Board prioritized new park purchases, proposing a total of nearly $2 million in purchases in August 1973. Eleven properties were included, the most important being the acquisition of additional buffer zone property immediately south of Garden of the Gods.

In June 1974, the Parks Advisory Board recommended another $2.6 million for the capital improvement budget, with priorities given to Acacia Park, Portal Park, Memorial Park, the Garden of the Gods, a new city golf course and construction of a community recreation center on the north side of Palmer High School gymnasium. Interestingly, "the board agreed that city neighborhood parks are no longer being developed exclusively for children. They explained that because of the rise in leisure time, adult recreation must be included in all park development."[30]

Top: The Garden of the Gods was designated as a National Natural Landmark by the U.S. Department of the Interior in 1971. Mayor Eugene McLeary received the award.

Bottom: Trail in Monument Valley Park.

Capital improvements were topped by the opening of the $1,200,000 Memorial Park Ice Rink in February 1975 (renamed Sertich in 1986).[31] In its first ten and a half months of operation, over seventy-nine thousand adults and children enjoyed public skating sessions. The twenty-seven-hole Patty Jewett Golf Course clubhouse was remodeled, and the new eighteen-hole Valley Hi Golf Course acquired.

Acacia Park, which lost most of its trees to Dutch Elm disease in 1975, was renovated. Pine beetle infestations had also contributed to devastation in the urban park forest, and over 1,300 new trees were planted by the Parks Department that year alone. A unique program, the "decade of trees," was initiated in 1975, which enabled homeowners to purchase trees at a minimal cost to plant in their right-of-way properties. The Parks Department obtained four hundred trees from a local nursery at $50 apiece and sold them to citizens to plant for $25 each.

In 1976, the old reservoir site in the northern part of Monument Valley Park was converted to a youth soccer field, over the objections of some immediate neighbors. Fred Simpson, Colorado Springs mayor from 1957-1959, had donated some acreage adjoining the park in 1970, but he and his neighbors protested the proposed use of the old city reservoir land, located next to his gift, as an athletic field. They were concerned over the lack of parking and a possible change to the neighborhood. All was resolved, however, as Tim Boddington relates in the story of the conception and development of the Boddington soccer field:

> *My father coached soccer at Colorado College as a volunteer for a bunch of years, taking the program from a club to varsity. During that time he watched a gazillion soccer balls go over the fence on Stewart Field into the creek. Half the team seemed to be in the creek looking for wayward balls, frustrating the volunteer coach! While walking his dog*

in the park around the old indent, he divined it would make a perfect soccer field. After some negotiating with the neighbors, it was agreed that the proposed field would be for Youth sports only. Adults and their beer and swearing would be prohibited. He and my mother donated the sod and I believe a small stipend each year in their will. . . . It's all pretty simple, soccer without chasing a ball into the creek was a natural choice for a field. The ball rolls up the embankment and back down, game on! [32]

Local and county residents continued to enjoy Monument Valley, North Cheyenne Cañon, and Palmer parks, as well as smaller neighborhood parks. At the White House Ranch, a Living History Pilot Program was begun in May 1978, attracting more than seventeen thousand visitors. The Horticultural Arts Society constructed the Rocky Mountain Arboretum at the ranch, featuring native and drought-tolerant plants. The Parks Department diligently cared for the athletic fields, turf grass, flowers, and trees in over seventy-five parks and medians. More than 3,800 acres of parkland were being maintained by hundreds of people and protected by park rangers who patrolled the parks, assisted visitors, and investigated crimes.

PLANNING AHEAD: 1976 COLORADO SPRINGS OPEN SPACE, PARK, AND RECREATION MASTER PLAN

Unquestionably, the surprisingly rapid urban growth that began in the 1960s had caused unexpected difficulties for the city. With an increasing population and sprawling geographical expansion, city leaders acutely felt the need for a comprehensive growth plan for Colorado Springs. It was likewise believed that the Parks Department required a new planning method for timely development of neighborhood parks, prioritization of programs and improvements, and projections of future growth and demands.

Boddington Field.

The use of Master Plans for park maintenance and development had become a widespread national practice in the previous decades, and the Colorado Springs Parks Department followed suit in the 1970s.[33] Nine master site plans were completed by the Design Division of the Parks Department in 1975 alone, including a master plan for the Garden of the Gods that was developed to determine how best to preserve and protect the unique red rock setting.[34] Ultimately, the number of design plans came to thirty-five. The department's ultimate goal was to design plans for all park sites, center parkways, open space areas, and golf courses.[35]

In the fall of 1974, the Colorado Springs City Council contracted with THK Associates of Denver to help the Park and Recreation Department develop the first overall Master Plan for the entire park system. The process was threefold: first, to develop possible concepts and ideas for the future direction of the parks; second, to survey city residents for their thoughts and desires; third, to articulate the actual master plan that would accommodate projected growth through 1990—a fifteen-year-span. The plan was ambitious and comprehensive. Acknowledging that Colorado Springs had an especially strong foundation upon which to build, it proposed thoughtful expansion, including new neighborhood parks, playfield areas, community parks, a citywide trail system, additional open space, and other special facilities.[36] It outlined in detail where new parks should be placed and what new recreational facilities might be needed, given the predictions for growth patterns in the city. It also noted the need for increased police protection for the "vast investment" in parks. The plan delineated the many ways in which the city could acquire parkland and open space, and it projected future budget needs, which it estimated could more than double in fifteen years.

Boys compete in youth soccer.

This was the first attempt (since General Palmer's) by Colorado Springs leaders to comprehensively capture the existing status and future needs of the park system. The city now had a "map." The plan analyzed the existing conditions and trends of the recreational programs, outlined deficiencies and opportunities with the system, delineated special considerations, recommended priorities, and included estimates of eventual operations and maintenance costs the system would incur. It concluded with several recommendations for implementation, including a variety of ways to ensure funding. It endorsed the establishment of a "voluntary, non-profit, tax-exempt corporation whose sole purpose would be to receive bequests of land, cash or securities to be used for the Colorado Springs open space and park system."[37] The plan's authors thought it fitting such a foundation should be named the Palmer Foundation after the city's founder, General William Palmer, remarking that:

> *Over one hundred years ago, Palmer dreamed of a beautiful city on the barren plain at the foot of Pikes Peak. His dream resulted in a city with wide, tree-covered boulevards, an institution of higher learning, and a basic park system. All of today's Colorado Springs residents should accept the responsibility for perpetuating and building upon that dream.*[38]

Union Meadows, between North Union and Austin Bluffs Parkway, was enjoyed by neighbors for several years before becoming official Colorado Springs open space in 2004.

Like so many others, those creating this plan were attuned to the remarkable legacy of Palmer's park system.

The Master Plan was enthusiastically endorsed by park supporters, city leaders, and advocacy groups. Many of the recommendations were already in progress or quickly acted upon. The concept of acquiring open space and establishing a "green belt" connecting the important areas of the city—an idea not dissimilar to that of Palmer's original plan for the parks—had taken hold during the 1970s, and city leaders were committed to this as a priority. In 1974, the Sunset Mesa Open Space had been added to the system, as had Broadview and Mesa in 1975 and Austin Bluffs in 1976. In 1977, the Santa Fe Railroad donated their abandoned right of way from Pikes Peak Avenue to near Fillmore Street, creating the opportunity to begin construction of a "hiker-biker" trail within the city. Planners anticipated this was the beginning of a loop through Monument Valley Park. In spring 1977, the city completed the "High Street Open Space" park near Corona and Bijou; another "linear" park along Shook's Run between Boulder and Willamette was planned for completion by 1980.

POLITICS AND CONFLICTS

The 1970s had brought a roller coaster of events to challenge the leaders of Colorado Springs and its Parks and Recreation Department—funding problems, disorienting growth, urban sprawl, more parkland, new recreational resources, expanding responsibilities, changes in organization and governance, demands and dissatisfaction, and a renewed focus on planning. Consequent personal dramas, disagreements, and dissension were an unavoidable part of the city's growing pains.

Since the 1947 vote that removed the Parks and Recreation Department from the oversight of the Park Commissioners and placed it under city governance, the Parks Department had become one of many units subject to the arguments and differing perspectives of City Council members. The nine members of City Council represented diverse needs, interests, and priorities; they did not present the united front that the former Park Commissioners had. Furthermore, they were concerned with all aspects of city functioning—not just the parks. And while City Council members formed alliances, argued priorities, and made political decisions based on the particular needs and demands of their own constituents, the relatively powerless Parks Advisory Board that had replaced the Park Commissioners often struggled to effect its own influence and agenda.

In 1970, a public outcry surfaced over an apparent agreement between certain members of City Council and the heirs of General William Palmer. Councilman Larry Ochs had independently arranged an agreement with Palmer's heirs regarding the purchase of their reversionary rights to Colorado Springs park property. When Palmer deeded the parklands to the city, the General conditioned that if any provisions of his bequest were violated, title to the lands would revert to his heirs. It was to be relieved of this possibility that Councilman Ochs initially engaged in talks to purchase these rights from the heirs for the city.

When others challenged the city's authority to make such a purchase, Ochs proposed a conciliatory amendment that would require a citywide election to approve the sale of any park property. This sparked vehement opposition from Councilwoman Betty Krouse and the League of Women Voters, who questioned the underlying premise of anyone having authority to sell any of the property—in particular city politicians. Ochs asserted "character assassination" as others challenged his presumption of the need to engage in talks with the heirs.[39] Two weeks later, the agreement was on hold.

This flare-up foreshadowed a second fallout the following year between Council and city residents over a related issue: City Council's consideration of dividing the northern end of Monument Valley Park and citizens' alarmed response. Suspicions spread that City Council intended to sell the northern end of the park to developers. When City Council planned to extend Fontanero Street across Monument Valley Park—a breach of the restrictions on the parks in Palmer's deed—the League of Women Voters took the city to court. On September 21, 1971, Mary Kyer and other representatives of the League of Women Voters and the Springs Area Beautiful Association (SpABA) filed a class action suit against the city. The suit's stated intent was to clarify the trust established by Palmer for the parklands and establish the duties of the trustees, i.e., the City of Colorado Springs.[40]

The city filed a motion to dismiss the action; this was denied by Judge Patrick Hinton on January 10, 1972. A *Gazette Telegraph* article at the time noted the suit also alleged the city planned to locate a filter plant and conduits for municipal water across North Cheyenne Cañon, intended to use part of Palmer Park for an access road to Academy Boulevard, and was engaged in negotiation for the sale of Monument Valley Park.[41]

A declaratory judgment on the case was rendered by Judge Hinton on February 14, 1974. Stating the City of Colorado Springs, as trustee of the parklands, had a fiduciary duty not to violate the restrictions set forth in the deeds, the judgment established the city would not "be a party to nor engage in any activities which will result in sale, disposition of, loss of or diminished use of said park lands solely as parks." With no admission of any violation of the trust, the city was charged to "preserve and protect the parklands" with "undivided loyalty" and the exercise of "reasonable care."[42] In effect, the court determined building a road through Monument Valley Park would be a violation of the deed's restrictions. The plan was dropped. Colorado Springs was confirmed in its obligation to loyally protect and preserve its parklands.

The earlier reversionary rights controversy simmered for several years before being resolved in 1977. That February, City Council agreed to buy the mineral and reversionary rights held by Palmer's heirs on Palmer Park and Monument Valley Park for a sum of $95,000. But Larry Ochs—by then mayor of the city—was criticized for the secretive manner in which years of talks with the heirs' attorney had taken place. Representatives of the League of Women Voters, the Parks and Recreation Advisory Board, the Springs Area Beautiful Association (SpABA), the Citizen's Lobby, the North End Homeowners Association, and the Northeast Traffic Committee all expressed dismay over the manner in which the deal occurred, and urged further consideration of possible implications. They feared the arrangement might threaten the protected status of Palmer's parks.

In support of the agreement Ochs had negotiated, the city's legal counsel opined that, even without the threat of reversion (that was to be removed), the city still could not change the park and recreational purposes of the land without a vote of the citizens. SpABA's attorney agreed in general with the city's counselor, but vigorously opposed the idea that even a citizen vote could change General Palmer's restrictions, which many believed sacrosanct, particularly in light of the 1974 declaratory judgment.

Other City Council members argued that the city would only benefit by getting rid of the reversionary clause, as the reversionary and mineral rights could have been sold to a third party who might decide, for example, to extract coal from below Palmer Park, where substantial deposits lay. The argument within the Council and between concerned citizens was heated and divisive, and it revealed a deep level of disagreement and distrust.[43] Two weeks later, facing a skeptical public, the mayor and four members of the City Council agreed to "set in concrete" its verbal commitment to preserve Palmer-donated parklands through a court order or the city charter, or both.[44]

Discord was obvious. City Council's disagreements over parks were many. Being held in a public forum, meetings revealed a dissension between members that left many residents with a skeptical and sometimes untrusting perception of their city leaders. To further confound issues, Council members were often at odds as to what was the appropriate funding mechanism for parks, and how best to distribute funds. In 1974, the Park Advisory Board almost officially censured City Council for infighting over distribution of park funds, as Council members argued over which individual's district was receiving "the biggest slice of the park budget pie":

> *The subject of where park and recreation money is spent broke into the open at a Council meeting last month. During the debate over a $135,000 transfer of funds, so that additional recreational facilities could be built into a new School District 11 high school, Councilman Don Willman charged "it's just not right" that so much money was being spent in the northeast quadrant of the city and so little in the southeast quadrant which he represents. Although Willman didn't mention it, others have pointed out that the district he represents has only 88 acres of public parks while, for example, Councilman Leon Young's district has more than 1,000 acres.*[45]

By 1982, a double row of shade trees had grown tall along the grassy medians of city avenues.

This kind of infighting seemed unavoidable given the nature of City Council. Furthermore, being a political entity responsive to the changing priorities of city residents, the Council inevitably shifted its focus and priorities with each election. In 1975, the voters made a 180-degree turn in their choice of City Council members, voting in members representing "pocketbook issues" over a "quality of life/sensible growth" platform. They rejected all but one of seven bond issues—approving only the bond for the city's airport. They overwhelmingly rejected the proposed 10 percent earmark for open space. It was an election in which city residents emphatically voted for conservatism and frugality. This naturally affected the Parks Department management. In 1977, Richard Buerkle resigned his position, and Larry Schenk was hired as the new Director of the Parks Department.

MOVING FORWARD

By 1979, winds shifted once again. That year Colorado Springs citizens passed a $2.5 million dollar bond issue to support their parks. Much was being accomplished. The White House Ranch was placed on the National Register of Historic Places, and the Living History Association was formed to provide volunteer support for special events and fund-raising for site restoration.[46] The new Pioneers Museum had opened in 1979, receiving 63 percent of its funding from grants and donations the first two years of operation.[47] Trail restoration at the Garden of the Gods had been ongoing since 1977, with the laying of new trails or upgrading old eroded ones, to help make the inner park more accessible to more people. In recognition of the Park Department's accomplishments, the Tree City USA award had been granted to the Forestry Program in 1977, the first Colorado program to be so recognized and an honor that would be repeated for the next thirty-three years.

The White House Ranch buildings adjoining the Garden of the Gods, 1980.

Serious problems had surfaced for Colorado Springs parks during the 1960s and 1970s—problems of unanticipated growth, lagging resources, conflicting citizen needs and expectations, reactionary planning, political infighting, and insufficient funding. But they were largely resolved through the genuine commitment, civic concern, and rational (though sometimes heated) communication of citizens and city leaders. City residents had determined what issues were important to them and clearly expressed their concerns and interests at critical moments. They rose to the challenge of funding their parks and passed important tax and bond issues. Leadership developed out of mutual cooperation between active citizens and committed city administrators. Conflicts were resolved. A map for the future was in place.

Ultimately, the robust development of recreational programs, acquisition of new parklands, responsiveness to the need for care and maintenance of existing parks, resolution of problems, and outreach to all segments of the population gratified many. City residents enjoyed the availability and accessibility of places and programs that met their needs as well as the continuation of a parks program that reflected the values of the city's founding father—service to others, civic duty, land conservation, the right to freedom expressed through play, and the preservation of natural beauty. As evidenced by citizens' active involvement in city politics, their votes in favor of park funding, and their enthusiastic daily usage of their parks, the community was thriving and the future for Colorado Springs parks looked bright.

A Junior Docent program developed as part of the Living History program at the White House Ranch.

Median design near Memorial Park features racing cyclist, 1980s.

The System Blossoms

1980–1990: A Carousel of Parks, Plans, and Programs

"The public park, more than any other component of the city, reflects the life and vitality of the city and its people."

—Galen Cranz, *The Politics of Park Design*

PROGRESS, PRESERVATION, AND PLANNING

On September 28, 1980, the Parks Department scheduled a marathon dedication of twenty-one new parks and facilities, demonstrating to the public how their money was being spent.[1] Many citizens had combined forces to advocate for their own neighborhood parks, and these volunteer groups participated in the day's programs enthusiastically. Neighborhood communities organized special events at each park, a reflection of their interest and willingness to work together for what they wanted.[2]

The Parks Department in 1980 had eighty-nine neighborhood parks, four community parks, and nine regional parks to manage—a total over one hundred—compared to just forty parks in 1970. Major purchases of open space during the late 1970s and early 1980s included Pulpit Rock (192 acres), Austin Bluffs (76 acres), most of Ute Valley, and additions to the Garden of the Gods. And more parkland was to come. The next official dedication would occur in September 1987, designated the "Celebration of Parks 1987," with the recognition of fourteen new parks.[3] By then, the Parks and Recreation Department held responsibility for 7,268 acres of parkland.

Nonetheless, the backlog of designated parks awaiting development remained a nagging problem for Colorado Springs. Citizens were frustrated by the roller-coaster ride of promises for neighborhood play areas and disappointments when they did not appear. In 1980, less than a month after the dedication of the twenty-one new parks, City Council was faced with a curtailed capital improvement program for 1981. Of the thirty-eight projects recommended for development, seventeen were deleted, including Sand Creek Park, just west of the municipal airport. Residents were dismayed:

> *"We have a lot of kids in the neighborhood, and the only place they have to play is in the street," said Victor Morales. . . . "[For] the people that drive down Fountain to the airport, the school children markers are just a waste of time. Everybody's hitting 50 mph or better."*[4]

The tension between those who were upset and dissatisfied over the lack of development of their local parks and playgrounds for their children and others who reported high satisfaction with the Colorado Springs Parks programs would surface repeatedly in the decades to come.

The parks' 1982 budget experienced an upswing, growing 8 percent over the 1981 figures, and prospects were promising. The *Gazette Telegraph* noted that "[i]n spite of problems, the system is growing," reporting that "[l]and deeds are being signed, designs drawn, trails built, swings installed, trees planted. From one end of Colorado Springs to the other, the city park system continues to grow and take shape."[5] Additional trail work in the Garden of the Gods was completed. The Parks Department extended Shooks Run Park from Willamette Avenue to Cache La Poudre Street, renovated and built trails in Palmer Park, developed other pathways according to the city's Multi-Use Trail Plan, opened and improved smaller neighborhood parks throughout the city, paved space for parking at the Four Diamonds Complex on North Nevada Avenue, and acquired and developed trails between Bijou Street and El Paso County's Bear Creek Regional Park.

Shooks Run Park playground, 1986.

As more was acquired, more needed to be done. Early on, Bill Ruskin, the Department's Superintendent of Design and Development, cautioned, "A park is never fully developed. There is always something that can be done to improve it. [The most difficult aspect of a park's development] is to keep it together. Every one has 100 problems."[6] More parks required more preservation, protection, and maintenance. Lawns had to be mowed, trees trimmed, playgrounds repaired, trash removed, flowers planted, gardens watered, playing fields groomed—with each new acquisition came increasing responsibilities. The Parks Department staff rose to the occasion, meeting daily challenges with optimism, dedication, and professionalism.

Neighborhood park playground covered with fresh snow, 1980s.

Vandalism remained a knotty problem throughout the parks, adding pressure to the ongoing need for maintenance. In 1980, City Council discussed a crackdown on people who littered and vandalized city parks, noting the difficulty in patrolling them. In 1982, Park Police Chief Cliff Howe reported that Palmer Park experienced problems with "school age people go[ing] there to drink and race cars"; Cheyenne Cañon was a "frequent scene of vandalism, shooting, climbing injuries, and drinking parties"; unknown vandals drove over grassy areas, shot bullet holes through signs, tore apart fence rails for late night open fires, and committed other destructive acts.[7] The 1983 Master Plan for Memorial Park, the site of the popular Fourth of July celebrations and Labor Day Hot Air Balloon festivals, remarked upon the "tension between Hispanic and Puerto Rican groups" using the park, and noted problems with congestion, unruly crowds, traffic hazards, damaged lawns and landscaping, excessive noise, and crime.[8]

Efforts to protect the vast investment in parks were genuine but limited. In 1962, there were two designated park patrolmen for twenty-five parks; in 1982, six police officers—two on duty at any given time—were responsible for one hundred four parks; in 1988 the Park Police Program was transferred to the City Police Department, and by 1990, city police could no longer designate patrolmen specifically for park coverage. Officials contended the parks were safe, that problems consisted primarily of damage and destruction. They called upon citizens themselves to be sensible, responsible, and trustworthy.

THE GIFTS OF VOLUNTEERS—GENEROSITY, BEAUTIFICATION, AND COMMITMENT

Many did show themselves to be not only responsible and trustworthy, but generous beyond expectations. Through the decades, the Parks Department had received numerous gifts of time, land, money, and materials offered by individuals, firms, and organizations. The Junior League of Colorado Springs had committed itself to enhancing the park system since the 1970s, when they developed a nature trail for physically disabled and visually impaired individuals at the White House Ranch. They later

Top: Bijou Street entrance to Monument Valley Park.

Bottom: Volunteers cultivate gardens on North Cascade Avenue.

established a docent program there for the blind and handicapped. The League had been amongst the coalition of sponsors for Spring Spree, the annual festival in Monument Valley Park and the downtown area first held in 1979, an outgrowth of earlier spring festivals. In 1980, the Junior League contributed $1,900 for a new playground in Monument Valley from the proceeds of that year's event.[9]

Indeed, the Junior League made many contributions to the parks during the 1970s and 1980s, reflecting their long-term commitment to the well-being of the community and beautification of the park system. In February 1981, the Junior League provided two years of funding for the first salaried volunteer coordinator to be hired by the Parks Department, Joan Vermaire, with the city providing the benefits package. In 1982, the Junior League and Silverado Savings and Loan Association joined with the Parks and Recreation Department to restore the formal gardens at the Bijou Street entrance to Monument Valley Park. With the Parks Department performing the work, the League assumed fund-raising responsibilities and Silverado donated $20,000 toward the first phase, sprinkler installation. The League's comprehensive fund-raising effort for the project comprised three areas: a volunteer program, a park matching fund, and the Parks Gift Catalog.[10]

On April 16, Arbor Day, Junior League members launched a $6,400 drive to purchase 165 trees for the gardens. A Parks Department spokesperson described the restoration, designed by landscape architect Gene Fuhlrodt:

> *When completed, the formal gardens will have beds of zinnias, daffodils, roses and begonias. Also planned are shrubs, hedges, a lawn area, gravel walkways and two daises which can be used for a number of different events, such as a symphony concert.*[11]

Many other local citizens also sponsored programs, assisted with renovations, and contributed to the parks. In 1981 alone, the Parks Department collected more than $150,000 in donations. Other citizens (including members of the Horticultural Arts Society who had long supported public gardens in Colorado Springs) volunteered to help cultivate and nurture the remarkable flowerbeds for which Colorado Springs had become famous. In 1983, nine local residents committed to provide care for many of the city's beds under the coordination of Bill Brandenburg of the Parks Department. Each volunteer was assigned one flowerbed for the season. Mary Garnhart, who weeded her Monument Valley flowers with her father every Friday morning, explained her motivation:

> *I feel I have a little part of it. They do such a good job making the city look pretty. If I can do just a little bit, that helps. It gives me pride, even if it means pulling weeds. I remember when I was a kid how the flowers [in Monument Valley] used to be. I want to help them get it back [at least] halfway. . . .* [12]

Volunteers assist with trail building in North Cheyenne Cañon.

People volunteered for a variety of reasons: some wanted to learn more about flowers, some wanted to help the city, others loved the gardens, and still other apartment-dwellers were eager for outside space and a garden to work in. They not only added to the aesthetics of the city through their own efforts, but also freed up Parks greenhouse maintenance crews to spend more time on other beds.

In 1986, volunteers gave 114,748 hours of free labor to the Parks and Recreation Department, the equivalent of fifty-five full-time employees. In 1987, the Department established a "People for the Parks" pilot program, which provided for neighborhood maintenance of small natural areas; this was expanded to the Residents Park Assistant Program in 1988. Volunteers also regularly donated their time to maintaining their locally loved retreats, rebuilding overgrown trails in North Cheyenne Cañon, for example, and assisting with small tree planting, installing benches and picnic tables, and completing other tasks.

By the end of the 1980s, the Parks Department facilitated the organization of the "Friends of . . ." Groups, a coming together of local residents with vested interests in particular parks and the willingness to become advocates for them. The Friends Groups not only cared for their parks but also acted as strong citizen advocates at City Council meetings. The Friends of the Garden of the Gods was the first such group, forming in 1991. The Friends of Cheyenne Cañon was formed in 1993 to provide assistance in that park. In cooperation with the Rocky Mountain Nature Association, they sold educational materials at the regional park visitors centers, a potential savings of $50,000 to the city.

The year 1988 also saw the beginning of the GreenSprings Project, a volunteer effort that would continue into the 1990s. Each year, around Arbor Day, hundreds of citizen volunteers helped plant thousands of trees and flowers in medians, interchange quadrants, and other areas throughout the city. Trees selected for planting—such as hackberry, honey locust, ponderosa pine, juniper, and piñon pine—were generally drought resistant and required minimal watering. Sponsored by individual groups, local businesses

Clockwise from upper left: Pink, white, red, and purple petunias in median; Bijou Garden median, a major entrance to downtown Colorado Springs; median on North Wahsatch by Bon Shopping Center; North End median in diamond-shaped design; an array of color in downtown median; GreenSprings volunteers plant saplings on Arbor Day.

and corporations, the Partnership in Community Design, and the Parks and Recreation Department, the volunteer effort succeeded in adding many new trees and flowers to the city's vistas.

PARKS AND PARKWAYS ENHANCE CITY IMAGE

Beautification of the city had been a priority for the Parks Department since General Palmer first established the system, and this emphasis continued during the 1980s. One of the many individuals who provided impetus to this program was Gene Fuhlrodt. Landscape designer for the Parks Department since 1973, Fuhlrodt was widely respected as "the master planner of the city's gorgeous flowerbeds."[13] Following a long tradition of floral creativity, his 1982 designs included ninety flowerbeds, and, for downtown, fourteen tubs of flowers, thirty-six hanging baskets, and one hundred planters. Using petunias, zinnias, marigolds, ageratum, alyssum, coleus, geraniums, flowering cabbage, and flowering kale—all grown in city greenhouses—Parks Department workers put the plants in around Memorial Day, creating a lovely show by July for all who drove the city streets.

Price Oden, foreman of the city's greenhouses, had worked with the Parks Department from 1941 to 1989—a period of forty-eight years. In a 1989 *Gazette Telegraph* interview, Oden noted that during his career the number of flowerbeds went from 20 to 147, with another 216 shrub beds planted. Designs and plans had evolved from off-the-cuff arrangements to carefully hand-drawn creations to computer imaginations. Notable were the beds in Memorial Park, in front of the velodrome, featuring a cyclist in silver, blue, white, red, purple, and yellow flowers, and the colorful Olympics five-ring logo. Upon retirement, Oden remarked his favorite was "[t]he four intertwined arcs of yellow pansies, orange spice marigolds, and red geraniums at the intersection of North Nevada and Willamette Avenues."[14]

Top: Flowerbed features Olympics five-ring logo at Memorial Park.

Middle: Pansies, marigolds and geraniums at North Nevada and Willamette Avenues.

Bottom: Price Oden, foreman of the city's greenhouses.

Planting and preservation of trees also beautified the city. The once tree-

Formal flowerbed in Monument Valley Park.

less Colorado Springs flourished with tree-lined boulevards in 1986, in large part due to the Urban Forestry Division of the Parks and Recreation Department. The division supported the City Landscape Ordinance that detailed landscaping requirements for every kind of residential and commercial development and extended assistance and advice to local residents.

The average street tree in Colorado Springs in 1986 was worth $1,000, "and we have several in the city that are valued at $30,000," City Forester Ron Morrow remarked in a 1986 interview.[15] The value was not in the lumber, but in the trees as living additions to property; they reduced air and noise pollution, sheltered homes, trapped dust and pollen, lowered urban temperatures, stabilized soil, and provided beauty to property. The Parks' Urban Forestry Division offered four street-tree programs to homeowners: The Decade of Trees, the New Subdivision Tree Ordinance, the Cooperative Tree Planting Program, and the Tree Replacement Program, all to motivate the planting and watering of urban trees.

Colorado Springs continued to be recognized with the Tree City, USA Award in 1988, an honor it had received annually since 1977. By then it counted over 85,000 trees in the street and park tree inventory, estimated at a value of over $1 million. More than a thousand trees were added each year through the home planting programs; in 1988, 110,000 flowers were planted in 280 public beds and planters—all the responsibility of the Parks and Recreation Department.[16] The flourishing urban gardens and forests were a pleasurable attraction valued both by those who lived in and those who visited the community.

1982 PARKS MASTER PLAN UPDATE

The 1976 Master Plan for Colorado Springs Parks had been adopted as a map for the next fifteen years, with the intention of revisiting and updating it regularly. Plans for the first revision began in March 1981 with a call for public comment. At a cost of $36,000, the revision would include a reworking of the overall Master Plan up through the year 2000, with a more detailed five-year plan to cover 1982 through 1986. Funded by the federal Heritage Conservation Action and Recovery Service with matching funds from City Services, Baldwin and Bauer Consultants were hired to oversee the update.

A random sample survey of six hundred city residents was conducted and several public meetings were held in March and April. The Open Space Advisory Committee also served as a forum for citizen discussion and input. Results showed that despite the occasional dissatisfaction of individual neighborhood groups over the lack of development of their local parks, most citizens were largely satisfied with park maintenance, accessibility, and program quality. They wanted additional programs, new facilities, and further acquisition of open space. Residents believed there was a strong need for Parks and Recreation services, but also felt that the system should be based upon the city's ability to pay for it.

Ideas abounded. Hopes were high. Initial proposals included a recreation center with an Olympic-sized swimming pool in Briargate; a community park in the Norwood subdivision; 150 acres of additional golf course land; a velodrome; proposals for land acquisition in the Houck estate property in northeast Colorado Springs; the construction of a visitors center and walkway system for the Garden of the Gods; and improvements to Monument Valley Park, Palmer Park, the White House Ranch, Patty Jewett Golf Course, and Memorial Park.[17] The possibility of a motorcycle park was discussed and strongly supported by several citizens, as was the acquisition of more land for trails for hikers, bicyclists, joggers, and horseback riders.[18] In many ways, the parks were being asked to provide all things to all people: recreation, leisure, special events, athletics, community services, trails, open space, garden retreats, and greenways. Some of these hopes would be realized. Others would not.

Left: The Colorado Springs Parks Department received the National Grand Award for "excellence in the field of park management" from the Sports Foundation in 1983.

Top: The Colorado Springs Veterans Memorial in Memorial Park bordered by geraniums, marigolds, and other blooms. The Memorial, of granite, marble, concrete, and bronze, was constructed in 1968 to honor the five military services.

The revised Master Plan was approved by City Council on November 24, 1981, as "a guide to the future for setting of future goals, not a policy."[19] It reaffirmed the goals and objectives of the 1976 plan, included a new five-year Capital Improvement Program (C. I.P.), and focused on meeting the needs of citizens and visitors alike. Its recommendations had been coordinated with three other important plans: the 1976 Garden of the Gods Master

Plan, the 1981 Monument Valley Trail Plan, and the 1981 Trails and Use Master Plan.[20]

The Master Plan's short-range proposals specifically addressed the needs for development and maintenance of new and existing neighborhood and regional parks and sports facilities. Long-range planning included considerations for open space acquisition and preservation, review of major subdivision developments, trail corridor acquisition in line with the Multi-Use Trail provisions, development of master plans for existing and regional parks, development of more sports facilities, attention to critical drainage issues, and administrative and planning issues.

Top: Cottonwood Creek Park, deeded to the city in 1985, under construction.

Bottom: Cottonwood Creek playground, 2010.

COTTONWOOD CREEK LEADS NEW PARKS

One of the immediate priorities highlighted in the 1982 Master Plan update was the creation of a large community park for residents in the northeast area of the city. Throughout the 1980s, the Parks Department acquired and developed neighborhood parks and open space as the city continued to grow, but the burgeoning population in the northeast section of the city still lacked a large recreational area to serve the entire community. This deficiency was addressed in 1985, when the city accepted a deed for seventy-seven acres of parkland and water rights for Cottonwood Creek Park from the developers of the Norwood area. The donation fulfilled the requirements of the Parkland Dedication Ordinance; the developers also agreed to pay an additional $39,000 for drainage improvements as well as provide topsoil and make other improvements—a generosity that exceeded the ordinance requirements.

Cottonwood was an important acquisition that provided significant recreational space for residents in the newer areas of the city. Plans for the park—on a scale similar to Memorial Park—were released that spring. They featured four soccer and three softball fields, two gyms, a recreation center, racquetball and tennis courts, a swimming pool, picnic and play areas, and ponds. Development began in 1986 with the construction of the playground, softball fields, soccer fields, and parking.

Bill Ruskin, superintendent of Design and Development for the Parks Department, noted at the time that a well-organized and enthusiastic group of soccer players "had a lot to do with moving [plans for the park] up. They did get council's attention."[21] Subsequent development of Cottonwood would include tennis courts, walking paths, additional restrooms, a disc golf course and a recreation center, an indoor swimming pool, gymnasiums, fitness rooms, and shower/locker facilities.

The designed median and arch on North Nevada honors the city's "sister city" relationship with Fujiyoshida, Japan, begun in 1962. Colorado Springs Sister Cities International (CSSCI) helps develop and coordinate international relationships for the city's artistic, educational, cultural, and economic benefit. In 2010, Colorado Springs partners with six sister communities around the world.

During the 1980s, several new parkland areas also were designated, community services were expanded, and the large variety of sports and athletic programs were extended.[22] But local frustration with the lack of neighborhood park development continued to plague the system. In 1988, of the twenty-six neighborhood park sites the city had acquired since 1970, fourteen remained undeveloped. Another eleven were only partially developed. In October 1987, Director Schenk explained to City Council the restrictions of the tightened 1988 budget that allowed for only a .08 percent increase:

> *"The department usually develops two to three parks annually," [Schenk] said. . . . "[But] that spending increase [in the 1988 budget] covers only a slight hike in employee salaries and benefits and provides no new money for park development. . . .[It] also would eliminate four Park and Recreation jobs that have gone unfilled." . . . Although painting a gloomy picture during his comments before the council, Schenk said afterward that the slow development of parks is merely a reflection of the poor local economy. Once the economy picks up, he said, the department will resume its normal park development schedule.*[23]

CREATIVE COMMUNITY PROGRAMS A BOON TO CITY

The Old Farm Community Center provided local residents daycare for their children.

In the face of financial limitations, the Parks Department nonetheless found ways to build impressive programs. One of the widespread benefits provided by Parks and Recreation during the 1980s was the development and expansion of community and service centers throughout the city. These centers extended comprehensive support and innovative programs to residents of all ages and across all income levels. They offered senior services, nutritional and food programs, social events and educational classes, emergency services, outdoor and indoor recreational programs, environmental programs, after-school programs, kindergarten readiness and pre-school activities, teenage activities, therapeutic programs, and human services programs. Activities emphasizing health, socialization, educational resources, and recreation were designed to support all neighborhood residents: preschoolers through adults.

Top: Meadow Parks Community Center.

Middle: Hillside Community Center.

Bottom : Playground at Otis Park.

By the end of the decade, facilities serving the community included four community centers: Deerfield Hills in the southeast section of the city, Hillside (originally in the old Sinton home on South El Paso and moved to South Institute in 1990), Meadow Parks in the Stratton Meadows neighborhood, and Old Farm in the northeast section of the city. Senior centers at Acacia downtown next to Acacia Park and in the Human Services Complex at Golf Acres and the Beidleman Environment Center in Sondermann Park served city residents as well. Otis Park in Knob Hill was one of the first centers to provide therapeutic services for persons with disabilities.

In the Knob Hill neighborhood, the wheelchair-accessible Otis Park Community Center housed programs for people with disabilities and offered a playground designed to encourage motor-skill development for children with special needs. The park earned the Parks and Recreation Department a National Sports Foundation award in 1986 for service to people who are mentally or physically challenged. In 1988, the Parks Department completed a Therapeutic Five Year Master Plan that established a two-fold purpose for Otis Park: to provide recreational and social neighborhood programs and to integrate persons with disabilities into community recreational programs.

Another landmark community project was the Colorado Springs Senior Center, housed within the Human Services Complex. It opened in the Golf Acres Center in 1986 to offer seniors a place where they could learn, visit, eat, and play. Located in the seventeen-thousand-square foot former Johanneson Supermarket on North Hancock, the comprehensive center offered a forum for services, classes, and programs. It became a catalyst for new ideas and information affecting seniors. Programs emphasized wellness—including exercise classes, walking and biking tours, lecture series, and a free medical clinic for screenings. Places were provided for organizations to meet, distribute information, or offer referrals. Educational programs included college level classes; dance, drama, computer, and music classes; travel opportunities and lectures; art programs, and social opportunities. There was a large area for arts and crafts—woodworking, lapidary, pottery, and painting—as well as a photographic gallery and darkroom. The center also scheduled dances with a live band each week.

Considering the Senior Center a "great asset to the city," research analyst Jim Alice Scott noted it "serve[s] as a great example of how the public and private sectors can create something very neat together."[24] The Golf Acres

Shopping Center building had been a gift to the city from the Community Council of the Pikes Peak Region. The organization Pikes Peak Seniors Inc. launched a major fund-raising campaign to raise half the cost of transforming the facility into the Senior Center—$350,000—which the city then planned to operate as a self-supporting enterprise fund. Malinda Groening, president of Pikes Peak Seniors, noted:

> *We've been working on this for about three years. . . . This will give elders an opportunity for sociability and learning new things. We've been in many other centers to look them over and there are few with as broad a program as we will have.* [25]

Nancy Lewis, then Parks Leisure Services Superintendent, praised the Pikes Peak Seniors' resourcefulness, commenting, "We raised $225,000 to complete Otis Park, and I have the same kind of confidence in people involved with this. The project belongs to them."[26] An early example of successful public-private partnerships, the Human Services Complex would ultimately lease space to several non-profit agencies in the Senior Center along with some commercial businesses, providing an array of services.

In the heart of Colorado Springs, the Beidleman Environmental Center in Sondermann Park was dedicated as an environmental area and educational forum in honor of Dick and Reba Beidleman on September 26, 1987.[27] Sondermann Park itself stood on the original Upton Gardens Nursery property, which had operated from 1918 to 1948.[28] The city purchased the land in 1982 and operated summer environmental education and adventure-play activities there for children. Fall classes and school programs began with the opening of the Beidleman Center, whose purpose was "to help people understand fragile ecosystems and a riparian life zone (unique to the area), to appreciate the land's beauty, and to become good stewards of the land so that this island of untouched nature in the middle of the city may be preserved."[29]

Environmental educational programs and adventure play activities engaged children at Beidleman Environmental Center.

The Center provided school programs, group programs, a meeting place, workshops, and camps for children. It offered classes for preschoolers, children and parents together, elementary aged children, adults, and seniors. Rich with flowers, birds, animals, foliage, and trails, it provided the community with many unique opportunities for environmental education and volunteering.[30]

Throughout the 1980s, the Parks and Recreation Department contributed numerous diverse resources for the recreation, learning, and pleasure of all members of the community. In addition to

Future Living History events at the Garden of the Gods would celebrate the bicentennial of the Zebulon Montgomery Pike expedition, 2006.

providing adult education classes, after-school activities, and early childhood programs, the Department was an active member of a "Very Special Arts Program" and supported a series of visual and performing arts. Productions of Shakespeare in the Park, the presentation of "Legends and Legacy" at the Garden of the Gods, and Fine Arts Center performances of children's plays took place throughout the city's parks. Square dances, jazz groups, and brown bag lunch series occurred in Acacia Park.

Lunchtime entertainment at Acacia Park bandstand.

Summer programs included Great Explorations (evolved from Tot Lots), Summerville for elementary children in low-income neighborhoods, and Quest, which offered a variety of classes in kitchen skills, art, and movement to spark the interest of children unfamiliar with these activities. The Day Camp Program provided education in outdoor living skills and recreational activities for young people. At the White House Ranch and Cheyenne Cañon, with support from the local volunteers and the Living History Association, the Parks Department provided visitor services and interpretive programs that treated visitors to historical, environmental, and informative education about the areas. Countless people attended and enjoyed the wide range of Parks and Recreation programs.

TRAILS FOR ALL AGES

While "urban" trails were a unique and relatively new phenomenon across the country, surveys showed that trail use had become the single most popular outdoor recreation activity in Colorado by 1986; those who bicycled, hiked, ran, jogged, and rode horseback were individuals of all ages and abilities. Their growing interests focused more demands on the city's Parks and Recreation Department.

Interest in developing a citywide trail system for Colorado Springs—a priority long promoted by the Pikes Peak Area Trails Coalition—had been strongly expressed since the early 1970s. Yet by 1986, less than 25 miles of multi-use trails had been built in Colorado Springs, despite the 1981 plan proposing over 120 miles of trails.[31] To improve that situation, a comprehensive Multi-Use Trails Master Plan (revised and released by the Parks Department and the Public Works Department in May 1986) identified opportune trail corridors, set a standard of trail design and maintenance, and addressed the issue of implementation for the city—how to make a quality trails system a reality.

The plan identified eighteen trail corridors totaling one hundred miles, a reduction from the earlier 1981 plan, yet still a major undertaking.[32] The corridors were selected to provide an interconnected system of loops along the central spine of Monument Valley that would provide access to parks, scenic areas, and open space, as well as create an off-street circulation system throughout the city.[33] Not formally approved, the plan was subjected to revision again in 1987.[34] The resultant 1988 Colorado Springs Multi-Use Trails Master Plan confirmed the proposed system of interconnected linkages that would tie elements of the city together through a system of trails located along natural waterways and across open space. It recommended one mile of useful trail per two thousand population, a National Parks standard.[35]

Urban trails would remain a priority for Colorado Springs residents and the Parks and Recreation Department in the years to come. A dedicated group of Colorado Springs citizens had worked persistently to create a visible, viable plan for a citywide trail system, knowing a system could be created within a reasonable amount of time, but only with a major expansion in the level of funding. In 1987, the Pikes Peak Area Trails Coalition legally organized as a non-profit citizens group created "to preserve open space and rural land and to create a network of trails, bikeways, and greenways in the Pikes Peak region." It would later be renamed the Trails and Open Space Coalition (TOSC).[36] The coalition would remain a strong advocate for trails and open space over the next twenty-plus years. Ultimately, when additional funding sources were obtained through the Greater Outdoors Colorado lottery fund (GOCO) and a voter-approved sales tax increase (TOPS) in the 1990s, a comprehensive urban trail system within the city would unfold.

Y.A.L. players pass and tackle.

SPORTS AND SPECIAL ENTERPRISES: QUALITY OUTDOOR RECREATION

Many local residents in the 1980s equated the Parks and Recreation Department with the wide range of sports programs for youth, ages four to seventeen. By 1988, Parks and Recreation organized 650 teams in nine sports: hockey, basketball, soccer, t-ball, baseball, tackle football, flag football, track, and girls' softball. More than 10,000 youth participated that year, learning and practicing fundamental skills and good sportsmanship in recreational settings, guided by trained volunteer coaches. Revenue-generating (through fees) adult sports programs included leagues for men, women, and combined (co-recreational) teams in softball, volleyball, flag football, basketball, and fast pitch softball. The two self-sustaining golf courses, Patty Jewett and Valley Hi, remained popular, with annual revenues providing for the operation and capital development of programs and facilities.[37]

In late October 1986, the city acquired Ski Broadmoor from the Broadmoor Hotel, which was about to close the facility due to rising insurance costs. The small, steep ski slope located on Cheyenne Mountain behind the Broadmoor Hotel had provided Colorado Springs residents daily skiing and nightly recreation during the winter months since the 1940s. Many local children first learned to ski in the Broadmoor's "hats" program, moving up to differently starred ski caps as their skill progressed. Hoping to retain the local ski area for the community, the city pledged to operate Ski Broadmoor as another self-sustaining program, similar to the golf course operations—funded with user fees and not tax dollars. With that charge, the Parks and Recreation Department was responsible for opening the ski area in four short weeks—by December 4—and achieved that goal to the praise of administrators and citizens alike.

Top: Girls Parks and Recreation SOCSY Team, 1984.

Bottom: Skiers stand at foot of Ski Broadmoor.

But in early 1987, department employees assigned to upgrade the ski area overspent their capital improvements budget by an unauthorized $350,000, funds that the city was forced to cover by drawing from other operations. In a typically tight budget year, with neighborhood parks sitting in disregard, citizens and city administrators were outraged at the overrun. As a result, Director Schenk and three others within the Parks and Recreation Department were reprimanded or dismissed.

CHANGES IN ADMINISTRATION

Nancy Lewis was named the new Director of the Parks and Recreation Department in December 1987. A twenty-two-year department veteran who had started as a $1.29-an-hour part-time recreation worker, Lewis was selected for "her experience in financial areas and control of budgets, plus her vision of how the Parks and Recreation Department will have to meet its needs in tight budget years, and how it has faced recent problems."[38]

Under her direction, the Parks Department worked to get Ski Broadmoor back into operation, ultimately returning it to the hotel in late 1988.[39] The operation divisions of the Parks Department were reorganized for increased efficiency, keeping maintenance levels high while holding the increasing costs of maintenance down. The four operating divisions included Park Operations and Construction, the newly created Natural Resources Division, Community Resources, and Recreation Facilities. These were administered and managed by two support divisions: Administration and Planning/Design.

Top: Palmer Park "hoodoos."

Bottom: Patty Jewett Golf Course, 1980s

Director Lewis expressed hopes to expand the existing park system, adding to the network of trails and neighborhood parks, and completing new community resources. "Principally, we're land managers," she said. "It's our responsibility to see that those lands are managed well, not just for this generation, but for generations to come."[40]

1980s BUDGET: LOTTERY OPPORTUNITIES

Park improvements in the early 1980s had been accomplished with dollars from the 1979 bond issue, as well as money from the city's capital improvement funds, federal matching grants through the Land and Water Conservation Fund, and donations. In November of 1980, Colorado state voters passed a state lottery motion, and the expected receipts to the city were anticipated to help grow and maintain the park system. Lottery funds kicked in by 1983. These moneys were deposited to the State Conservation Trust Fund and distributed annually to local government organizations on a pro rata population basis.

The first "share" of lottery funds that Colorado Springs received—$1.7 million in fall 1983—was used for capital improvement projects.[41] Officials expected $735,000 more in lottery money by September 1984. Some wanted to use it for acquisition of additional open space; others were in favor of developing lands already owned.

Top: Parks and Recreation playing field.

Bottom: Prospect Lake in fall, Pikes Peak in the background

Many expected state lottery revenues to solve the funding problem for smaller neighborhood parks, but this possibility was limited. Every new neighborhood park development added to future maintenance costs—$5,000 per acre annually to water and mow grass—causing park administrators to pause on new development. The department's capital improvement budget was already stretched to cover all its capital expenses: renovation and repair of existing parks and park buildings, planting trees, performing asphalt overlays of park roads, installing irrigation systems, even paying for street and sidewalk construction around its park sites. Any new development guaranteed new ongoing obligations.

Further complications came from state guidelines that stated lottery receipts given to individual governments could only be used for capital construction projects, such as park development, and not for maintenance. Maintenance funds had to come from the city's general fund. Eventually, it was determined that some lottery funds could be used for maintenance, but only the maintenance of those parklands originally obtained and developed with lottery funds.

So lottery receipts were spent on other park needs: improvements to existing parks, park equipment, and restroom construction. Only 14.2 percent—about $1 million—had gone to build up the existing vacant neighborhood parkland.[42] Gradually, due to a clause in the original bill allowing for some diversion of money, many lottery dollars would be used for other governmental capital construction projects outside of parks. Still, the lottery had provided a significant boost to the parks budget. Overall parks funding (including lottery moneys) grew 72 percent from 1983 to 1988—from $8,975,331 to $15,456,864—providing important support to the parks and their programs.

1980s BUDGET: INCONSISTENT FINANCES, INSUFFICIENT DOLLARS

Prior to the availability of lottery funds, the Parks Department had relied primarily on bonding and allocations from the city's general fund for capital improvements. Up through the late 1980s, these sources continued to support important projects, and in 1987 and 1988, new capital improvement support for Parks and Recreation came from the voter-approved ½ cent C.I.P. city sales tax and the Bed and Car Rental tax. Special funds from the department's self-sustaining enterprise programs (e.g., Patty Jewett and Valley Hi golf courses, the Human Services Complex, and Ski Broadmoor) supported those efforts.

Nonetheless, a looming problem simmered. City receipts were largely dependent upon sales taxation (also dependent on tourist dollars) rather than property taxes, which remained remarkably low in Colorado Springs; consequently, the city general fund was inevitably subject to the cyclic rising and falling of economic prosperity. Every slowdown in the local economy impacted allocations for Parks and Recreation operational funding. At the same time, local economic conditions even affected the ability of the Special Funds programs to break even: residents naturally curtailed their recreational activities whenever they felt the need to tighten their belts. While revenues from the State Lottery and the Parkland Dedication Ordinance were projected to grow, they would not necessarily keep pace with the projected land increase and population growth, and would not be sufficient to maintain necessary funding levels for the Parks and Recreation Department.[43]

In the economic slowdown of 1986 and 1987, the Parks Department experienced consecutive reductions in its maintenance and operations budget. As some positions went unfilled and others were eliminated, new neighborhood parks were cut. Residents complained. Like others before them, representatives from the Mountain Shadows Community and Piñon Valley Neighborhood Associations argued before City Council for money to develop their neighborhood land designated for parks, sitting unimproved and overgrown with weeds. But the department, only having sufficient funds for renovations and maintenance of existing parks, denied their requests. Citizens felt ignored and neglected.

In 1988, City Council made a half-hearted attempt to solve this problem. Agreeing to designate 10 percent of its sales and use tax revenues for parks and beautification, the Council flip-flopped two weeks later, declaring the city "shouldn't earmark capital improvement funds for specific departments without first considering other department needs."[44] The 5-4 split on Council reflected council members' disagreements over priorities. Councilwoman McNally protested, "I get calls from people who have young families . . . who move into an area because it's supposed to be next to a park and it ends up being a weed patch for ten years."[45] Others argued drainage work and other city improvements were more important.

Tensions were exacerbated with Council's decision to use $500,000 from its 1987 and 1988 lottery receipts to renovate the deteriorating grounds at Pioneer Square Park (formerly Alamo Park), home of the Pioneers Museum in downtown Colorado Springs. The expenditures were justified as being both a necessary improvement and a boost to downtown, but many residents criticized politicians for opting for showy improvements over sorely needed small neighborhood park development.[46]

Colorado Springs Pioneers Museum.

Further disagreements with City Council surfaced in 1987, when the city, looking for ways to increase funding for the parks, advertised in *The Wall Street Journal* for proposals to build a new, privately operated visitors center in the Garden of the Gods. The plans called for a lavish center next to the Gateway Rocks, gift shops, snack bars, some kind of tram, and a 350-car parking lot east of the rocks. Local citizens were outraged at the prospect of commercializing the Garden. Hundreds of angry residents deluged city hall with phone calls and packed meetings to denounce the plan. The city quickly retreated from the idea. Clearly, the public was adamantly opposed to any commercial development within the Garden, yet a plan for its management remained at bay. It would be seven years before the park's ecological deterioration was reversed in a massive restoration project.

While City Council prioritized beautification projects and more development of neighborhood parks in its 1989 budget, they knew they were still only plugging holes.[47] Foreseeing more financial problems, the 1988 Parks and Recreation Department Master Plan urged that "[t]he Parks and Recreation Department, City Council and City residents must continue to work together to seek alternative funding and implement programs so that the park and recreation needs of present and future residents can be met."[48]

1988 COLORADO SPRINGS OPEN SPACE, PARKS, AND RECREATION MASTER PLAN UPDATE

Work began on the 1988 Parks and Recreation Master Plan Update in 1986, a follow-up to the 1982 plan. By then, the Colorado Springs system consisted of 7,171 acres, including 114 parks, 2 professional-length golf courses, 3 recreation centers, 4 community centers, 2 senior centers, 5 special-use centers, 25 miles of multi-use trails, and 25 miles of streetscapes-parkways.

Top: Adult league play.

Bottom: Joggers run along Monument Creek, Monument Valley Park.

A citywide user survey revealed that citizens on the whole were pleased. They felt their parks were well maintained, clean, accessible, and convenient, offering a variety of recreational opportunities, though some were deterred from using them by lack of restrooms, crime, and distance. Older citizens favored maintenance and development of their neighborhood parks and lower taxation; younger respondents, who used all the parks more heavily, overall were more receptive to the idea of taxation for park purposes. Generally, people preferred turf grass areas of parkland, despite its higher cost, to native grass areas. Predictably, those awaiting development of their neighborhood parks continued to be dissatisfied.

The reported interests and desires reflected the nature of the community. Colorado Springs was home to many outdoors-oriented, health-conscious, environmentally aware individuals who enthusiastically endorsed the recreational opportunities and outdoors activities that the Parks Department provided. They wanted more: more neighborhood parks, more open space, more trails, more regional parks, and more community sports activities.

PARK AND RECREATION GOALS

In forming the 1988 Master Plan, the eleven-member steering committee and Parks and Recreation administrators reaffirmed those objectives and goals from the two prior master plans, but gave particular emphasis to these four goals:

- To provide both physical and visual continuity to the overall open space system
- To provide a broad range of conveniently located, quality recreational opportunities for all citizens of Colorado Springs and visitors to the city
- To develop an adequate level of financing, including alternative funding methods, for an expanded open space system and additional park and recreational facilities
- To provide a consistent, high level of maintenance for all elements of the Open Space, Park and Recreation System

Y.A.L. football players compete on local playing fields.

Authors of the Master Plan applied National Recreation Park Association (NRPA) standards to its assessment of Colorado Springs' current resources and programs, using the standard of 25 acres of parkland per 1,000 population as a desired benchmark. Except for the years from 1970-1982, the city had maintained this ratio (or better) for eighty-seven years. The challenge city leaders and park administrators faced in 1988 was to continue to acquire and develop parks to keep pace with the growing population, thereby meeting that standard, while also maintaining the department's current properties and programs.[49]

For the first time in the Colorado Springs Parks and Recreation Department history, the department officially defined categories of parks and their usage according to NRPA definitions in the 1988 plan: i.e., neighborhood, community (with playfields), regional, open space areas, urban trails, special parks (such as arenas, nature centers, street medians), active, and passive. While this promoted efficiency in analyzing, planning, and prioritizing, it also opened the door to a mindset that fostered homogenization of parks and formulaic, lockstep development. The implications of this would be felt in future years, as predictable play equipment and pre-programmed park designs were installed in both new and renovated parks.

LOOKING AHEAD

The 1988 Master Plan clearly described future challenges and reflected the resolve to meet them with commitment and energy. The Colorado Springs Parks and Recreation Department had impressively managed the increase in park resources, community services, and recreational opportunities. But as the city continued to grow, the list of immediately needed projects for parks and facilities was greater than could be realistically accomplished in the next six years. To address this dilemma, the 1988 Master Plan recommended a Capital Improvement Program (C.I.P.) rating system and seven-year development schedule.[50]

Top left: Basketball players at Cottonwood Creek.

Top right: Park playgrounds were soon to feature standardized equipment, as in the Cottonwood Creek playground developed in 2000.

The plan proposed a prioritized system for acquiring and developing new parks, developing existing parks, expanding the trails system, and upgrading and renovating older parks and facilities. It also recommended shifting from the intensely developed neighborhood parks to establishing smaller neighborhood parks that incorporated natural features, while concentrating on larger community parks for more intense active recreational use.

Even with prioritized planning, the Master Plan warned that "[w]ithout significant increases in the Parks and Recreation Department Capital Improvement Funding sources, the City's Parks and Recreation could continue to fall behind in meeting the needs of City residents."[51] It presented other funding methods and addressed the possibilities of using special districts for funding park development.[52] The emphasis was apparent: alternative methods of funding expansion were sorely needed.

Some solutions would surface in the 1990s through the Greater Outdoors Colorado (designated lottery) funds and a voter-approved sales tax increase dedicated to trails and open space. But the special metropolitan districts that were to evolve in the next two decades would not necessarily solve the financial problems for the Parks and Recreation facilities and programs, and, indeed, would create some unexpected backlash. Funding for capital improvement, maintenance and operations would continue to be supported largely through sales tax receipts, leaving these expenditures vulnerable to cyclical economic conditions. Local anti-tax movements would rise to stymie city spending on park improvements. Indeed, funding problems would plague the city and its Parks Department over the next two decades.

The Hot Air Balloon Festival, held annually over Labor Day weekend in Memorial Park, 1986.

The annual Garden of the Gods Run, begun in 1976, continues in 2010.

Something for Everyone

1990–2000: Purpose, Preservation, and Growth

"The very setting aside of ground for park activities is a collective recognition of the need for play . . . and parks will always be associated with the related ideas of spontaneity and freedom."

—Galen Cranz, *The Politics of Park Design*

The Colorado Springs parks system was poised to provide many benefits to citizens throughout the community at the beginning of the 1990s. From youth playing t-ball to adults competing in soccer leagues, from seniors in community centers to pre-schoolers in after-school care, from elementary kids learning to swim to toddlers playing on swings, from hikers venturing into open space to mountain bikers and skateboarders trying new moves to local residents picnicking at the Fourth of July fire-works—a thriving community anticipated partaking in many diverse park services.

But there was much to be done to meet everyone's needs and conflicting opinions as to how to accomplish goals were in play. Upcoming political maneuvering, new legal entities and voter-approved ballot measures ultimately complicated the system and fragmented the focus of the community. The parks were sustained through the dedicated efforts of park staff, local volunteers, and generous residents, who personally extended themselves time and again to redirect, recreate, and preserve a system that would provide the greatest good to all who lived in and visited the community.

BUDGET ADAPTATIONS

In 1989, the "wish list" for capital improvements was long and many desires remained unfulfilled; the needs list of projects totaled $90 million, while the parks department capital improvements budget amounted to only

$2.1 million annually. How to realistically balance hopes and expectations with income and expenditures remained a conundrum.

When the local economy was impacted by the 1991 recession, the Parks and Recreation Department responded to a city-required 5 percent cut in operating funds with prudent reductions. Various services—trash collection and disposal, weed spraying, and fertilizer application—were privatized. Public-private partnerships were explored. The department developed relationships with school districts, hospitals, sports organizations, the Olympic Training Center, Pikes Peak Library District, the Y, various church organizations, El Paso County Extension Office, UCCS Theatreworks, and others to offer programs and facilities to the public at the lowest possible cost to the user.

The department was responding to both a tightened annual budget and a general community resistance to public spending, which ultimately manifested itself in the 1992 passing of legislation called the Taxpayer's Bill of Rights, otherwise known as TABOR.[1] TABOR would hinder city planning and budgeting well into the future. A complicated law, TABOR "capped" government spending at whatever was spent the prior year, plus inflation (based on the Denver-Boulder consumer price index, essentially ignoring the real costs of such items as energy and insurance) and growth (defined as net new construction). If a city wanted to set aside savings to draw on in tough economic times, any money set aside would be included in the maximum spending allowed in following years—eliminating any budgetary benefit.[2]

Unforeseen consequences of TABOR would include what is now known as the "ratchet-down effect," the restricting of governmental receipts to a small increase in years following a recession. Essentially, when budgets dramatically decreased due to lowered tax revenues during recessionary periods, funding was prevented from returning to the stronger levels of healthier economic years upon economic recovery because TABOR would not allow it.[3] However much the budget may have dropped the previous year, it could only be increased to the limit allowed by inflation and growth indices during the next fiscal year.

In 2009, Rocky Scott, former head of the Colorado Springs Regional Economic Development Corporation, remembered the mood at the time TABOR was passed:

> *"I think what people thought they were voting for was 'let me vote on an increase in taxes,' [but] it's a little bit like doing an appendectomy with an ax."*[4]

TABOR would have a profound effect on all Colorado governmental spending in the coming decades. It generated endless ballot issues that asked voters to function as government accountants, spawned special interest advertising campaigns that further muddied issues, and resulted in asking voters to designate taxes to fund favorite causes, designations that neglected more mundane but still vital expenses—everyday needs like park maintenance and payroll.[5] Inevitably, its effects were felt by the Parks and Recreation Department.

THE RISE OF SPECIAL DISTRICTS

As the emerging complications of TABOR restricted the city's ability to finance new parks, drainage, and streets, developers of new property subdivisions in Colorado Springs adopted the practice of creating special districts to fund and manage the public infrastructure necessary to support their projects. This enabled developers to proceed with their developments; it would also further confound funding for citywide park and recreation programs.

By forming a special district, the developer acquired an effective financing tool and the city had its unfunded obligations for new public infrastructure met. The process was relatively easy. A service plan was created for the district, which was then subject to approval by the city (if the property was within city limits) or the county (if property extended beyond city limits). Once approved, the district acquired equal and independent standing with the city and other local governments, and could only be dissolved by the state.

Yucca Flats in Palmer Park.

Special district status conferred a range of powers to its independently elected board of directors: the authority to assess a property tax mill levy, collect public improvement fees, issue bonds, condemn property, enter contracts, sue or be sued, construct and operate facilities, and enforce covenants. The developer who formed a special district could obtain tax-exempt financing, while shifting costs to future property owners. Indeed, sometimes new residents would be paying back bond financing arranged through the district long after the developer was no longer involved.[6] By 1995, metropolitan special districts proliferated throughout the newer developing areas of Colorado Springs.[7]

The practice of creating special districts had unforeseen long-term negative effects for the city. The city's approval of their use inadvertently contributed to the balkanization of city neighborhoods and the consequent difficulty gaining communitywide support for city initiatives. Residents of special districts invariably paid higher taxes than those in other neighborhoods and therefore were less inclined to support general purpose taxes proposed by city government.[8] So proposals to raise funds to benefit older parks and neighborhoods often failed. Residents began to see themselves as separate from other neighborhoods, and the possibilities of a citywide vision were diminished. As Barry Noreen stated in his 2009 *Gazette* column:

> *When it comes to parks . . . the special districts do a good job providing for their residents. There's a question, though, about whether these separate enclaves are the best way to build a community for all.*[9]

GREATER OUTDOORS COLORADO FUNDS

The effects of voter initiatives and legislation were not the only issues to complicate the funding of parks. During the same 1992 election that saw the approval of TABOR, restricting government spending, voters overwhelmingly passed Amendment 8, allowing for the creation of the Greater Outdoors Colorado (GOCO) fund, to which lottery funds were redirected. Amendment 8's passage would enable the purchase of land for open space and wildlife habitat and the acquisition of water rights to ensure stream flows for boating and fishing. The 1992 GOCO fund was charged specifically with making investments in parks, wildlife, outdoor recreation, environmental education, open space and natural areas throughout the state.[10]

GOCO funds enabled the development of an extensive urban trail system; here a local resident enjoys the Mid Shooks Run Trail section in fall 2010.

While the original 1982 voter approval of the lottery system had directed that lottery moneys be used for acquisition of open land and the provision of outdoor recreation, a clause in the language had allowed legislators to spend these funds for other projects. Consequently, much of the Colorado Lottery receipts had been used to pay for prisons and other capital construction projects rather than open space, parks, and recreation.[11] The 1992 GOCO rectified this. It phased in a six-year repayment of the state's obligation on prisons, during which time $7 to $10 million was allocated to a parks and outdoors project fund. Then by 1998, all lottery profits were designated for four specific areas: state parks, local parks, open-space purchases and projects, and wildlife enrichment—each receiving 25 percent of net lottery proceeds. The GOCO fund was to be distributed through grants by a thirteen-member board of citizens from across the state. In a little over a year's time, the state board began spending GOCO funds.

GOCO would provide great benefits to the Colorado Springs Parks and Recreation system over the years, allocating funds annually for important projects that ranged from small neighborhood parks to significantly large land purchases and new development. In Colorado Springs, Vermijo and Woodmen Valley Parks; bike trails, shade structures, and other improvements in the Garden of the Gods; the "Goose" Gossage Youth Sports Center; Sinton Pond; Confluence Park; Palmer Park improvements; the Pikes Peak Greenway; Stratton Open Space; and Red Rock Canyon offer just a few examples of projects that would receive GOCO grant money.

"Goose" Gossage Youth Sports Center.

TABOR, special districts and the GOCO amendment set the stage for a complicated funding environment for the city. And, at the same time Colorado voters had passed Amendment 8 and TABOR, Colorado Springs voters chose to eliminate the city sales tax for capital improvements, phasing out a critical source for citywide capital construction projects—including parks—by 1996. This immediately restricted available funding for capital construction projects. No doubt, the financial message for parks was mixed.

PARKS: DEVELOPMENT AND MAINTENANCE

In the midst of financial uncertainties and jockeying for funds, the Parks and Recreation Department continued to work carefully to manage the burgeoning responsibilities of its many services. In 1988 and 1989, five new neighborhood parks were developed.[12] By 1991, another four were added.[13] A 1989 festival celebrated the renovation and reopening of Prospect Lake, revitalized with sod, sand, and new landscaping. The bathhouse was painted, docks improved, new picnic tables installed, and a second basketball court opened. A local Neighborhood Policing Unit was established to discourage criminal activity and restore the park to families and the community. Memorial Park gained six sunken volleyball courts in 1990, as well as new landscaping, sod, trees, and flowerbeds. The 1990 White House Ranch Master Plan focused on the restoration of historical elements and improvements in the interpretive program at the ranch.[14]

More projects were completed at numerous parks in 1991: renovating the Earl Bryson Fountain in the Formal Gardens at Monument Valley Park, replacing sidewalks and improving the band shell at Acacia, restoring the plaza and pavilion in Antlers Park, paving walkways in the Garden of the Gods, and renovating Palmer Park's Lazy Land picnic reservation area. The Patty Jewett Clubhouse restoration was completed in May 1992. Interpretive programming was improved at North Cheyenne Cañon's center as well as at the Garden of the Gods and the White House Ranch, where restoration of the 1907 Orchard House continued.

A particularly notable improvement was the completion of the Starsmore Discovery Center in North Cheyenne Cañon in 1992, following the dramatic move of the two-hundred-ton Starsmore home from South Nevada Avenue to the Cañon in April 1990. The Starsmore house, an Arts and Crafts–style structure built from Cheyenne Cañon river rock between 1918 and 1922, was purchased from Mary Starsmore by the Colorado Springs Parks and Recreation Department in 1989.[15] Once it was moved to North Cheyenne Cañon, the city funded initial renovation with approximately $250,000 in lottery funds. When additional money was needed, Mary Starsmore and her late husband's brother Larry donated $175,000 to complete structural renovation; Mrs. Starsmore subsequently donated $100,000 more toward exterior and interior remodeling. Neighboring Seven Falls in South Cheyenne Cañon donated $80,000 toward the parking lot and remodeling. The Starsmore Center in North Cheyenne Cañon opened to the public in May 1992, providing a natural history museum, visitor center, and informational resource to complement the century-old park.

Top left: Mayor Robert Isaac, Mary Starsmore, Parks Director Nancy Lewis, and Larry Starsmore at the opening of the Starsmore Discovery Center, 1992.

Top right: Moving the Starsmore house from South Nevada Avenue to North Cheyenne Cañon, 1990.

Three more parks were dedicated in 1993: renovated Vermijo Park with a new playground and restrooms, the seventy-eight-acre Rampart Park next to Rampart High School, providing baseball, football, and soccer fields, as well as natural terrain, for the joint use of city leagues and the school; and Woodmen Valley Park, the first in the Peregrine development—five of its thirty acres being developed into volleyball, baseball, and soccer fields, tennis courts, and a playground. At Cottonwood Creek, a professional level disc golf course, built in cooperation with the Colorado Disc Sports Association, also opened that year.[16]

Responsibility for Evergreen and Fairview Cemeteries had been assigned to the Parks Department in 1991, bringing the department's total acreage of parkland and cemetery grounds to 7,552. The department continued to plant 105 flowerbeds, growing 129,774 plants in the city greenhouse and overseeing 230 baskets of flowers. It managed an urban forest counting over seventy-six thousand trees, maintained forty-two miles of medians and center islands, and beautified downtown streetscapes.

The forestry division of the Parks Department promoted the established street tree program, working with homeowners to purchase and plant shade

The Starsmore Discovery Center, North Cheyenne Cañon

In 1910, the Evergreen Chapel was built to provide a place of shelter and comfort in Evergreen Cemetery. General William Jackson was buried at the cemetery in 1909.

or ornamental trees in their neighborhoods.[17] Forestry also removed and replaced dead trees; in 1992, a thousand street trees were destroyed due to disease and the 1991 winter cold spell, an unusually high number. "This is the first time in twenty years we've lost so many trees to mortality and decline from cold weather," Bill Stookey, Supervisor of Forestry and Natural Resources for Parks and Recreation, observed at the time.[18]

Citizen volunteers continued to support their parks. In 1991, thirty-seven parks, fifty-five city blocks, and twelve flowerbeds were "adopted" by local residents through the "Adopt A Park" program. The "Teens for Trees" program facilitated a survey of the city's forest by local teenagers trained to detect tree disease and insect infestation. The Mountain Shadows neighborhood group created a gravel trail link to the Garden of the Gods. Overall, in 1991 alone, 5,540 volunteers provided over 90,000 hours of service, a value of approximately $450,000.

SUPPORT FOR TRAILS AND OPEN SPACE: THE PIKES PEAK GREENWAY PROJECT AND SECTION 16

Work on multi-use trails continued. In 1989, the city approved purchase of the unused portion of the Denver and Rio Grande Western railroad that ran east-west along Constitution Avenue between Templeton Gap and Academy for development into a linear park and trail.[19] By 1991, a gravel trail was constructed from North Monument Valley Park to Fillmore Street, and another three sections of trails were constructed with street millings, in cooperation with the Transportation Department.[20] Yet connecting parks with a greenbelt corridor was still more dream than reality, a glaring drawback to the city's economic appeal, according to the director of the Colorado Springs Convention and Visitors Center:

> *Without such a network, Colorado Springs has fallen behind other Colorado cities. . . . "We need to work on some identity," [Terry] Sullivan said. He suggested that as a tourist destination, Colorado Springs has stood still during the past twenty years while towns like Boulder, Vail and Breckenridge have blossomed.* [21]

Others agreed. Enthusiasm for creating an urban trail system was high. The Multi-Use Trail Master Plan was in place. Formal planning for the Pikes Peak Greenway project soon began, with approval of the Pikes Peak Greenway Master Plan occurring in January 1994. The Greenway Plan delineated a thirteen-mile-long, north-south corridor that followed the Monument/Fountain Creek system through the heart of the Colorado Springs urban area. The trail offered access to the creek corridor and connection with east-west trails, parks, and other recreational amenities. It also enhanced the natural beauty of the area, promoting water quality and watershed management, protecting natural vegetation and wildlife habitat. Through a combination of city funds, GOCO grants, generous donations, and El Pomar and other grants, the department was able to make considerable progress turning the idea into reality.

In 1995, Castle Concrete donated thirty-five acres of property, a half-mile stretch north of Highway 85-87, to link Colorado Springs to the Fountain Creek Regional Park via Fountain Creek Regional Trail, which became part of the Greenway Project. "Development of the entire Fountain Creek Regional Trail corridor is the direct result of the generous contributions of either easements or property by local businesses and private citizens," remarked Kurt Schroeder, El Paso County Parks Department.[22] By then, only two small segments of trail between Colorado Springs and Palmer Lake remained unfinished. Sinton Pond, a fourteen-acre wetland located between Garden of the Gods Road and Fillmore Street, was acquired by the city in May 1996 for $300,000. The purchase helped complete the Sinton Trail, an east-west route linked to the American Discovery Trail.

Top: Shooks Run Creek.

Bottom: GreenSprings Volunteer's t-shirt illustrates the Greenway Trail Map.

In October 1996, a $2 million GOCO grant enabled the city to pay for the last two properties to complete the thirteen-mile, ten-foot wide Greenway Trail, connecting forty miles of trails from Palmer Lake to Fountain Creek Regional Park. City Senior Planner Craig Blewitt commented, "Walking and being outdoors is growing in popularity and it's so important to have this asset accessible to families. It's more than just a trail."[23] By then, $5.7 million had been spent on the Greenway project. It would take several million dollars more to complete the interpretive signs, rest areas, benches, and wetlands, as well as purchase land to develop Confluence Park (later renamed America the Beautiful Park), designed to be a focal point in the trail system.

Coincidentally to development of the city's urban trail system, a strong citizen voice calling for increased efforts to preserve and protect open space vulnerable to further development throughout the city was making itself heard.[24] While Mayor Robert Isaac discounted the movement as bordering

Section 16 Open Space trail.

on "hysteria," in June 1995 City Council members responded to these concerns by creating an eleven-member citizen task force, consisting of park and trails activists and other interested parties, to study and recommend strategies for open space acquisition.[25] At the same time, city staffers were charged with completing a study on how much open space the city should have based on its population and needs. Another citizens group—a coalition of interested business and environmental individuals organized under the label TOPS (for Trails, Open Space and Parks)—hoped to get a proposal for a city sales-tax increase to pay for open space acquisition on the November ballot.

The heightened movement had been triggered by the State's announcement that it was considering selling off a square mile of foothills property, Section 16, that was located just west of El Paso County's Bear Creek Park, between Colorado Springs and Manitou Springs. El Paso County had held the lease on the property, which was highly prized by local residents for its hiking trails, rugged terrain, proximity, and unhindered vista. The county had initially decided not to renew the lease in 1994; when County Commissioners subsequently changed their position, the State Land Board had already determined to entertain development offers. Residents were alarmed at the possibility of losing the valued area and anxious to find a way to preserve it. They rallied to the cause, forming the group Section 16 Intact. The concerned enthusiasm did not surprise Paul Butcher, appointed Director of Parks and Recreation in 1994, who explained:

> *There have always been open-space advocates in this county, but there has never been as identifiable a rallying point as Section 16 has been. . . . Open space hasn't materialized out of nowhere. It has come out of the closet a little bit because there's an issue to rally around.* [26]

Without funds, private citizens and local governments remained in a quandary as to how to resolve the issue, which was defused when the State Land Board agreed in 1995 to continue the lease of Section 16 to the county, eventually reassigning it to the city in 2004. But the organized movement for the preservation of open space—areas permanently maintained in their natural state for their natural, aesthetic, or cultural qualities—had taken a strong hold. This would profoundly affect the face of Colorado Springs parks in the coming years. As Dan Cleveland, then Director of Pikes Peak Area Trails Coalition, remarked:

> *Section 16 is only going to be the first one. It's got a lot of people's interest in open space up. After this is resolved, I would hope the open-space issue wouldn't go away.* [27]

NEW ACQUISITIONS STACK UP

Meanwhile, the Parks Department worked to develop and maintain the parks system as new properties came online. In fall 1991, the Parks and Recreation Department completed the master plan for Ute Valley Park, a 343-acre natural sanctuary in northwest Colorado Springs that it had recently acquired. Ute Valley featured grassland, brush land, and coniferous forests, offering a wilderness retreat in the midst of the northwest urban development. The department planned to preserve its many natural attributes as a "regional, natural open space park" that emphasized its natural ecology, geology, wildlife, and flora.[28] The plan for Ute Valley included building a trail system for hiking, jogging, and mountain biking, as well as a signed interpretive trail that was wheelchair accessible.

Ute Valley Park.

During the 1992 public hearings on park priorities, hundreds of residents had requested more sports and recreational facilities. In response, City Council approved the purchase of 82 acres near I-25 and Fillmore Street that year for a proposed sports complex.[29] The future "Goose" Gossage Youth Sports Complex was acquired for about $450,000—some of it from state lottery proceeds and some from the city's 1993 capital construction budget.[30] It would eventually provide comprehensive youth sports resources, as well as link the Monument Valley Park trail to trails heading east along Templeton Gap and west along Douglas Creek.

And in 1993, City Council accepted title to Jimmy Camp Creek, the future site of a 693-acre regional park, northeast of U.S. Highway 24 and Marksheffel Road. The transaction resulted from a 1988 agreement in which the city annexed the 23,000-acre Banning-Lewis Ranch.[31] Jimmy Camp Creek was dedicated to the city as open space, an acquisition additional to any parkland dedications that would be required for future neighborhood and community parks as the area was developed. Jimmy Camp Creek would be the city's fourth largest park—behind Garden of the Gods, North Cheyenne Cañon, and Palmer Park—yet it still remained without improvements or access in 2010. Home to deer, pronghorn antelope, and other wildlife, the area consisted largely of rolling hills, rock outcroppings, and some timber.

Programs were in place, parks were being acquired, and growth was being managed as new plans were being developed. In January 1994, Nancy Lewis, Director of Parks and Recreation, announced her retirement after twenty-seven years of service to the department, six as director. An internal search was conducted for her replacement, and Paul Butcher, who started with the department in 1984, was selected for the position. At the time Director Butcher was appointed, the name of the department was changed to the Department of Parks, Recreation, and Cultural Services, to reflect the department's responsibilities for the Pioneers Museum and other cultural programs.

RESTORATION OF THE GARDEN OF THE GODS

Perhaps the most significant parks projects during the 1990s were the restoration of the Garden of the Gods, resulting from the 1994 Garden of the Gods Master Plan, and the construction of an extraordinary Visitors Center outside the park entryway, developed through a unique public-private partnership.

Internationally renowned for its stunning natural beauty, the Garden of the Gods was suffering severely from overuse by the early 1990s. Between one and two million visitors a year tromped across the 1,360-acre park. Mountain bikers bushwhacked through scrub oak and mountain mahogany, gouging the sandstone with their knobby tires. Automobiles stacked up bumper to bumper in front of the aging Hidden Inn and the crumbling High Point visitors center. Hikers and picnickers wandered at will in search of a peaceful resting spot. Some rock climbers ignored regulations and scaled fragile sandstone walls. Occasional horseback riders departed from specified trails to explore vulnerable territory. Parking lots consumed more and more space. The damaged Garden was showing significant wear, and badly needed a plan—and funding—to save it from the many who arrived daily to absorb its beauty.

The last Master Plan for the park had been completed more than fifteen years earlier, in 1976, and while some components of that plan had been implemented, many had not. Widespread support existed for a new program to counteract the park's deterioration, particularly following the public outcry in 1987 rejecting the city's proposal to build a new visitors center in the middle of the park. Determined to restore the Garden, the Parks Department and the Parks Advisory Board began work sessions on a new Master Plan in February 1993, deciding upon an open "fish bowl" process in which no designated committees would be used and all interested parties would be invited to participate. The final plan was ultimately devised by hundreds of citizens who loved the Garden. The first meeting took place on June 9, 1993, at the Chuckwagon Pavilion. [32] From that core organizational meeting, fifty-one public meetings were held over the next year. More than four hundred people participated.

The Chuckwagon Pavilion was removed from the Garden of the Gods after restoration.

Comprehensive studies of the Garden were completed and five critical areas of concern were decided: traffic, rock climbing, management, trails, and interpretation. [33] The driving principle agreed upon for the Master Plan stated:

> *Conservation, preservation and restoration are overriding principles, and, within those principles, the ultimate aim is to allow uses in the park which will not conflict and which are appropriate to the setting.*[34]

The last meeting of the group was held on April 7, 1994, with the updated Garden of the Gods Master Plan presented on April 28, 1994. Final approval of the plan by the Colorado Springs City Council occurred on August 9, 1994.

The plan called for comprehensive changes to the park trail system and management policies; a revised traffic plan for the Garden that closed Gateway Road, converted most roadways to one-way traffic, downsized parking lots, improved on-street bicycling, opened 4.6 miles of trails to bicyclists and equestrians, and provided pathways for pedestrians; a renovation that removed the existing visitors center, the Chuckwagon Pavilion area, the High Point building, and closed or redesigned parking areas; the endorsement of a new visitors center, already approved by City

Improved one-way traffic patterns and bicycle lanes in the Garden enhanced visitor's experiences.

Southern Ute Elder Austin Box performed a traditional blessing at the Visitors Center opening, May 1995.

Council, being built outside of the park; and ecological restoration of the Garden through revegetation with indigenous plants and erosion control. A decision on the fate of the old Hidden Inn was delayed until 1997; the Inn was ultimately removed from the Garden, in accordance with the 1909 Perkins deed that prohibited the construction of buildings within the park.[35]

The costs of renovations for the Garden were estimated to be about $1.2 million, the biggest share of which was for road improvements. Another $22,000 was allocated for building demolition, $101,000 for trails development, and $286,000 for paving parking lots. A 1995 GOCO grant to the Garden of the Gods restoration project for $100,000, matched by $383,000 from the city, gave a strong start to the construction timeline. "It's going to help us implement much more quickly the master plan," said Parks Director Butcher. "We probably cut what we were going to do over five years to three."[36]

Volunteers pitched in to help. In June 1995, 250 individuals from Volunteers for Outdoor Colorado came to the Garden to help repair and reroute major trails, install stone steps, build retaining walls, and add water bars to help fight erosion—backbreaking work shoveling heavy gravel and lifting rocks in slippery red mud. Residents from Denver as well as Colorado Springs participated in the team effort between the organization and the city. "There is at least two months of planning by trail experts—the design work is invaluable," said Bill Stookey from Parks and Recreation. "And the labor, if you want to calculate 250 people working eight to ten hours a day for two days, you can see what the city is getting for free."[37] It was a clear expression of how many loved this park.

GARDEN OF THE GODS VISITORS CENTER

Concurrent with the development of the Garden of the Gods Master Plan was the conceptualization and construction of a new $3.5 million visitors center outside of the Garden, the gift of philanthropic entrepreneur, Lyda Hill. In 1993, Hill offered to build a new center on property she owned directly east of the park. In exchange, she requested exclusive concessionaire rights for the park, a swap (for other land Hill owned) of 4.9 acres near the proposed center to accommodate parking, and the realignment of a 2,000-foot segment of Thirtieth Street.[38] She further committed to donate $75,000 the first year to a new non-profit foundation to help support the Garden of the Gods, increasing that amount by 3 percent every year thereafter.

Hill, a lifetime summer resident of Colorado Springs, whose family owned and operated Seven Falls and built the Garden of the Gods Estates, the Garden of the Gods Club, and the Kissing Camels Golf Course, explained her offer was in the spirit of American volunteerism. "My 'why' is to protect the park," she said. "This is a way for me to walk my talk, a way to do something that will last."[39]

Park supporters immediately recognized the value of what Hill proposed. Community activist Jeanne Mathews praised the idea, commenting, "If we want anything like this in the city in the future, it's going to have to come from people like Miss Hill."[40] Hill also offered to provide a tram service that would reduce the impact of automobile traffic in the park, to include park naturalists on her payroll—freeing the city of that expense, and to pay all maintenance on the center. Some initially doubted Hill's motives or the merit of the plan, but Hill's attorney, Bruce Warren, noted, "She wants this to be the very best quality. The bottom line is that the community gets a world-class visitors center and a flow of money to the park."[41]

The Garden of the Gods Visitors Center welcomes thousands annually.

City Council approved the plan in December 1993, and construction immediately commenced, despite two lawsuits filed by opponents to the project.[42] Progress was swift and the new Garden of the Gods Visitors Center opened to enthusiastic reviews on May 15, 1995. "It was very cool," said thirteen-year-old Bryan Turner. "I never knew the park was so big," remarked ten-year-old Katie Skinner. "It's beautiful," commented Bill Stookey of Parks and Recreation.[43]

Offering a panoramic view of the Garden's red rocks, the new visitors center featured a three-dimensional model of the park inside a two-story atrium; displays with interactive computers explaining the park's history and geology; dioramas; life-sized wildlife models, dinosaur exhibits, and huge murals; and a twelve-minute movie, "How Did Those Red Rocks Get There?" presented in the Gateway Theatre. Other amenities for visitors included a cafeteria, seating one hundred indoors and another one hundred on a large deck overlooking the park, two gift shops, 210 parking spaces and a guided bus service through the Garden. Landscaping reflected the variety of habitats within the park.

The Center welcomed all who came to see the park with a unique combination of educational and interpretive displays, combined with

Native American dancers perform during the Annual Earth Day Celebration at Garden of the Gods Visitor & Nature Center, 2010.

services to meet all the basic needs of visitors, presented in a setting that reflected the stunning beauty of the Garden itself. "This is the culmination of a nineteen-year-old dream, and it's much better than I ever thought it would be," said Nancy Lewis, former Parks and Recreation Director. "This is a true partnership between the public and private sectors—probably unequalled anywhere else in the United States."[44]

The restoration of the Garden of the Gods and the construction of the new visitors center reflected a shift in public thinking—a growing public awareness that respected the importance of protecting the environment and assumed responsibility for nurturing our ecological heritage—a value also expressed in the burgeoning open space movement. The 1994 Garden of the Gods Master Plan provided a blueprint that balanced both present use and future preservation of the Garden. The new visitors center offered in-depth educational resources that developed understanding and appreciation for the unique park. The Garden of the Gods Foundation that was created with the opening of the visitors center promised to be a resource to protect the park into the next century.[45] Bonnie Frum, who managed the old visitors center and transitioned to the new one, had seen both the neglect of the past and hope for the future. She remarked:

> *It works out wonderfully. I really feel this visitor center came out of the same generosity as [that of] Perkins. The vision to see something worth protecting and the willingness to do something about it. . . . It's a miracle how it turned out. For years we watched this park degrade. It used to be painful to just watch all the social trails and traffic. Today it's quiet. It's peaceful. You can sit right in the center and listen to the birds.* [46]

Palmer Park's 1997 Master Plan accommodated all users.

MORE PLANS FOR PARKS

The Parks Department produced several more master plans for individual parks during the 1990s, including Palmer-donated Acacia Park and Palmer Park.[47] The 1994 Master Plan for Acacia Park, Colorado Springs' historical town square, was designed to return the park to a wider public use. It eliminated the cement slab and steps that had become a popular skateboarder destination, removed the iron fences surrounding the shuffleboard courts, eliminated the horseshoe pits, and upgraded existing restrooms.[48] Other improvements included rounding off the band shell to the form of the original stage built in 1893, fronting the shell with planters, replacing cement with sod, improving seating options along Tejon Street, and modernizing play equipment.

The 1997 Palmer Park Master Plan responded to problems created by heavy trail use and "off-trail traffic of hikers, leisure walkers, mountain bikers and horseback riders." It addressed the need for accessibility for disabled persons, provision of on-site information and education about the park, and, in the spirit of Palmer's deed, finding a balanced common ground to accommodate all users—particularly hikers and mountain bikers.[49] Recommendations included rebuilding and widening trails, organizing them into an easy to understand system, improving trail signage, completing the Meadows area as a community park with a restroom and playground with shade trees, and renovating the Lazy Land picnic area. Road, parking, and picnic area improvements throughout the park were also planned.

SPORTS COMPLEXES SERVE THE CITY

More citizen needs generated more development. As the demand for recreational sports fields grew, the city turned more and more to the development of the "sports complex," an area specifically designed for high-intensity sport activities, including baseball, softball, football, and soccer fields; tennis court complexes; in-line skating rinks; recreation centers; aquatic centers, and skateboard parks.The first sports complex—Four Diamonds on North Nevada Avenue—had been built in the 1980s. Designed to specifically accommodate league and tournament play, Four Diamonds was shared by teams from the nearby University of Colorado at Colorado Springs and city league users.

Four Diamonds Sports Complex on North Nevada Avenue, the first sports complex in the city.

More facilities were to come. In 1996, the acreage on Mark Dabling Boulevard (purchased in 1992) was developed into a youth sports complex, helped by a large infusion of funds from the state lottery. When the Richard M. "Goose" Gossage Youth Sports Complex opened, it featured five kid-sized baseball diamonds, nine soccer fields, trees, parking, restrooms, an announcer's booth, and a concession stand.[50] The Gossage Complex was described by Parks and Recreation planning and development manager Terry Putman as "the biggest [sports] thing that has happened to us in quite a few years. It's really the first sports complex we've built since Four Diamonds. It's the first youth complex we've ever built."[51] Construction of a playground was soon to follow, as were additional restrooms and lights.

Players at Leon Young Sports Complex.

Subsequently, the Sky View Sports Complex off South Powers Boulevard, catering exclusively to adults, opened, and the Leon Young Youth Sports Complex on South Chelton Road became available in 1997, offering baseball and softball fields in the Pikes Peak Park area for local youth.

The Sports Complexes helped meet the growing demand for sports and recreational space. In 1995, nearly five thousand kids played t-ball through the Parks and Recreation program. Youth soccer drew 10,134 players, and over 1,500 adults played in soccer leagues that year. In 1996, 291 residents between the ages of eight and eighty-seven participated in the city's Special Olympics program, which included baseball, softball, volleyball, tennis, cycling, soccer, and figure skating events.[52]

In a 1997 *Gazette* interview, Director Butcher predicted even more demand for sports facilities:

> *Beyond the outdoor sports, there is a growing interest in indoor facilities and recreation centers. That's going to be a need that the community will have to address because of increasing demand for indoor space. It's up to us to come up with some solutions, and everybody's working on the issue of addressing indoor recreation and youth activities to offer kids alternatives.* [53]

BUDGET PRESSURES

Plans are one thing, and budgets another. As master plans were being created, recreational use growing, and citizen expectations pressing, the Parks and Recreation Department's budget was suffering familiar financial pressures. The aging playground equipment in the neighborhood parks offered one simple example.

In 1995, most of the old wooden playground sets needed to be replaced. Considered ecologically inspired when first installed, in twenty years the railroad tie and rope play sets had splintery timbers and worn-out tires that were injuring children. The cost to replace old playground materials with metal frame structures covered in recycled plastics and composite was $10,000 to $25,000 each. So Parks and Recreation requested $500,000 over five years to replace play equipment in twenty-five city playgrounds. The new ones, expected to last twenty years or more, would only need changes in swing seats and *S* hooks for ongoing maintenance. Jon Pitzer, superintendent of parks, explained the request:

> *We definitely get fewer injury complaints from parents with the newer [playgrounds]. They're also wheelchair accessible, which is required by the ADA, and the repair costs are low. With wood, whatever kind, it has to be treated and sanded yearly. And you can't just come in with a 2-by-4 to fix them. You have to order parts from the company, so it's more costly. When I started with the Parks Department 29 years ago, everything was metal. I guess we've come back to those days.* [54]

Maintenance of 144 neighborhood parks and over 8,000 acres of parkland was an enormous daily task. And allocations were dropping. The city still depended primarily on inconsistent sales-tax revenue for its operating budget. The half-cent C.I.P. sales tax approved in 1987 to help pay for city construction projects was about to be lost; in 1991, tax-aversive city voters withdrew their support of the tax, voting it out over a scheduled five-year reduction. As a capital improvements funding source, it would disappear in 1996. This would have a huge negative impact on the city's budget, including funding for development of its Parks and Recreation programs.

Adult play at Parks and Recreation ball field in northern Colorado Springs. Adult user fees were increased in 1996.

In 1995 the Parks and Recreation Department proposed increasing recreational fees to gain additional income over a three- to five-year period. At the time, about $8 million of the Parks Department's $12 million annual general fund budget covered programs and services that did not raise money—parks, tree maintenance, nature programs, and the like. Another $4 million was spent on youth and adult sports and other programs, for which fees from program participants covered about half the costs. The plan was to not add any fees where none were currently charged, nor to make a profit, but to try to close the gap between cost and revenue.[55]

While several people objected to the prospect of increased costs, the proposal reflected the reality of the difficulties of making ends meet. In 1996, adult user fees were increased with the approval of the Parks Advisory Board, with the hope of recovering some of the costs of sports and leisure programs. When the city contemplated ending adult sports in 1998 to save money, participants quickly organized a Save Our Sports (SOS) movement, pointing out that there were 1,750 adult sports teams, 21,000 people playing, and 6,817 games played annually. The programs were retained, but fees again increased.

The Parks Department worked to come up with other creative solutions to their financial problems, looking for private enterprises, charitable groups, and citizen volunteers to help support programs. The department coordinated with the Colorado Rockies Foundation to refurbish the Ellis Burks baseball field on South Chelton Road. In October 1997, 500 volunteers signed up to build the first playground ever at Palmer Park, with $100,000 for equipment donated by Phil Long Dealerships Community Fund and the Denver Broncos. The department's long-range plans to build more sports complexes featuring multiple fields at one site also increased efficiency and reduced costs. Park administrators were searching for every possible way to balance budgets, sustain programs, and meet citizen expectations.

Urban trails enjoyed active use from diverse groups, accounting for the 1997 approval of the Trails and Open Space tax.

TRAILS AND OPEN SPACE TAX (TOPS) AND THE COLORADO SPRINGS OPEN SPACE PLAN

The citizen demand was diverse. Just as parents and participating athletes were advocating for the preservation and expansion of sports programs, environmentalists and trail users rallied around the open space movement. While Section 16 backers had been given a reprieve in 1996, with that property being leased for at least another ten years, the open space movement in Colorado Springs had only gained momentum, following a strong statewide trend toward open space preservation.

Local supporters were well aware of the urgency to protect open areas before they would be lost to development. They argued that natural settings—grasslands, stream corridors, foothills, bluffs, and mesas—were essential to the quality of life in Colorado Springs and warranted permanent protection. After mounting an unsuccessful measure to increase the city sales tax by .1 percent to fund open space in 1995, they succeeded with another try two years later. On April 1, 1997, voters approved a .1 percent sales-tax increase, known as the Trails and Open Space tax (TOPS), by a narrow margin. Advocates for open space now had the means to obtain and preserve important properties well into the future.

Why did the 1997 TOPS tax pass in fiscally conservative Colorado Springs, just when the C.I.P. sales tax had been eliminated? There were several reasons. TOPS had widespread popular support; people anticipated a direct benefit from it. Economic times were good, land preservation was promoted in the context of healthy urban growth, a strong campaign had been launched in favor of the proposal, people saw a direct connection between the tax and the programs they wanted, and homeowners were genuinely alarmed at pending development of nearby scenic areas:

> *"We're reaching the critical mass with people moving to town . . . seeing building up on the hillsides, and lots that you thought would be vacant forever all of a sudden have bulldozers on them," said Anne Oatman-Gardner, campaign manager for the non-profit group that proposed the tax. "People are really feeling the heat."*[56]

The first tax increase in the Pikes Peak region in twenty years, TOPS was designated specifically for the acquisition of trails, parks and open space. Raising a penny for every $10 spent in Colorado Springs, it was projected to generate between $5 and $6 million annually through 2009, its expiration date. The program allocated 20 percent of revenues to parks, 20 percent to trails, and 60 percent to open space. It mandated a citizens group be appointed to recommend land purchases and preservation to City Council.

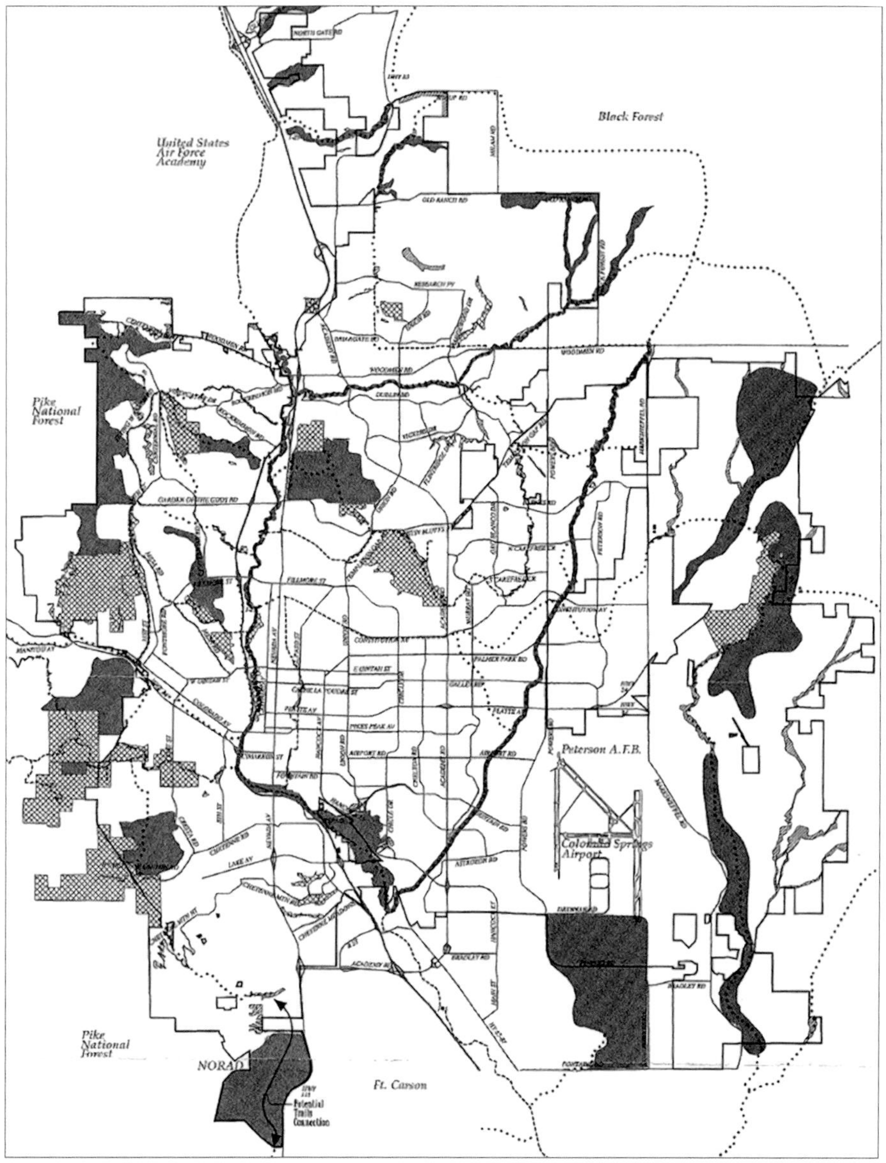

Proposed Open Space properties, 1997 Open Space Plan.

TOPS was timely, arriving just in time to advance the goals articulated in the recently completed Colorado Springs Open Space Plan. The plan was begun in January 1996, when a sixteen-member citizen review committee responded to a City Council directive to create a guide for future land conservation in and around the city. When submitted in December 1996, the plan provided the community an information resource, policy document, vision for the future, and a road map of how to get there. The Colorado Springs Open Space Plan was unanimously approved by the City Planning Commission on February 6, 1997, by the Parks and Recreation Advisory Board on February 13, and by the City Council on March 25—six days before the passage of TOPS.

The Colorado Springs Open Space Plan defined and described the city's open space holdings:

> *Open space areas in Colorado Springs are designed primarily to preserve the natural landscape. Certain types of recreation, such as hiking,*

Stratton Open Space, acquired 1998.

running, bicycling and horseback riding, are ideally suited to many open space areas, but are accommodated only to the extent they are compatible with the protection of the natural environment. [57]

It noted that of the city's total parkland (8,495 acres—including regional parks, community parks, open space, and trails), over 6,500 acres (75 percent) could be counted as open space in 1996. Over fifty miles of 159 miles of planned trails were extant in the city, providing critical linear open space for both human and wildlife movement.

The plan emphasized developing individual open space areas in the context of the entire city. Recommendations endorsed establishing a public program for open space conservation, using a multi-year funding source (which TOPS would provide), establishing an open space geographical information system (GIS) as public information source, organizing a non-profit Open Space Coalition (a function the Trails and Open Space Coalition would fill), applying standards for conserving open space to new developments, requiring dedication of open space as part of new annexation agreements, and partnering with the Palmer Foundation (a local land trust) to acquire conservation easements.[58]

TOPS IN ACTION

Colorado Springs now had a city plan and a city program specifically dedicated to open space—a first. The pending influx of considerable sums of money from TOPS required new organization and thoughtful management. With increased open space acquisition, the Parks and Recreation Department would assume a new workload that would include developing policies and procedures; analyzing parcels based on wildlife habitat, vegetation, visual quality, and water resources; acquiring appraisals; and surveying public opinion. TOPS campaigners called for the appointment of a full-time Parks and Recreation staff member to oversee open space within the department.[59] A TOPS citizen advisory board (required as part of the TOPS sales tax passage) would recommend which land parcels should be acquired for open space or developed into trails and parks.

In June 1997, City Council appointed the Trails and Open Space Working Committee (TOPS Working Committee) to review applications for land acquisition and set priorities for purchases.[60] Their recommendations would go to the Parks and Recreation Advisory Committee and then to City Council for final decisions. That same month the Trails and Open Space Coalition (TOSC) combined with the existing Pikes Peak Area Trails Coalition as a private non-profit support and advocacy group for open space; they would strongly influence the development of open space in the years to come. And in 1998, City Council established an Open Space GIS and revised city codes for conserving open space in subdivisions, zoning, master plans, and annexation.

The first urban trails expenditure came in September, when the TOPS Working Committee recommended $410,000 be spent on connecting trails within the city. The proposal included the development of the Rock Island Trail between Academy and Murray Boulevard, further construction of the Rock Island Trail from the Pikes Peak Greenway to Shooks Run, the design and construction of a one-mile stretch at Cottonwood Creek from the Greenway trail to Academy Boulevard, construction of a trail segment to connect Bear Creek Park to the Greenway project, and the construction of the Sinton Trail, the western segment of an east-west trail across the city and part of the American Discovery Trail, envisioned as a cross-country route.

Urban joggers.

The first TOPS open space acquisition followed in 1998 with the purchase of the 318-acre Myron Stratton property adjacent to North Cheyenne Cañon. When plans for private development of the Stratton property loomed in 1997, a local community group, Cheyenne Commons, organized to protect and preserve the scenic area—an area of grassy meadows and woodlands that supported an abundance of wildlife. They gathered signatures, raised funds, and lobbied for protection of the treasured space. Faced with a June 1998 deadline, the group worked furiously to raise the necessary funds: they needed $1.5 million to add to the city's $4.4 million contribution—TOPS money the city had pledged that January. Richard Skorman, who helped lead the drive, called it "the biggest fund-raising effort for a natural area the city has ever known."[61]

Cheyenne Commons "raised $1.05 million in cash from 758 contributors, ranging from dimes from children's lemonade stands to a $288,000 grant from The Gates Family Foundation."[62] When the remaining funds were secured with a $502,000 GOCO grant, the purchase of the property as city

Bicycling on the Pikes Peak Greenway.

open space was assured. The Trust for Public Land (TPL), a national non-profit, helped bring parties together, obtain purchase options on the parcels, and negotiate a complicated purchasing agreement. El Pomar Foundation pledged $300,000 for building infrastructure—parking lots, trails, and signage—for the property when the transaction was finalized. Stratton was saved as open space in perpetuity.

The following year, City Council unanimously approved spending $3.65 million of TOPS funds toward the purchase of the J.L. Ranch south of Colorado Springs as a state park, the acquisition of thirty acres to complete the Monument Creek trail system, and the purchase of seventy-four acres of open space in University Park, a subdivision being developed on the former Houck estate.[63]

TOPS would continue to provide invaluable support for open space acquisitions into the future. By 2009, TOPS would have protected open space that exceeded 6,178 acres, built over thirty-two neighborhood parks, and constructed over forty-six miles of urban trails.

SPRINGS COMMUNITY IMPROVEMENTS PROGRAM (SCIP)

In 1997, the same year that TOPS passed, City Council launched an unprecedented effort to involve the public in governmental decision-making. The program was called Springs Community Improvements Program (SCIP) and was based on a forty-year-old model in use in Phoenix, Arizona. The city faced an enormous backlog of capital projects, a list growing larger and larger since the 1991 revocation of the C.I.P. half-cent city sales tax. City officials hoped SCIP could help solve what was an alarming deficit. Council members called on local citizens to serve on eight committees to assess the city's improvement needs, prioritize projects, and recommend funding mechanisms. The city clinched the deal by vowing to follow the committees' recommendations—whatever they might be.

"It's a philosophy change in council and management," explained Elena Nunez, city budget analyst who helped devise the new program. "We know citizens want to be involved, based on the criticisms we've heard—in letters, phone calls, the newspaper, talking to our own relatives and neighbors. We're spending their money and they don't know where it's going." [64]

City Council appointed Lou Mellini as chair and Nancy Lewis as vice-chair of SCIP's Executive Committee, and individual community leaders to chair each of the remaining seven sub-committees: drainage, transportation, public safety, parks and facilities, community enhancements, finance, and public information. Everyone was welcome to participate. Hundreds did. The first SCIP town hall meeting was held in early 1998, at which committees of interested citizen volunteers were formed. Volunteers had signed on for a hefty task. Recommendations were due to City Council in June. As the SCIP Executive Summary observed:

> *Those involved in the process [were made up of] a broad spectrum of people, with fresh perspectives and a strong belief in the future of Colorado Springs. This was not a process undertaken exclusively by those who frequently volunteer for public service. 'Can do' encompasses the spirit of those who came to work the SCIP process, both old hands and newcomers.* [65]

Both El Pomar Youth Sports Complex (above) and the America the Beautiful (formerly Confluence) Park (below) were recommended as top priorities in the 1998 SCIP process.

More than 250 local residents participated. Provided by city staffers with a project list of those city projects that had no potential funding sources—about $200 million worth—the committees met weekly for three months, researched the issues, discussed the priorities, visited on-site locations, and, by June 1, 1998, ultimately recommended thirty-three projects as top priorities to the city. Recommendations had been carefully analyzed and justified. SCIP's efforts represented over 1,640 hours of volunteered work. Richard Box, a public affairs professor at University of Colorado at Colorado Springs, praised the project, observing it could be a way "to permanently institutionalize citizen self-governance that's real and ongoing, where they're assisting in making decisions."[66]

Many projects were recommended. Some were surprising. The wide-spread grassroots movement prioritized a new road in the Roswell neighborhood, just south of Fillmore Street, to redirect industrial traffic along Monument Creek away from neighborhood homes. It recommended a new shelter to replace the crumbling home of the Humane Society of the Pikes Peak Region.

Those SCIP projects prioritized by the Parks and Public Facilities Subcommittee included three proposed community recreation facilities in the southeast, northeast and northwest quadrants of the city; a youth sports complex already site-planned on fifty-four acres near Harrison High School, south of Circle Drive and east of Janitell Road; the expansion and upgrade to meet code compliance of the Memorial Park Aquatics and Fitness Center; and a two-phase renovation of the Sertich Ice Center at Memorial Park.

The SCIP Community Enhancements Subcommittee prioritized funding for the completion of Confluence Park (later renamed America the Beautiful Park), including acquisition of additional land, relocation of existing businesses, and expansion of the size and scope of the park to include a connection to the Pikes Peak Greenway, an artisan's district, and resources for community events.

SCIP volunteers had spoken up for the kind of city they wanted to live in, for the critical improvements they saw as necessary for a gratifying quality of life for Colorado Springs citizens.

Cottonwood Creek Recreation Center opened its $4.6 million SCIP-funded pool in 2001.

SCIP FUNDING VOTER APPROVED

To fund the SCIP projects, which crossed all aspects of city governance, City Council determined to ask voters to approve an $88 million bond issue, and to allow city retention of both 1997 and 1998 surplus taxes (which were to be returned to city residents per TABOR requirements). The bond issue—a financing method that required no additional taxing because its incurred debt was backed by sales-tax revenues—would be voted on in April 1999. The request for retention of 1997 surplus tax money ($6.6 million for five key SCIP projects) was on the ballot for November 1998, while the retention question of the 1998 tax surplus was held for the April 1999 ballot.[67]

On November 3, 1998, for the fourth time in five years, voters agreed to let the city keep the surplus tax revenue, $6.6 million for 1997 that would otherwise have gone back to local taxpayers; the huge El Pomar youth sports complex, already under construction, would receive $1.8 million. The following April, the SCIP $88 million bond issue narrowly passed by a margin of 1,028 votes, out of 60,448 votes cast. At the same time, voters decided to keep their 1998 tax surplus, denying the city $790,600 in 1998 surplus collection. This lost by another narrow margin—1,166 votes out of 65,364 total cast on that question.

With the approval of the SCIP bond issue, the city was able to do what historically it had been unable to do: plan, fund, and complete significantly large projects, citywide. Up to that point, city officials had been largely confined to a pay-as-you-go, do-what-you-can, ignore-what-you-can't process. Many large park projects were included in the effort. For parks, the

SCIP bond funded the first stage of a new recreational center on Centennial Boulevard in northwest Colorado Springs; improvements at the Northeast Recreation Center at Cottonwood Creek Park; a multi-purpose use facility at Memorial Park and renovation of Sertich Ice Center; improvements and staff for the Youth Sport Complexes; and site and design plans for the thirty-acre Confluence Park near Interstate 25 and Highway 24.[68]

Why did the SCIP bond issue pass in such a fiscally conservative community? Years later, Marylou Makepeace, mayor of Colorado Springs at the time, reflected on the results:

> *If people feel ownership, they get more interested in participating. People need to be involved in their government. I think [SCIP] passed because so many people were involved in creating it. . . . A whole lot of citizens were saying the same thing.* [69]

PARK PROGRAMS

Parks and Recreation staffers continued to support the traditional park programs. In 1998, more than 130,000 flowers had been planted in 119 flowerbeds around Colorado Springs. Still cultivated in the city greenhouse—a practice that had begun with General Palmer—begonias, geraniums, snapdragons, lobelia, and other flowers were soon blooming in city beds, as well as in flower baskets in Old Colorado City, along Union Boulevard and in downtown areas. Weeding, trimming, and watering was done by the city's horticultural crew, with the help of volunteers, many of whom came back every year, motivated by a sense of pride, ownership, and pleasure. Running on an annual budget of around $245,000, the floral program had begun drawing on business and organizational sponsors the previous year, offering them the opportunity to have their logos created in floral displays at a price competitive with a billboard advertisement—and on a product much more pleasing to the eye.

Top: The greenhouse donated by General Palmer in 1907 remained in use into the twenty-first century.

Bottom: Nancy Lewis Park, on the grounds of the old turf farm at Union Boulevard and Fillmore Street, dedicated in 1996.

The Legacy of Trees Program in 1996 was a new take on the established urban forestry program. The brainchild of hospice-volunteer Susan Martz, the program represented a combined effort between the Parks and Recreation Department and Pikes Peak Hospice to plant trees and raise funds for the hospice program. It offered individuals the opportunity to purchase and plant a tree in Nancy Lewis Park in honor of their loved ones. They made

145 trees available (in 63 species) at a cost ranging from $300 to $1,000. All were about six feet tall and could grow to forty feet. Benches and gazebos were also an option, as was a complete playground set for $35,000.[70]

Many individuals continued to make contributions to their parks. Residents of Colorado Springs' north-end neighborhood committed in 1997 to raising funds to build a half-acre park immediately south of their local school, Steele Elementary. With approval of the plan from City Council, pupils raised pennies, homeowners and parents solicited donations, and businesses pledged architectural, construction, and clean-up services. The Phil Long dealerships donated $30,000 to the project from a fund set up for community contributions. It became the first park to be built in Colorado Springs "solely by homeowners and without taxpayer dollars."[71]

The Phil Long dealerships and the Denver Broncos also contributed a Fantasy Playground to Cottonwood Creek Community Park, which was dedicated in 2001. That same year, Taylor Park was opened south of Patty Jewett Golf Course. Left an unfinished dirt field when Taylor Elementary School was built in the 1940s, Taylor Park was another result of parent and neighborhood organization. Committed to developing the park as a community resource, local residents organized in support of the project. They secured grants to help install soccer and kickball fields, a community walking path, nature education stations, native plants, and improved parking area.[72]

Tennis at Cottonwood Creek Recreation Center.

Recreational programs continued to offer sports activities to thousands of residents. Organized baseball for youth and adults, softball programs, basketball, volleyball, and soccer, football leagues, tennis, golf and swimming programs, ice skating, and in-line hockey leagues were all enthusiastically enjoyed by residents at parks throughout the city. In 2001, the city received a $100,000 GOCO grant to build one regulation in-line hockey rink at El Pomar Youth Sports Complex, the fifty-four-acre site under construction along Fountain Creek east of the World Arena.[73] A project prioritized during the SCIP process, this sports complex was created through public/private partnerships with the Gates Land Company, El Pomar Foundation, the

Colorado Rockies Foundation, El Pomar Youth Sports Park, Inc., and the city itself. It offered fourteen baseball fields and ten soccer fields in addition to the in-line skating rink. The complex also provided walking trails, a playground area, and concession facilities.[74]

INTO THE NEXT CENTURY

Prospects seemed promising for the Colorado Springs Parks, Recreation, and Cultural Services Department programs at the beginning of the twenty-first century. A solid funding source for acquisition of trails, open space and parks was in place. Residents had endorsed and approved funding for critical capital improvement projects through the SCIP process. Traditional park programs were continuing. The parks enjoyed strong backing from local citizens, City Council, and city administrators. While all the challenges to the city and its programs had not necessarily been resolved—the loss of the C.I.P. tax in 1996 was particularly vexing—the momentum of thoughtful planning, citizen participation, and strong leadership was encouraging to those who loved their parks and believed in their importance to the community.

Corral Bluffs east of Colorado Springs would be one of the many open space acquisitions in the next century.

Young and old share a hike during the Beidleman Environmental Day Camps, 2000. Programs were discontinued in 2002 when Beidleman Center and its programs were cut from the budget.

From Bloom to Bust

2000–2010: Parks Struggle as Funds Dry Up

"Our trees and parks and gardens must be renewed constantly if we are to leave a decent world for those who follow us."

—S. R. DeBoer

Despite the possibilities for growth, prosperity, pleasure, and preservation, the Colorado Springs parks system would encounter daunting problems in the next ten years. A combination of natural misfortune, poor tax policies, economic downturns, political neglect, contesting priorities, community fragmentation, and citizen inertia would thwart the healthy cultivation of the system. By the end of the decade, the city's extensive programs supporting parks, trails, recreation, open space, cultural resources, and community service for the citizens of Colorado Springs would be on the verge of collapse.

THE 2000–2010 COLORADO SPRINGS PARKS, RECREATION, AND TRAILS MASTER PLAN

On January 4, 2000, the Parks and Recreation Department presented its Master Plan for the next ten years, the first since the 1988 plan.[1] The Parks Department now managed 11,449 acres of parkland, as well as 44 miles of park trails and 65 miles of urban trails. In total, it was responsible for 132 parks, 29 open space areas, 28 park trails, 34 city trails, 7 sports complexes, and 13 centers for environmental education, recreational and community activities. And future growth was undeniable. As urban development continued, the department would acquire more new parkland through the Parkland Dedication Ordinance, and thousands of acres of open space would be added to the system through TOPS acquisitions.

The Master Plan stated the department's overall goals:

- To provide for a wide range of opportunities for all citizens and visitors to Colorado Springs
- To equitably distribute parks, recreational facilities, and trails throughout the city
- To develop an adequate level of financing for trails, parks, and recreational facilities
- To develop parks, recreation, and trails system in an environmentally sensitive manner

The Julie Penrose Fountain in America the Beautiful Park, 2010.

Within that context, recommendations of the Master Plan were specified: an updated classification system for parklands and new park locations; an appropriate management framework for various types of properties to be acquired; additional development of the urban trail system to complete the core trail network and link the system together; and the development of more recreational facilities. Some specific projects included parks for Stetson Hills and the new Briargate communities, the ongoing development of Confluence Park (renamed America the Beautiful Park in June 2005), the development of open space in accordance with the 1996 Open Space Plan, and the addition of approximately 153 urban trail miles over the next twenty years.

The plan recommended three more recreational centers (in addition to those three and the one renovation funded by the 1999 SCIP bond). It delineated a need for more senior center development and analyzed what additional sports facilities were needed to meet current as well as anticipated future recreational demand in Colorado Springs. It also argued for more staffing, noting: "[The department] is operating at a staff level well below the norm. . . . In addition to maintenance staff, additional staff will be needed to provide planning and design services, interpretation and environmental programs, open space and trail maintenance, and facility reservations and recreational programs associated with new parks, recreational facilities and trails."[2]

Facility at "Goose" Gossage Youth Sports Complex, 2010.

Success would require adequate funding. Projected park revenues would come from the TOPS tax, lottery funds, GOCO awards, and other grants, but in the year 2000 those programs were scheduled to sunset by the end of the decade.[3] The SCIP bond was assured, but already fully allocated to specific projects. The Parks operational budget was allocated by City Council from the city's general fund; this fund was primarily reliant on sales-tax revenues, and therefore variable.

Overall, the Parks Master Plan predicted a funding shortfall over the next ten years of approximately $54 million, not including funding needed for special projects such as additional recreational centers. To address this need, the plan recommended the adoption of a parkland development impact fee (in addition to Parkland Dedication Ordinance funds), the passage of an additional SCIP funding measure, and strategic partnerships and collaborations with other agencies and service providers. But a clear-cut solution to the funding gap was not to be had. While the vision was ambitious, city parks administrators would be faced with insurmountable challenges ahead.

SCIP REVISITED, FUNDS DENIED

The 1999 approval of the SCIP bond funded the highest priorities for capital improvements in the city, but a backlog of nearly $315 million in unfunded projects still remained. Backers recognized that the bond issue was not a long-term solution for the city, but a "jump-start" to funding infrastructure priorities.

Plans for a second SCIP program, "SCIP '01," began in 2000, with citizens developing a proposal for $250 million in construction projects to be funded by a city sales-tax increase—the largest spending package to be submitted to voters in the region's history. Co-chairman of the committee Lou Mellini argued that was what was needed.[4] "This is a twenty-year-old list," he said, blaming much of the backlog on the voters' 1991 decision to phase out the C.I.P. tax earmarked for city construction projects.[5]

Using the same process of citizen input as had worked with the first SCIP project, the SCIP '01 committees reviewed over $1 billion in requests. The final recommended list of projects and public safety services was presented to City Council on December 12, 2000. The Council made some adjustments and presented the request to voters on the April 2001 ballot. The total price tag was $758 million over a dozen years, to be funded with a .9 percent sales-tax hike.

This time, voters soundly rejected the proposal. SCIP '01 was overwhelmingly defeated by a margin of 57 percent to 43 percent, despite a strong "YES" campaign to garner support. Apparently, in a weak economy, Colorado Springs residents objected to the lack of a sunset clause on the tax hike and the all-or-nothing aspect of the measure, which included funding for all city projects—fire, police, roads, and drainage, as well as parks and community enhancements.[6]

City Council tried to gain funding approval again in the November 2001 election, dividing their proposals into six separate tax or bonding questions on the November 6th ballot. They hoped to gain about $142 million a year for city projects through a variety of measures: a permanent sales-tax increase, increased fees on city services to pay back a bond issue, a temporary sales tax, and a one-time expenditure of excess sales-tax revenues. They offered several options that would allow residents to decide what—if anything—they wanted to fund. But park administrators were to be disappointed again. In a strong turnout, Colorado Springs voters approved a .4 percent Public Safety Sales Tax for new police and fire hires, but they resoundingly rejected any new tax hikes for open space, roads, and parks.

Perhaps it was uncertainty about the poor economy or worry resulting from the September 11th terrorist attack in New York, but while Colorado Springs voters gave a big boost to their police and fire departments, they denied the .01 percent sales-tax increase for parks and recreation by 64.4 percent to 35.6 percent. The lost funds would have amounted to about $42 million. As a result, the Parks Department suspended plans for three recreation centers, two family fun pools, the Briargate Sports Complex, and renovations to the Pioneers Museum. Director Butcher reflected on the outcome: "I think some [projects] will probably fall by the wayside. We haven't looked and said, 'This is a project we don't ever see funding.' It'll just take a long time to come up with $42 million."[7]

Bluestem Prairie Open Space, 2010.

OPEN SPACE GROWS, TRAILS DEVELOP THROUGH TOPS

While traditional park projects suffered rejection, citizen groups continued to urge preservation of open space, and the TOPS funds offered a means to do so. In September 2000, with the help of the Trust for Public Land, the Trails and Open Space Coalition, and $8.2 million in TOPS receipts, the city acquired 650 acres surrounding the county's largest body of water—Big Johnson Reservoir—southeast of the city.[8] The purchase of the mid-tall grass and tall grass prairie stopped a proposed development of 2,400 homes and preserved prime habitat for migratory birds, while offering visitors sweeping views of the distant Pikes Peak.[9] Jane Titus, a TOSC member who had advocated for the acquisition, remarked upon the preserve's quality, saying, "Part of the beauty is the reservoir's site. You can't see Colorado Springs from its shores. It's a wonderful way to experience the prairie and the peak."[10]

It was hoped Big Johnson would be the keystone in the ultimate preservation of 3,000 acres of open space between the city's airport and the southern communities of Widefield and Security. The area—renamed Bluestem Prairie Open Space when it opened to the public in 2003—provided visitors a parking lot, trailhead, and trails around the perimeter of the area, while preserving large interior areas for wildlife. Commenting on Bluestem Prairie's value, Terry Putman of the Parks and Recreation Department explained, "The tall grass prairie and mid-tall grass prairie are really historically what people saw before they got to the mountains. This was an opportunity to preserve some of that heritage and historical grassland."[11]

High Chaparral Open Space.

Following Bluestem Prairie's acquisition, two more open space purchases were completed with TOPS money: Blodgett Peak and High Chaparral—both in prime growth areas also slated for development. Blodgett Peak, 167 acres of trees and trails just south of the Air Force Academy, offered visitors a mountain setting with streams, Douglas fir and ponderosa pine, access to Pike National Forest, and undeveloped, unsigned single-track trails. High Chaparral in Stetson Hills included seventy-three acres of bluffs and grassland.[12]

These last two purchases essentially drained the TOPS open space budget.[13] Only $118,000 was left, considered contingency money for an emergency. Yet more open space projects were in the sights of TOPS supporters—specifically the south peak of Cheyenne Mountain, Section 16, Red Rock Canyon, and Union Meadows. Open space advocates were looking for more ways to generate funds before these lands were lost to more development.

Citizens did not always agree on where limited revenues should be spent. Some prioritized land protection, others open space, and others recreation. While many saw the need to provide people with things to do, others were mindful of the urgency for preservation of historic areas. Even TOPS supporters differed on the relative importance of large open spaces on the perimeter of the city and smaller parcels within city limits. "We're always having tough decisions to make," said Kent Obee, chairman of the TOPS Working Committee. "There's much more land to buy than money we have to buy it with."[14] Many were already talking of extending the TOPS sales tax beyond its 2009 sunset date.

Extending and connecting the urban trails system was seen as a high priority. With 20 percent of TOPS funds specified for trails, Colorado Springs park planners had spent money and energy acquiring urban trail land from 1997-2002. Then in 2003 their focus shifted to trail construction, and a record $1.6 million of TOPS money was designated for trail development. "First tier" projects included developing the Midland-Creekwalk Trail, built along an old railroad bed aside Fountain Creek from downtown Colorado Springs toward Manitou Springs. The schedule also included portions of the Rock Island Trail along Constitution Avenue, the Pikes Peak Greenway, the Sand Creek Trail, and the Cottonwood Creek Trail.[15] "Second tier" development included a gravel trail linking University Park to the Four Diamonds Sports Complex. Ultimately, the city planned a 164-mile urban trail system. Should a TOPS extension be passed, TOSC advocates estimated the entire trail system could be completed by 2023, providing a way for pedestrians, in-line skaters, hikers, and cyclists to enjoyably navigate the city without encountering the hazards and discomfort of automobile traffic.

Hopes to acquire Red Rock Canyon as open space helped pass the extension of TOPS in 2003.

TOPS EXTENDED: A 2025 SUNSET

The extension of the TOPS sales tax was proposed in 2003. Trails and open space advocates carefully planned their campaign, surveying citizen perspectives and generating support. They were assisted by the Trust for Public Lands and the Trust's lobbying affiliate, the Conservation Campaign, in communicating, organizing, and advocating for the measure. They emphasized the importance of understanding that although the original TOPS tax was not set to expire until 2009, all of its funds were committed, making it impossible for the city to leverage any more open space acquisition without the guarantee of additional future revenues.

Red Rock Canyon, 2010.

The measure to extend the TOPS tax to 2025 was placed on the April 2003 ballot.[16] The timing was prime. Colorado Springs citizens highly valued the open space that they had already preserved through TOPS measures. They were well aware of the pending private development of Red Rock Canyon, and they were eager to preserve that unique area for future generations. Voters validated their belief in TOPS with an emphatic 68 percent vote in favor of the sales tax extension.[17] The city again had a guaranteed stream of funds for open space acquisition, and administrators and local environmentalists quickly acted to secure the prized Red Rock area.

Red Rock Canyon had long been prioritized as prospective open space; in 1997 it was identified as one of eighteen preservation "candidate areas" in the city's open space plan. Located along the foothills between Colorado Springs and Manitou Springs, the 787-acre area had been slated for extensive development, including a convention center, high-rise buildings, luxury homes and a twenty-seven-hole golf course. Open space advocates argued its natural and historical significance warranted preservation. It was a geologic wonder, featuring sandstone rocks that swept upward in cathedral-like spires. White limestone outcroppings—hogbacks along the eastern perimeter—bracketed south-to-north running valleys that offered spectacular scenery, including two man-made lakes.[18] Native Americans had camped here, protected by the heat-retaining rocks and sheltering canyons. A Colorado College geology professor, Dr. Jeffrey Noblett, emphasized the area's importance in a local interview:

> *No city in the United States has more geological history located within the city limits than Colorado Springs. . . . [The region] from Garden of the Gods through Red Rock Canyon to Section 16 should be set aside and preserved as one of the most geologically important parts of the natural history of the West.* [19]

Abandoned quarry site in Red Rock Canyon, 2010. Stone from Red Rock Canyon had been used in buildings throughout Colorado and in some northern Texas courthouses. The last large quarried project was stone provided for the ripapping of Monument Creek after the 1935 Memorial Day flood.

Colorado Springs purchased Red Rock Canyon in fall 2003 for $14.5 million, using Certificates of Participation to finance the transaction.[20] About $13.5 million came from TOPS money; in December 2003 the city received a substantial GOCO grant of $1 million to help pay off the purchase.[21] The Trust for Public Land negotiated and managed the transfer of the land from the owner, Mrs. Joan Bock, to the city, a complicated transaction in which the Trust played a critical role.

The property was opened to the public in September 2004, following the completion of the Red Rock Canyon Master Plan by the Parks and Recreation Department and the construction of a parking lot, restrooms,

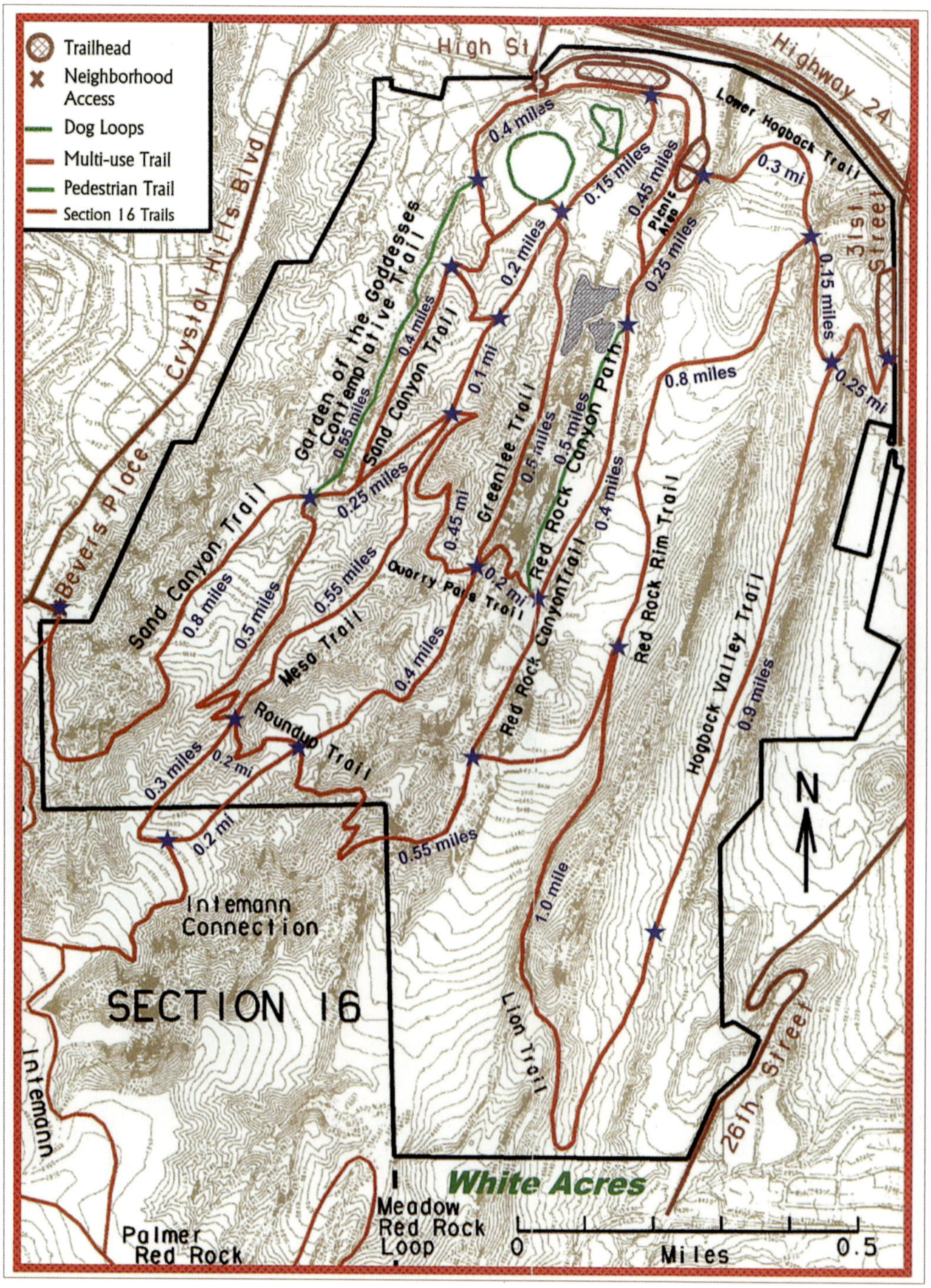

Trail map for Red Rock Canyon, Colorado Springs Parks and Recreation Department, 2010.

and some of the planned trails; construction continues in 2010. When completed, Red Rock Canyon will offer seventeen miles of trails in three loops—the "history loop," the "geology loop," and the "contemplative loop"—of which many miles will have been built by volunteers. Included in the Master Plan are equestrian trails, free-ride mountain bike trails, and off-leash dog parks, as well as picnic areas and designated technical rock climbing locations. Red Rock Canyon soon became a locals' favorite, attracting crowds on weekends, offering a surprising quietude during the week.

The next open space property purchased with TOPS funds was much the opposite of Red Rock Canyon—small, intimate, centrally located, lacking in geological significance. Union Meadows is a thirty-three-acre stretch of land between North Union and Academy Boulevard that had provided local residents a quiet retreat and leisurely strolls on wooded hiking trails for well over a century. Somehow the oasis had remained undeveloped as the city grew up around it. A true neighborhood open space, the preserve of bluffs and grasslands was enjoyed daily by local residents who had argued for years to protect it. In May 2004, after five years of organizing, advocating, and fund-raising, residents finally secured their longtime public gathering place as a preserved retreat amidst a sea of development and traffic. The city acquired the property with $320,000 from TOPS money, to which neighbors contributed another $55,000 raised through private donations.

Top and Bottom: Union Meadows Open Space, 2010.

TOPS money was a powerful tool. It enabled ongoing negotiations for future large purchases: Section 16 and the privately owned south peak of Cheyenne Mountain. It provided a means to leverage other grants and funding. Particularly important to the Parks Department was the 6 percent of TOPS money allocated for maintenance of TOPS-funded properties. These funds helped the department maintain neighborhood parks, at least those acquired through TOPS funding. Even though the 6 percent was not sufficient to cover all maintenance costs, it was sorely needed as departmental budget cuts became more severe.

GROWING PARKS SUPPORTED BY STRETCHED STAFF

Maintenance was a daily task, and the Parks Department staff worked hard and efficiently to keep up city parks for citizens' pleasure and recreation. The department prided itself on its maintenance of city-owned athletic fields and neighborhood parks—picking up trash, mowing lawns, chalking soccer fields, checking playground equipment—and the staff took their responsibilities to heart. Dan Gieck, the Parks North Athletic Field Supervisor, explained their motivation:

> *A well-dragged field gives kids the confidence to get in front of the ball. It makes you feel like you're something special. If kids see a manicured lawn, just like the ones the pros play on, it makes them feel like they're in the World Series. That's the impression we want each kid to have, like that kid is playing in the World Series.* [22]

But the parks staff was being stretched tighter and tighter. In 2002, when in a ten-year time span the city had increased its holdings by 31 parks and 379 acres—as well as 16 open space areas—it had added only 4 people to its

Parks Department staff.[23] When Director Butcher argued for a budget for more hires, City Council denied his requests. Sales-tax revenue was plummeting and demands for other services heightening. The Parks Department director cautioned that no new staff would result in a halt to the development of new parks, a reduction in maintenance, and/or new charges for the use of parks and trails that were currently free, but to little avail. As City Councilman Richard Skorman noted: "[I]t had been easier to curry favor with voters by buying and building parks than by putting money aside to maintain them."[24] The Colorado Springs Parks and Recreation Department now had approximately one employee for every twenty-two acres of parkland the city owned, a dramatically higher ratio than other Colorado Front Range cities.[25]

Two years later, prospects were no better for Parks and Recreation staff. While the city added employees to police, fire, public works, and other departments, the number of parks workers continued to be reduced, going from 142 full-time employees in 1997 to 127 in 2004. Community Center services were scaled back, and adequate maintenance was threatened. Councilman Skorman underscored the situation, saying: "I just don't think people have a sense of what's really happening. We're putting a strain on a certain kind of infrastructure we have, and I think the community will be very uncomfortable when they see the results."[26]

Athletic fields required ongoing maintenance, such as this soccer field at El Pomar Youth Sports Complex, 2010.

DROUGHT DRIES UP PARKS

The 2002 statewide drought, the worst on record, did not help matters. Anticipating a long hot summer, the city initiated a voluntary water reduction plan that spring. In June, City Council enacted mandatory water restrictions that would last until October 2005. The Parks and Recreation Department was required to reduce its water usage by 10 percent, and it pondered the possibilities. It planned to continue watering high-use athletic fields, flower-lined medians, and high-profile parks such as Acacia Park and Pioneer Square, but anticipated cutting back or eliminating irrigation where it might not be absolutely necessary. "We're looking for areas that are not used very regularly that maybe we could, for lack of a better word, sacrifice," explained Kurt Schroeder, the department's Maintenance, Trails, and Open Space Manager.[27]

By June the Parks Department had reduced watering in most parks to three days a week; some parks were to be watered only once a week; areas of native grass that were sparsely used were not to be watered at all. Sprinkler heads were replaced with more efficient models, and sprinklers were to run only overnight, from 7 p.m. to 9 a.m. Sports complexes that saw more use would be watered four times a week. But by August, fields were being watered just two days a week, and sports areas were losing grass and beginning to feel as hard as concrete. Turf became thin, weeds took over, hard bare spots surfaced, and exposed sprinkler heads dotted parkland. Officials worried that the fall sports season would be cut short, as hardened field conditions began to pose a serious threat.

The effect of reduced watering on Colorado Springs' urban forest was profound. Many trees died. The city's tree population numbered 122,000 in 2002; in 2004 it was reduced to 118,500. Over 10,000 more trees were estimated to have died the following year, and another 2,500 in 2006. In five years, the city had lost almost 14 percent of its trees. The considerable expense of repairing the long-term damage to the city's grounds, medians, and urban forest loomed over the department.

BUDGET WOES UPROOT MEDIAN GARDENS

Problems compounded. A national economic downturn was being felt in Colorado Springs, the city continued to face declining sales-tax revenues, and City Council made police and fire service its clear priority. In 2004, the Parks Department budget was drastically reduced; the department lost $1.1 million in operating funds, twenty-four full-time positions, and about 100 seasonal employees. In an unprecedented move, the 130-year-old tradition of city beautification was cut. City Council eliminated $120,000 of funding for the median-planting program, leaving it to volunteers recruited through a program called "Springs in Bloom" to plant and maintain city medians.[28]

As park-lovers had done for so many years, individuals and groups of volunteers pitched in, adopting 98 of 105 public flowerbeds. But the costs were high, flowers looked sparse, and some were so discouraged that they failed to return to weed their beds. Judy Finley, a longtime parks supporter and volunteer who argued for the return of city funds to the program, questioned, "Why would citizens want to reinvest their time and money if public government won't show the city it cares about its flowerbeds?"[29] Members of the Parks Advisory Board praised the spirit of volunteerism, but some concurred that the flowerbeds were unattractive and needed professional oversight. While others disagreed with Finley's perception of the program, her view held some sway. The following year, City Council

In 2005, the city again used the city greenhouses to grow flowers for Springs in Bloom volunteers to plant.

budgeted $60,895 so the city greenhouses could resume growing flowers, but it still chose to rely on volunteers to plant and maintain them, essentially turning over the management of the city's medians and streetscapes to a goodhearted but underqualified and overworked volunteer workforce.

Individuals, couples, Girl Scout troops, churches, corporations, organizations, and school groups all offered their services. In 2005, sixty-nine medians were planted and cared for by residents, businesses, and local organizations. Workers planted petunias, zinnias, and geraniums they picked up from the city greenhouses. The Parks Department provided irrigation to the planted areas, and volunteers were responsible for weeding. By the end of the 2005 growing season, Springs in Bloom volunteers had given thousands of hours of service.[30] But despite volunteers' formidable generosity, the beauty of Colorado Springs roadways would not approach their earlier glory again.

CREATIVE ATTEMPTS TO SOLVE DIMINISHING SUPPORT

Other daily aspects of the Parks and Recreation programs were suffering as well. Important repairs to City Auditorium were put on hold, despite the advocacy of the organized Friends of City Auditorium.[31] Prospect Lake was running dry; the lake had been receding since March 2002, when, during the drought, the city shut off a water pipe that kept it full. New neighborhood parks were delayed as city lottery receipts that would have paid for their development were transferred into general operating funds to cover salaries and maintenance.[32] Only TOPS money was available for the construction of two new parks.

Park administrators argued they had no other choice—pointing out their reduced general budget had already failed to keep up with inflation. Without taking lottery funds to cover staff salaries, they would have had to eliminate programs and cut maintenance, even though that meant no new parks. Council member Jerry Heimlicher argued City Council's position: "Parks are not expendable, but parks are not an absolute essential situation. It would be far worse to create new parks that we can't maintain and let our existing parks become cesspools."[33] And yet, local children were playing football in the streets, while parents and grandparents questioned the lack of adequate playing fields.[34]

In the face of diminishing financial support, the department had consistently searched for creative ways to keep parks open and programs running. It reached out to community organizations to create public-private partnerships, developing a westside play area and ball field, for instance, that remained the property of the Boys and Girls Club of the Pikes Peak Region. It teamed with the YMCA to build a facility for southeast Colorado Springs, a partnership in which the city offered land and $4.6 million and the YMCA raised an additional $7.3 million. Upon completion, the YMCA managed the pool and recreation center, serving ten thousand people. These and other innovative strategies helped keep programs running and parks maintained during difficult times. But some programs could not be maintained. The Beidleman Environmental Center was transferred to the Colorado Springs Utilities when the Parks Department no longer had funds to maintain the program. When the Utilities funds were cut as well, the Department leased the facility to a local, private non-profit with a focus on outdoor education, the Catamount Institute.

Hot air balloons drift above Prospect Lake and Memorial Park.

The year 2005 brought some brighter developments with slightly improved allocations. Portable toilets were removed from parks as finances enabled maintenance of permanent structures, a city forester and additional workers were added to care for trees and cut weeds, funds for trail building and visitor centers were allocated to North Cheyenne Cañon, and the leaky, nearly dry Prospect Lake was restored that year—in time for the Labor Day weekend Colorado Balloon Classic.

The Prospect Lake renovation was largely triggered by neighborhood activism, a common theme in the history of Colorado Springs Parks. The victim of the drought, a leaky clay liner, and budget reductions, Prospect Lake was turning into a mud hole when Prospect Lake Partners formed in 2004. The lake had not been used for swimming in over two years, and some were discussing simply filling it in. The partners, a group of residents organized by Jean Ferguson, started the momentum to save the lake, ultimately convincing voters in April 2004 to allow the city to retain $1.9 million in tax refunds for the restoration of Prospect Lake.[35] With that impetus, the El Paso County Commissioners contributed $200,000 to the cause, the Division of Wildlife provided a $160,000 grant, and another $430,000 came from savings on utilities to help fund the project.

By July 1, 2005, Prospect Lake received a new liner, and it was filled with water in time for the Hot Air Balloon Classic. Prospect Lake Partners offered continued support for the area, helping improve trails and plant grass, and providing support for the restoration of the beach house. A pleased Nancy Goodbar, president of the advocacy group, commented, "I think people are going to come back to the lake. We have a very caring community. They care about their resources because they care about their community."[36]

Top: Plaque celebrates the placement of Monument Valley Park on the National Register of Historic Places, 2007.

Bottom: Guided visitor hikes have been supported through the Garden of the Gods Foundation.

In similar spirit, many others supported their parks. The Historic Preservation Alliance and the Friends of Monument Valley Park worked to nominate Monument Valley Park to the National Register of Historic Places, for which they received approval in 2007. The Friends actively participated in the development of a Monument Valley Park Master Plan in 2004, the first such plan for Palmer's jewel in over sixty years. Other citizen advocates contributed to the North Cheyenne Cañon Master Plan, published in 2003. By 2004, the Rocky Mountain Field Institute (RMFI) had managed 837 volunteers who gave 3,713 hours of work in the Garden of the Gods.

A ten-year Master Plan for Memorial Park was approved in 2007, resulting from Parks Department collaboration with citizens in four public workshops. Of eighteen proposed improvements, highest priority was given to a professionally designed skate park, two handball courts, a tennis-center enclosure for two courts, a handicapped accessible playground, expansion of the Sertich Ice arena, Prospect Lake restrooms, and security, safety, and pedestrian improvements. While funding for individual projects would be determined on a year-to-year basis, enthusiasm was high for enhanced facilities.

The Garden of the Gods Foundation, the beneficiary of 100 percent of the profits from the Garden of the Gods Visitors Center, continued to support trail maintenance, erosion control, fire mitigation, school programs, and other activities in the Garden. By 2005, the Garden of the Gods Visitors Center had provided $858,726 to the Foundation. By 2010, the Visitors Center had returned $1.6 million to the Foundation—100 percent of its profits—for the benefit of the historic park.[37]

Despite all this generosity, unpaid ongoing volunteerism was down in 2004, and this was also impacting the underfunded Parks Department. Volunteer hours that had numbered 216,548 in 2000 had shrunk to 149,861 in 2004, the equivalent loss of thirty-two full-time workers. The loss was significant—volunteers were relied upon to coach kids' sports teams, build trails, adopt flowerbeds, clean up, pick up, and keep an eye on parks. Much of the loss of volunteers was attributed to the discontinuation of the city's contract with the Keep Colorado Springs Beautiful organization. The group managed the Adopt-A-Park program, organizing volunteers to clean parks, but their contract with the city was eliminated in 2003 because of budget cuts. With less volunteer help, programs inevitably suffered while department staff tried to fill in all the gaps.

SLIM DEVELOPMENT UNDER SHRINKING BUDGETS: 2006-2009

Even with dim funding prospects, the Parks Department made its best effort to meet expectations. The final 2006 budget included $9.1 million for capital improvements—$7.3 million less than requested—providing for seven new trails and three new neighborhood parks.[38] City Council contributed $250,000 toward the new athletic center at Saint Mary's High School, located a distance from the school above the Templeton Gap floodway, in exchange for city use when Saint Mary's teams were not playing there. TOPS money that had been tied up in litigation was released in 2007, and the department scheduled new neighborhood parks for development.[39] But Chris Lieber, the Parks Department program administrator for TOPS, cautioned the funds would not go as far as hoped; inflation and lengthy wish lists limited what could be accomplished, how many would be satisfied. The backlog of new park construction stood at twenty-one parks, and this was expected to extend for more than a decade.[40]

The Susan G. Komen Race for the Cure in the Garden of the Gods, 2010.

Nonetheless, residents continued to enjoy their parks and neighborhood events, participating in the Garden of the Gods 10K run, biking under moonlight during the Starlight Spectacular, golfing at Patty Jewett and Valley Hi courses, competing in organized sports, and hiking through wild and dramatic preserves only minutes from the city.[41] In 2007, Colorado Springs residents celebrated with a "disc-a-palooza" festival on the eighteen-hole disc golf course at Cottonwood Creek Park, introducing locals to the game

Skateboarders at Memorial Park Skate Park, 2010

that combined disc-throwing skills with golfing rules. Bicycle races, softball and baseball games, soccer competitions and tennis matches, peewee football and hockey games, Memorial Park's annual Fourth of July festival and the Labor Day weekend Hot Air Balloon Festival all attracted participants and spectators from throughout the city.[42]

The contributions of volunteers also stabilized. Volunteers in the Adopt-A-Park program, the responsibility for which returned to the Parks Department in 2004, helped with ninety-five parks. The Church of Latter Day Saints assisted with a large one-time project in 2008. Many others assisted with one-time projects, especially at Red Rock Canyon, in 2005 and 2006. Indeed, in 2009 parks volunteers provided the equivalent hours of seventy-two full-time employees.

Some selected development continued. The city joined financial forces with the county to build the Deerfield Hills Community Center spray ground, an array of fountains, sprinklers, and spray devices north of Drennan Road, in 2006; this was the first time the City and County Parks Departments had worked together to build a facility. In 2008, residents of the northeast Briargate Development were gratified to have the John Venezia Community Park Master Plan finally approved for development, after over seven years of campaigning.[43] And the Memorial Park Skate Park opened to rave reviews in December 2008.[44]

TOPS AND GOCO OPPORTUNITIES

While the Parks Department juggled to balance its shrinking budget, TOPS funds and GOCO grants nonetheless provided more opportunities to acquire new trails, parks, and open space. In December 2007, Greater Outdoors Colorado grants enabled the purchase of sections of the 962-acre summit of Cheyenne Mountain, providing residents with open space that reached from the Cheyenne Mountain State Park through the Pike National Forest to Mueller State Park on the west side of Pikes Peak. Funds were also reserved to purchase Section 16, the 640-acre parcel connecting Red Rock Canyon, Bear Creek Regional Park, and Pike National Forest.[45] In November 2008, the city initiated the first of several purchases of the Corral Bluffs open space on the eastern edge of the city, whose 522 acres of cliffs, mesas, and sandy valleys had been used as a cattle-drive stop in the late 1800s.[46]

TOPS and GOCO funds also made it possible to further develop the Rock Island Trail, Pikes Peak Greenway, and Midland-Creekwalk Trail. In 2007, the city purchased twenty-eight acres covering two and a half miles along the Rock Island Trail, widening the narrow trail between Murray and Powers Boulevards and extending it to points east. The widening of the trail corridor to up to two hundred feet in some places preserved dramatic rock outcroppings and open space for the benefit of the trail's users—humans and wildlife alike.[47] In 2008, the Pikes Peak Greenway between America the Beautiful Park and El Pomar Youth Sports Park was upgraded and expanded, using a combination of GOCO funds, city funds, and county funds.[48] Later that year, another GOCO grant enabled Colorado Springs to complete plans to extend the Midland-Creekwalk that paralleled Fountain Creek from Twenty-First Street to Manitou Springs. The additional GOCO funds, combined with TOPS money and funds from Manitou Springs and the Department of Transportation, would support the project.

Corral Bluffs Open Space, purchased in 2008.

The purchase of Section 16 was finalized in 2010.

In ten years, from 1997 through 2007, the TOPS sales tax had generated $59 million. With these funds, Colorado Springs had acquired more than five thousand acres of open space, completed more than one hundred miles of multi-use trails, constructed twenty-four neighborhood parks, and funded over forty park-related projects, such as picnic pavilions and playgrounds. TOPS funds had also leveraged another estimated $39 million in matching grants and donations. As Chris Lieber, manager of the TOPS program for the Parks and Recreation Department, explained in a 2008 interview, "That's just shy of $100 million in value to the community in terms of quality of life as a result of TOPS. We're pretty proud of that."[49]

2009: THE BALLOON BURSTS

Economic worries for the city and its departments did not abate, however. Following the 2008 nation-wide economic collapse, city revenues shrunk again in 2009, and the Parks Department bore the brunt of budget cuts. Not only were their operating funds reduced, but costs had escalated. The general fund budget for Parks and Recreation plunged 22 percent in one year, and at the same time water rates were hiked 43 percent.[50]

The department struggled to fund necessary maintenance. As new neighborhoods were developed, new parks came on line. New open space was acquired, and more trails built. Everything required maintenance. Having no other financial source, the Parks Department relied increasingly on the lottery fund—the Conservation Trust Fund moneys—for basic maintenance. Kurt Schroeder, the department's Parks, Trails and Open Space Manager, explained:

> *Any of our new parks in the last five years or so have all been brought on with TOPS money, but TOPS has not been able to provide the maintenance dollars. . . . [W]e've been falling behind the curve every year.* [51]

Beset with financial difficulties, many officials were tempted by the TOPS funds, arguing more TOPS money should be designated for maintenance. To that end "Ballot Issue 1C" was placed before voters at the city's municipal election in April 2009. The issue proposed increasing the maintenance fund proportion of the TOPS tax from the existing 6 percent to 15 percent, and allowing those moneys to be spent anywhere in the parks system for the following five years.

Members of the Trails and Open Space Coalition opposed the measure, perceiving it as a city raid on funds specifically designated by voters for new acquisitions. Others agreed—1C failed by a narrow margin of 49 percent to 51 percent. The Parks Department strategized how to make ends meet.

The department cut forty seasonal maintenance workers and searched for more volunteers for its Adopt-A-Park program, hoping to increase participation by 140 percent.[52] It locked up restrooms and slashed its irrigation spending by $767,000, reducing all but fifteen parks to half of the recommended watering ration, at the risk of permanently losing park grass. In summer 2009 City Councilwoman Jan Martin argued for other alternatives—closing city pools for the summer, for example—to preserve the parks:

> *"There are 135 neighborhood parks that we risk, literally, dying off this summer if we don't give them adequate water, [and it will cost] $6 million next year to reseed and replace those parks," Martin said. "I personally feel that it's irresponsible of us not to go back and consider options."*[53]

Matters worsened in subsequent months, and by fall 2009 the city warned of even more dire financial circumstances in 2010 as sales-tax revenues continued to plunge. What had been a shrinking budget was soon to be a collapsed budget. In 2010, the Parks Department faced a 75 percent reduction in its operating funds, on top of the 22 percent cut in 2009.[54]

Friends of the Garden of the Gods' "Trail Volunteers" trim trees, pick up trash, and work on trails every month..

In an attempt to avoid extensive cuts to city services, Councilwoman Jan Martin and her colleagues introduced Measure 2C to the November 2009 ballot, a modest mill levy increase on property that would be phased in over a five-year period.[55] The measure received strong support from City Council and city administrators, local media, park advocates, and many other concerned citizens. Yet it was overwhelmingly rejected by tax-aversive city voters. The proposed mill levy increase lost by a margin of nearly two-to-one, depriving the city of an estimated $27.6 million in additional revenue—funding that would have allowed the continuation of services in 2010 at 2009 levels.

Why were Colorado Springs citizens so opposed to increasing their property taxes to save services? Apparently, many voters believed city administrators had been using "scare tactics" to try to convince them to support the increase, that the situation was not as dire as presented. Many agreed that belief, combined with an extremely poor economy, distrust of government officials' handling of the budget, and a general conservative attitude within the community, brought about the defeat of the measure.[56]

2010: SCARE TACTICS OR NOT?

The subsequent impact on the Colorado Springs Parks and Recreation Department was profound. Without needed funds in 2010, City Council was compelled to eliminate services and reduce the size of its government. City departments were reorganized.[57] Facing a $24 million deficit on a $185 million budget, Council made severe cuts to the Parks Department budget, reducing it a stunning 80 percent.[58] By January 2010, 79 parks employees (out of 215) were laid off, and another 15.5 positions were on notice to find alternative funding. Trashcans were removed from city parks; volunteers were entreated to step up to maintain their local neighborhood parks; watering was planned to be reduced and in some places eliminated.[59]

City officials turned to volunteers and the private sector to try to salvage programs. The Parks Department worked to organize Volunteer Stewardship Plans for TOPS open spaces, broadening volunteer responsibilities.[60] Established volunteer groups—Friends of the Garden of the Gods, North Cheyenne Cañon, Stratton Open Space, and Red Rock Canyon, for instance, and Guardians of Palmer Park and the Corral Bluffs Alliance—provided extended support services to those areas.

By April, volunteers had provided trashcans for 37 of the city's 128 parks; some paid for porta-potties, irrigation and fertilizer. Others weeded, built trails and kept an eye on the parks. But excessive reliance on volunteers was not a viable solution. The ability of the Parks Department to even manage the volunteer programs, given its drastically reduced staff, was uncertain. The potential of volunteers being able to sustain parks over the long term remained in question. Furthermore, the reliance on volunteers had the likelihood of creating inequity:

> *Dave Munger, president of the Council of Neighbors and Organizations [CONO], which includes about 180 neighborhood groups [in Colorado Springs], worries that neighborhoods with fewer resources will fare worse than those that are affluent or better organized. "We're looking at the possibility of a culture of haves and have-nots if this lack of income extends," he says.*[61]

While citizen-volunteers clearly cared about their parks and were willing to donate their time, money, and energy to help preserve them, the over-reliance on their efforts represented an unsustainable strategy. The parks system of Colorado Springs, a very large urban system, required professional care, planning, and oversight to deliver the many benefits residents needed and expected.

UNCERTAINTY PREVAILS

But professional resources were rapidly disappearing. Many staff were gone. People questioned what programs might be able to continue with what funding. In a stopgap effort to salvage what it could for its parks, City Council determined to provide three months of funding for several programs while citizens and the remaining parks staff searched for other support.

Both the Aquatic and Fitness Center (AFC) at Memorial Park and the Cottonwood Recreation Center remained open under city support from January through March. Then in the spring, the Colorado Springs Swim School, a private operation, reached an agreement with the city to operate the AFC and the Wilson Ranch and Portal Park outdoor pools for five years. By summer, Monument Valley and Valley Hi outdoor pools and the Prospect Lake swimming area were closed. The city provided funds to keep the Cottonwood Creek Recreation Center afloat through the year, but by September Cottonwood reported it was running out of money, with "expenses running higher than estimated."[62] Deerfield Hills spray ground was open through the summer, and Julie Penrose and Uncle Wilbur Fountains operated on a slightly reduced schedule.[63]

Top: The Cottonwood Creek indoor pool remained open for swimmers, 2010

Bottom: The pool at Monument Valley Park was closed in 2010.

The four community centers—Hillside, Westside, Meadows Park, and Deerfield Hills—also received city funds for the first three months of 2010, while supporters tried to raise private funding. Eventually, the Westside Community Center was taken over by the Woodman Valley Chapel, but generally large non-profit organizations did not have the resources to replace the Parks Department subsidization of the community centers. Efforts by Meadows Park to generate income to save their programs fell far short of their goal. The center, serving a low-income neighborhood in southwest Colorado Springs with about fifty thousand visits a year, "sponsored everything from pizza dinners to jewelry-making classes to bake sales. A chili cook-off 'didn't make more than $50,' [Director Brian] Kates sa[id] with a sigh, 'but it did bring a lot of people in.'"[64]

The community centers were particularly vulnerable because poor neighborhoods lacked the resources to raise sufficient money to keep the popular programs going. But the services provided were critical, as described by *The Colorado Springs Independent* in February 2010:

> *Located in relatively poor neighborhoods, centers are places to pick up donated food, access affordable preschool and day care, work out, attend classes, meet neighbors, and forge friendships. On a typical day you may find seniors line dancing, or families hauling away boxes stacked with cereal, meat, bread and frozen fruit. Last year, the four centers, which together cost $1.7 million a year to run, saw 228,492 visits.*[65]

In March, City Council extended "bare-bones funding" from the city's reserve fund to keep the community centers operating until year's end, cautioning that they would have to have other established financial sources for ongoing support in the next year. With Council providing $450,000 to Hillside, Deerfield Hills, and Meadows Park, the Parks Department searched for another $125,000 to close the gap for full funding in 2010.

The Senior Center received an anonymous $20,000 donation at the beginning of the year and utilized endowment funds, gift trust accounts, and revenue to support operations throughout 2010—a successful short-term strategy but an unsustainable process for the long term. Consequently, in fall 2010 the Parks Department initiated the process of transferring the Senior Center and the Human Services Complex—its property, services, and dedicated funds—to the Colorado Springs Housing Authority.[66] The goal was to have the agreement completed by December 31, 2010 with the transfer effective January 1, 2011.[67]

The Living History Association at Rock Ledge Ranch increased fund-raising efforts to support programs in 2010.

City Council also drew on its reserves to allocate $365,000 to the Pioneers Museum so it could remain open for the year, with the charge to the Museum to search for different sources of support by year's end. The Friends of the Pioneer Museum, a strong, established support group, helped keep the museum's doors open. "Fifty very dedicated volunteers are at the core of the organization, and another one hundred devote time to the museum," explained the city's public program assistant, Rhonda Wooten. "Without them, we couldn't stay open."[68] In September, Mary Mashburn of the Museum Board said they were discussing establishing 501(c)(3) status for the museum.

At Rock Ledge Ranch, the Living History Association increased their fund-raising efforts to help sustain their program, as did the Friends of North Cheyenne Cañon for the Starsmore Discovery Center. The Garden of the Gods Foundation, funded by the Garden of the Gods Visitors Center, provided support for the maintenance and development of the Garden's programs. In March, the Garden of the Gods Foundation and Friends of the Garden of the Gods pledged $80,000 to fund staff positions that were cut from the city budget, keeping educational programs at the Garden operational.

The Youth and Adult Sports Programs, City Auditorium and Sertich Ice Center managed to maintain their programs by generating sufficient revenues to match expenditures. This cost recovery basis enabled them to generate enough support to cover daily operations, but provided no funds for capital investments. In April, the United States Olympic Committee provided Colorado Springs with a $125,000 grant specifically for youth, to be used for sports programs and summer camps offered through the community centers, with the promise of another $125,000 the next year. Sports programs were well utilized and appeared to be holding their own by year's end.

The Garden of the Gods Foundation and Friends of the Garden of the Gods provided support for educational nature hikes within the Garden, 2010.

TREES, TURF, MEDIANS, AND MAINTENANCE

Colorado Springs' tree inventory had grown to one hundred thousand plus street trees and twenty thousand park trees (not including the trees on hundreds of acres of open space), and a depleted workforce made its best effort to manage them. The Forestry Division was reduced from fourteen full-time positions to four and a half positions; it also lost two of its three hourly positions. Those employees remaining provided inspection for diseases, removal of dead and diseased trees, and maintenance of healthy ones. They focused on tree-related emergencies and mitigating hazardous tree situations, but the staff was clearly reduced to the point of being unable to meet its former responsibilities.

Concerned about the impact of reduced watering on valued trees and expensive turf in the parks, City Council directed the Colorado Springs Utilities to modify the water rate structure for the Parks Department that spring.[69] The Utilities provided a revised rate structure featuring a tiered program that encouraged water conservation by giving rate reductions when total watering was kept below a certain threshold. The new structure provided some relief to the Parks Department, enabling it to water at 2008 levels. The department established a watering schedule to focus on the trees most impacted by heat and the lack of moisture, and the City Forester applied a chemical on American Elm trees to promote slower growth. However, the revised rates only provided little relief and the department is still uncertain on how to manage water in upcoming years.

Downtown medians received some maintenance in 2010 when City Council approved $170,000 from salary savings for the effort. The department provided limited bi-weekly maintenance on the developed medians and worked on the irrigation system, and the median flowerbeds were sprayed for weeds. The same level of effort is planned for the next year, providing for some planting and maintenance, but the flowerbeds will be but a shadow of their former beauty.

The two ponds in Monument Valley Park were disappearing. The duck pond off Glen Avenue needed water. The southern pond had been leaking for years and, without any supplemental irrigation, had run dry. When rain came, it turned to a mud hole; in drier times, weeds grew waist high; when the wind turned, one could catch a stench rising from its bottom.[70] Despite the $125 rental fees for the pavilion that overlooked the pond, the Parks Department had no immediate plans to repair the vanished lake. "We really don't have the money to do it," explained Kurt Schroeder, "and you need money [to get] matching grants. We're hoping for support. Over the winter the department hopes to piece something together."[71]

Monument Valley Park's south pond (with pavilion in background) had run dry in 2010 (Top), and the park's duck pond water level was significantly lowered (Bottom).

DRAINED STAFF CONTINUE WORK

In the face of overwhelming responsibilities, the Parks Department staff worked tirelessly to preserve and maintain the city's legacy of parks. As Parks Director Paul Butcher remarked in a 2010 interview:

> *I really am proud of the staff. Problems started in the late 1990s, but they just went out and did their job. They loved their job. They are such a dedicated workforce, in face of the repeated message "you are not essential."*[72]

But as the work wore on, the department was to suffer the loss of key people. Several upper-level managers resigned or retired in the spring of 2010. Chris Lieber, Manager of Design, Development and TOPS, departed May 21, 2010 and Clay Shuck, Aquatics Supervisor, left on April 16, 2010. Paul Butcher, the Director of Parks, the Recreation and Cultural Services Department, chose to retire from the department April 30, 2010, after twenty-six years of service to the City of Colorado Springs, sixteen years of which he had served in the director's position. Others followed. [73]

With the wave of resignations, city departments underwent reorganization again. The Parks, Recreation, and Cultural Services Department, along with Public Works Team, Planning and Development Team, and Public Communications, was assigned to report to Assistant City Manager Nancy Johnson.[74] On an interim basis, Kim King, Manager of Parks Administration, and Kurt Schroeder, Manager of Parks, Trails and Open Spaces, were given responsibility to direct the Parks Department in a joint acting capacity.[75]

Despite all the difficulties and disruption, the Parks Department staff managed some significant accomplishments in 2010. An urban garden to grow vegetables for community need was established at Dorchester Park, at no cost to the city.[76] Two other new urban gardens offered plots for families to plant at Vermijo Park and Westside Community Center, in addition to the existing community garden at Old Farm and the demonstration garden at Harlan Wolfe Park. The Therapeutic Recreation programs, Wounded Warriors, and U.S. Paralympics, took place, funded by a U.S. Paralympics grant, and construction of the universally accessible playground at Memorial Park, a welcoming play area for all children including those with disabilities, began in March, with completion in May.[77]

A number of trail projects moved forward, with the help of federal funds and matching TOPS funds. Plans for the Midland Trail from Twenty-First Street to Manitou Springs were completed, with construction to begin in late summer/fall. The Cottonwood Creek Trail from Cottonwood Creek Park to Union Boulevard was scheduled for completion by the end of August; a small trail was built on Cottonwood east of Academy; and Parks staff worked with other city departments to connect a section of the Cottonwood trail from the Pikes Peak Greenway under I-25 east along Woodmen Road. Further work was done to resolve issues regarding the Sand Creek Trail. A Transportation Enhancement grant was received to complete improvements for a section of the Pikes Peak Greenway from I-25 to Cottonwood.

ACQUISITIONS DESPITE DIFFICULTIES

Despite the harsh reality of lost funding, more property came under the purview of the Parks and Recreation Department. In July, the Palmer Land Trust donated to the city a private lot it had acquired adjacent to the Garden of the Gods, helping preserve the western backdrop to the Garden. By the end of the summer, the TOPS Working Committee voted unanimously to approve the acquisition of the Anderson property, approximately seventy-four acres adjacent to the Corral Bluffs Open Space. The property provided land to complete a "rim" trail, providing Corral Bluffs a more sustainable trail system with impressive views of the Front Range.[78] In October, City Council approved the purchase, using $186,000 from TOPS funds.

Perhaps most significantly, the long-desired Section 16 would finally be acquired as preserved open space by the end of 2010. A decades-long goal of open space advocates, outdoors enthusiasts, hikers, and residents, the property more than once had seemed on the verge of being lost, but determined groups repeatedly stepped up to preserve the possibility of acquisition. The city and State Land Board had worked together closely to acquire and convey Section 16 to the city since 2005. After many negotiations, an authorization for the city to purchase the property for $3.8 million was finally approved in October 2010. The purchase of Section 16 was to be funded primarily by TOPS funds and a GOCO grant that had been set aside for that express purpose. Additional funding came through the pledges of El Paso County, the Palmer Land Trust, the City of Manitou Springs, the Trails and Open Space Coalition, and the Intemann Trail Committee.[79]

The "poster property" that had been used to argue for extending TOPS through 2025, Section 16 enjoyed overwhelming public support. Over 150,000 people visited Section 16 annually, where the Trails and Open Space Coalition led frequent guided hikes on trails built and maintained by the Intemann Trail Committee and the Colorado Mountain Club. With Section 16 guaranteed in the system, a contiguous open space would fill the western foothills between Red Rock Canyon, Bear Creek Regional Park, and Pike National Forest

It was a gratifying accomplishment in a year of struggles and disappointments for supporters of Colorado Springs parks.

Hiker in Section 16, 2010.

THE SEARCH FOR SOLUTIONS

Park prospects for the future were grim. There was no funding available for renovation and repair of existing park facilities. All the Conservation Trust Funds (allocated lottery moneys) were needed for parks maintenance and paybacks. What funds remained in TOPS were allocated for Section 16, and only those programs in the Recreation Services Division that were self-sufficient (cost-neutral/revenue generating) would have adequate funding. There appeared to be minimal funding available for the community centers, North Cheyenne Cañon, Rock Ledge Ranch, and the Garden of the Gods, public swimming pools, Therapeutic Recreation, and community sports.[80]

View of Red Rock Canyon, Colorado Springs and Black Forest from Section 16, 2010.

In an effort to garner more funds for park maintenance, City Council placed a proposal on the November general election ballot that would modify the use of the current TOPS sales tax receipts, similar to the 2009 issue that failed. The proposal changed TOPS allocations to allow no more than 15 percent (rather than 6 percent) to be used for stewardship and maintenance of all city-owned trails, open space and parks for a period of two years, from January 1, 2011 through December 31, 2012.

The ballot issue passed, with 57 percent of voters supporting the move. Its passage assured an additional \$500,000 to \$550,000 for parks, but parks advocates questioned its effectiveness in the face of a \$9 million need. "Our biggest fear is that people would vote for this and then think the problem is solved," remarked Susan Davies, director of the Trails and Open Space Coalition.[81]

Sign posted at Monument Valley Park bathhouse, 2010.

The Trails and Open Space Coalition had spent much time and energy during the year brainstorming possibilities for a "sustainable parks initiative" that they hoped would provide a long-term solution for Colorado Springs parks. They considered three possible proposals: a "regional service authority"—a countywide entity with its own elected board of directors and citizens; a "legislative district"—a governmental entity with dedicated tax dollars; or a "TOPS model"—a system including a voter-approved tax increase with dollars dedicated to specific purposes. Each possibility offered advantages and drawbacks, and all would cost more money to be acquired through increased taxes. But extensive surveying of Colorado Springs voters made it clear citizens were not prepared to support any increases in taxes in upcoming elections, and TOSC efforts remained in the conceptual stage at year's end.

As the city looked ahead to 2011, the Parks and Recreation Department was in disarray. Almost half of its staff had been laid off, and many other people in critical positions had resigned; those remaining were stretched to the limit to try to keep the parks and programs functioning. Pools were closed, programs privatized, community centers farmed out, and traditional park locations dried up and shuttered. Loyal and generous citizen groups who loved their parks formed organizations to try to save favored locations and programs, but fragmented volunteer groups were insufficient to assume the duties and maintain the overall vision that a professional parks department backed by committed politicians provides.

Clear and inspired leadership was lacking. City leaders, park administrators, volunteer groups, city residents—taxpayers all—disagreed on the relative importance of their parks and open space, their significance to the identity and economy of Colorado Springs, preferred priorities for the many diverse programs that served the community, and workable funding strategies to sustain a system that was unraveling before their eyes.

The parks of Colorado Springs were in crisis. Whether community leaders and city residents could and would make the decisions that would lead to the preservation of an exceptional and enduring public park system remained to be seen.

Red Rock Canyon, 2010.

Xeriscape gardening offers water-wise options for landscaping throughout the southwest. Demonstration garden at the Colorado Springs Utilities Mesa Road facility, 2010.

A Future of Possibilities

"It is politics that makes a great park system—
politics based on the muscle of grassroots support,
the brains of sophisticated leadership,
and the nerves of elected politicians who know when
to stand firm and when to compromise."

—Peter Harnik, *Urban Green*

THE LEGACY RECEIVED

It was with a clear vision, generous spirit, and inspired imagination that General Palmer originated the Colorado Springs park system. Palmer valued what was both purposeful and beautiful, and he fully realized the impor-tance of the parks to the health and well-being of the Colorado Springs community. From the pastoral playgrounds of Monument Valley Park to the scenic respite of North Cheyenne Cañon, from the red rock wonder of Garden of the Gods to the congenial gatherings in downtown Acacia Park, the early residents of Colorado Springs found solace, sustenance, and pleasure in their built and natural surroundings.

This was not an aside or an afterthought. This system was consciously and deliberately created for the benefit of all, when a common aspiration to the public good was understood as a way for individuals to realize the best within themselves. Because Palmer had intentionally established a connected and cultivated parks system, because Colorado Springs was blessed with stunning natural beauty, because local citizens arrived and remained to live healthful and vigorous lives, the parks grew to be a central source of personal pleasure, communal prosperity, and civic pride.

An expansive system evolved over the following 140 years. Under the attentive care of those who made Colorado Springs their home from generation to generation, the parks grew and changed to meet shifting needs, hopes, interests, and expectations. Neighborhood parks were added and

Clockwise from top left: Playing cards in Acacia Park, early 1900s; Swimming at Prospect Lake, 1960; Bluestem Prairie birdwatcher, 2009. Two-wheeling at Memorial Park skatepark, 2010; Memorial Park Olympic velodrome, 1980; Rock climbing in the Garden of the Gods, 2008; Center: Children swinging in Monument Valley Park, 1976.

playgrounds built. Medians planted and cultivated for urban health and visual aesthetics. Lakes, ponds, and pools designed for swimming, fishing, boating, and ice-skating. Community and individual recreation provided through athletic fields and tennis courts, shuffleboard courts and skate parks, spray grounds and basketball courts, golf courses and hiking trails.

The natural beauty with which the city was blessed was preserved through open space acquisitions and conservation easements, and a cultural consciousness developed and sustained through museums, living history presentations, educational facilities, and informational programs. As varying needs of the community arose, they were acknowledged and addressed—

The Orchard House at Rock Ledge Ranch, 2010.

from daycare and toddler programs to community service offerings and senior centers. Youth were provided opportunities for play, development, education, and growth; adults opportunities for refreshment, recreation, and public service. Where there has been a need, a joy, an interest—the people of Colorado Springs have responded through their parks.

As the city grew, the park system naturally did as well. Parks evolved to serve the community. What was essential for one generation could become outdated the next. What was unimagined in one decade could be critical many years later. Details varied. But one critical element remained throughout: the people involved expressed an ethic, inclusive and democratic, that was committed to the public good, that valued what had been given, that resolved to pass on this gift intact and enhanced to future generations.

AN INHERITED IDENTITY

"A park is an idea expressed in terms of place," said Denis Galvin, National Park Commissioner.[1] Palmer's vision was one of vigor and intelligence, generosity and quality. The parks of Colorado Springs have expressed his intentions and the like-minded ideas of local citizens—how they care for themselves, their families, their friends and neighbors—since the city's founding. In this sense of shared well-being, the parks have been integral to the identity of Colorado Springs.

Acacia Park, 1908.

Colorado Springs is, and always has been, a city of heart and beauty and strong character. Known as the City of Sunshine since its early days, the city was a beacon to tourists seeking delights, homesteaders seeking opportunity, adventurers seeking experiences, stricken patients seeking a cure. People came here to become well, to find a new life, to search for adventure, to learn and grow, to absorb a new and expansive panorama. They healed, they settled, and they stayed. They lived a productive life, they knew and cared for their neighbors, and they nurtured the extensive park system for the generations to come.

Early residents of Colorado Springs recognized health and tourism as the mainstays of their hometown economy. Today these appeals remain a natural focus on which the city can continue to build and prosper. A thriving park system—one that supports people, attracts business, promotes social well-being, advances personal health and fitness, satisfies aesthetic yearnings, and stewards the environment—goes hand-in-hand with this focus and consequent prosperity. A healthy and prosperous community needs its parks. They are not a luxury. In Colorado Springs, the parks are integral to the community's identity and the attractive, healthful life that can be enjoyed here.

Today, this system that has been essential to the city's well-being is facing a critical challenge. Overburdened and underfunded, the park system as it exists is proving to be unworkable. In 2010, programs have been eliminated, diminished, or transferred. Maintenance is lacking. Responsibilities have increased while staff have been drastically reduced. Vandalism is increasing. Priorities are unresolved. Without visionary political leadership, local citizens are indifferent, distracted, unaware, or ineffective. No long-term solution is in sight.

Questions are pressing. What is best about these parks, and what can be done to preserve these qualities for the generations yet to come? What actions will balance land use, cultural needs, economic well-being, healthy social relationships, and common history in ways that reflect essential principles and purposes? How will citizens choose to think about the problems with which the community is faced? What will serve the community now?

A RENAISSANCE IN URBAN PARKS

Across the country, others have been working to revitalize their cities and re-imagine their parks. Indeed, efforts to revive city park systems have gained momentum since the 1970s, when the urban lifestyle began to develop a new attractiveness. Particularly innovative solutions have emerged in the last decade. Communities across the nation have recognized parks as a clear ticket to promoting the health and vitality of their cities and infrastructures, and, as individual cities addressed their own unique situations and challenges, a wide array of successes resulted. Much of what has been achieved can be instructive to those Colorado Springs' citizens committed to revitalizing their own parks, open space, and recreation system.

Downtown bicyclist crosses Monument Valley Park bridge, marked with grafitti, 2010.

CARETAKING: CONSERVANCIES, CORPORATIONS, VOLUNTEERS, AND GOVERNMENT

Finding a strong funding stream has always been an essential priority. No doubt, insufficient and unreliable funding has consistently plagued public parks, especially in terms of maintenance. As in Colorado Springs, in cities across the country local citizens regularly responded to impending park system financial crises and consequent losses by joining together. In the 1980s, fledgling neighborhood groups began forming to advocate for their city parks, and new partnerships developed. From these gatherings came established conservancies—creative partnerships between individuals, non-profit groups, corporations, and governments—that became an effective force for working together to build better parks and better communities.

The Central Park Conservancy, organized in New York City in 1980, was the first to offer a new approach to old problems, providing the backbone to the 1990s activism of the urban community park movement. Since then, other conservancies have developed, leveraging public land and money that turn parks into self-sustaining enterprises, promoting public-private partnerships that generate pleasure for users and prosperity for investors.

Examples of these partnerships abound: Manhattan's Madison Square Park is paired with Shake Shack, a popular and profitable concession that pays back a percentage of its take for park maintenance and programming. The new Highline Park on Manhattan's West Side is supported through special arrangements with the city for concession revenue and security. The Brooklyn Bridge Park benefits from revenue from an associated restaurant and small hotel with a conference center—though some critics have objected to the Brooklyn Bridge Park Development Center's pre-emptive planning, pointing out that planners shifted development from more commonplace amenities to elements such as yacht berths that benefit wealthier patrons.[2]

Indeed, some dispute the advantages of conservancies and public-private arrangements, arguing these practices create a two-tiered system, benefitting high-profile parks while neglecting hundreds of others that rely solely on city support. Others point out local neighborhoods are vulnerable to losing control of their parks when overreliance on private money kicks in. But when individuals form neighborhood groups—from gardening clubs to independent non-profits—to provide maintenance and support, they often find that their efforts are simply not enough. The amount of work and the never-ending need for an ongoing effort eventually discourage most well-intended individuals.

The alternative of reliable governmental funding, such as systems developed in Chicago and Minneapolis through a citywide tax specifically for parks, may promise a more equitable system. But these are difficult to put into place. Taxpayers regularly reject such proposals. They look instead to the conservancies and other innovative public-private partnerships and non-profit organizations to solve funding issues.[3] The best solutions remain elusive.

A 2010 "Love Your Parks" Summit in Dallas convened the city's most dedicated parks supporters to explore ways to bring more volunteers, more funding, and more stability to the system. Facing a difficult bond proposal and recognizing the need to change funding strategies, the Park Board president explained the idea of shifting focus away from traditional approaches. "We've been running parks in a facility management way, and what it really needs to be is institution to institution," Mike Rawlings said, explaining the search for working with corporations and other funders.[4] Park supporters recognize that while steady and sufficient funding is critical to the realization of parks' potential, the best methods for insuring that funding are yet to be agreed upon. Solutions will likely be individual, involving a balance of different approaches best suited to each community's unique situation.

IMAGINATIVE DESIGNS DEFINE REGIONAL IDENTITY

This search for viable long-term funding is motivated by the successful, exciting, and economically stimulating urban parks emerging nationwide. Across the country, new and renovated parks featuring a range of fascinating gardens, theaters, concerts, fountains, recreational activities, and community gathering centers have breathed new life into cities. In his recently published book *Urban Green*, Peter Harnik explains how, in the midst of suburbanization and sprawl, the new urban park design harkens back to the principles of human scale, walkability, efficiency, respect for ecological principles, and democratic ideals.[5]

In the last decade, new parks in Boston, Atlanta, Cincinnati, Denver, and Santa Fe, and older parks in cities such as Pittsburgh, Brooklyn, and San Francisco, have generated an exciting urban dynamism, creating downtowns that are places to live, not just work.[6] In Chicago, the Millennium Park opened along the city's lakefront in 2004. St. Louis' Citygarden was completed in 2009, as was the High Line Park built on abandoned elevated railways on Manhattan's West Side, and Discovery Green in sprawling Houston.[7]

Residents walking their dogs in Monument Valley Park, 2010.

High praise and admiration have been forthcoming for these imaginative park designs that have enlivened the city experience. In the middle of downtown Detroit, the privately funded Campus Martius Park opened offering simple pleasures—movable chairs, a fountain, regular arts programming, and greenery—spurring renewed urban development. In Louisville, Summit Fields replaced turf grounds with native prairie grasses and mowed paths to delineate movement through the space. Plants were used as art pieces. Parks in Santa Barbara provided sunset-viewing platforms and built-in lounge chairs to protect cliffs from erosion.

When Oklahoma City leaders gambled on rejuvenating the river (formerly the North Canadian River, now renamed the Oklahoma River) running through the city in 1999, the result was not only a powerful economic stimulus but also a Mecca for athletes competing in elite water sports. A series of dams and locks were built along the trickling ditch that transformed it into a genuine waterway. The city added thousands of trees and developed wetlands and walking trails along the banks. Now, the Oklahoma City river park draws top rowing teams, including that of Harvard, to its annual regatta. In 2008, competitive trials for that year's Olympics in kayaking and canoeing were held there. A new Dell office complex overlooks the waterfront, and a multi-million-dollar American Indian Cultural Center is being built along the site.[8]

Monument Creek in downtown Colorado Springs, 2010.

In Denver, the old Stapleton Airport was de-paved to restore original land contours and create the city's largest park, adding to Denver's significant parkland growth. The economic value added by parks is clear. According to the Trust for Public Lands (TPL), urban parks contribute to clean air, clean water, tourism, local recreation, improved health, enhanced property values, and a greater sense of community, all of which can be measured. TPL analysts in 2010 determined that parks in Denver "delivered annual revenue of $7.1 million for the city, municipal savings of $3.6 million, resident savings of $517 million, and a collective increase in resident wealth of $48.7 million."[9]

In nearby Boulder, Colorado, the thoroughly integrated greenway has solved many of the city's transportation problems. A 1990 Transportation Master Plan promoted a transit system that included bicycles, pedestrian facilities, and a greenway in place of widening roads and constructing interchanges. In 2010, there is no doubt that the resulting hybrid trail-park has enhanced Boulder residents' quality of life. In addition to providing an efficient, safe, and enjoyable venue for rollerblading, cycling, and walking, the greenway offers residents appealing setbacks where they can relax—reading, reflecting, wading, and observing at their leisure along Boulder Creek. Particularly notable was the manner in which Boulder's Transportation Department, park planners and environmentalists worked together to achieve these results.[10] Similar trail systems have developed in Minneapolis, Seattle, and Washington, DC, as well as other cities.

THE ECOLOGICAL PARK, AN EMERGING TREND

These are but a few examples of the many various ways in which the nation's citizens have re-imagined their city parks, reflecting an evolving vision of parks and their importance to civic life. Besides benefitting infrastructure and revitalizing everyday city affairs, new park designs invite residents to take a distinct perspective on their environment. The most acclaimed new city parks reflect a growing awareness of the vital connection between human and natural life, and their designs are intended to offer people a more sustainable relationship with their natural resources.

Union Meadows Open Space provides relief to urban congestion in the middle of Colorado Springs, 2010.

In her most recent research, University of California professor Galen Cranz points to the "ecological park" as an emerging type.[11] She explains that this latest evolution in park design, one that neither opposes nor dominates nature, has embraced a system that incorporates humans into the "ecological whole." These new "sustainable parks" use native plants, restore streams or other natural features, promote recycling, and generate community-based stewardship. The ecological park connects fragments of open space into a comprehensive network, and harkens back to the older vision of the city as a garden, just as General Palmer had once envisioned.

Cranz delineates how ecological parks serve to promote the health of the city itself and all who reside therein. Today's best parks employ modern technological methods to minimize urban runoff, air pollution, and traffic noise. They help collect, store, and clean storm water and gray water. They serve as "the lungs of the city," using native plantings to minimize water demand, improving soils with compost from park maintenance activities, and championing the sustainable design of buildings and surrounding infrastructure.

As Cranz points out, the scope of this latest development in urban parks has multiple benefits. She argues that revitalized parks offer "a continued attention to fitness and sports, contemplation and appreciation of nature, community building and celebration, culture and art." The most visionary, aesthetically inviting parks feature "body-conscious" benches and play equipment that encourage people to experience their surroundings with their whole bodies, not just their eyes.[12]

Open-minded and innovative park designers, with broadened community involvement, have found exciting ways to solve urban problems and express a new vision of community through the imaginative parks that have opened in the last decade.[13] Where does Colorado Springs fit into this vision? Colorado Springs has extraordinary natural resources in place. With inspired leadership, clear-headed thinking, and committed grassroots support,

Colorado Springs could seize the same opportunities to renew and recreate its legacy of parks today.

AN EXPLORATORY FORUM

Those who care about the parks of Colorado Springs face opposing possibilities: the first, the evolution of an invigorating, revitalized, and visionary parks system emerging from the current solid—though shaken—foundation; the second, the continued deterioration of the presently scuttled and fragmented system, limping along piecemeal in the absence of clear leadership, creative imagining, and a broad community commitment. There is, of course, a range of variations between these polar opposites, but the extent of what truly can be accomplished depends on the imagination, resourcefulness, open-mindedness, and flexibility of those who dedicate themselves to the task. The future of the city's parks depends upon the people of Colorado Springs.

In September 2010, the authors met with four other concerned residents in an exploratory forum to discuss ideas and approaches that could forge a positive direction for the city's parks, open space, and recreation system. The four had long and distinguished careers serving Colorado Springs: Mike

Educational signage at Red Rock Canyon Open Space, 2010.

Anderson, retired Deputy City Manager; Paul Butcher, recently retired Director of Parks, Recreation and Cultural Services; Jim Colvin, retired City Attorney; and Bill Ruskin, retired Superintendent of Planning, Design, and Development for the Parks and Recreation Department. They brought together years of experience in city and park management and a lifetime of commitment to the city parks to discuss the possibilities of what could be. Ideas abounded. Analyses were realistic. Optimism was high.

Forum Participants Jim Colvin, Bill Ruskin, Mike Anderson, and Nancy Lewis imagine possibilities, 2010.

FIRST WHAT WENT WRONG

The benefit of hindsight is that it enables one to see more clearly patterns that developed and undermined goals. With a system as large, comprehensive and complex as that of the Colorado Springs parks, there is no one simple definitive answer to the question of what led to the present crisis. But several points were considered.

Certainly, the lack of reliable and sufficient funding has been and remains a critical problem. Programs were discontinued, facilities shut down, maintenance delayed, and fees raised because the funds were not there to provide services. But why has the city been unable to fund its public parks?

"We are slowly pricing people out of recreation. When the city says they see no value in subsidizing youth in sports, more and more drop off. Swimming is a survival skill. We are obligated to provide more recreation."

Paul Butcher, Forum Participant, September, 2010.

The city's over-dependence on sales tax has been an Achilles heel. Colorado Springs has a remarkably low city property tax rate; it depends instead on sales-tax revenue to fund necessary city functions. When recessions come, sales tax income drops, and all city functions suffer.[14] But there are other complications unique to Colorado Springs. Providing necessary city services is particularly difficult given the inefficient suburban sprawl that characterizes the city; the proportion of the city budget needed to fund police and fire is relatively high simply because of the manpower, time, and energy need to cover required travel distances.[15] And just as sprawl contributed to problems of service delivery, it continually added new neighborhood and community parks to the system without assuring necessary funds to build and maintain them.

Furthermore, sales tax dollars have not been used as effectively as they could be. The city, with a population over four hundred thousand at the end of 2009, had incurred no general obligation debt (other than the SCIP debt) to fund its infrastructure; it instead has operated on a "pay-as-you-go" basis.[16] Bonding debt (not the same as engaging in deficit spending) to build future infrastructure is a sound and strategic approach to creating prosperity. The city could operate more effectively than it has by issuing a large bond with small annual payments to maintain and retire that debt. However, tax-aversive citizens have voted down those options.

"The biggest problem is complacency. People are going to accept things as they are because they don't know what it used to be like."

Paul Butcher, Forum Participant, September, 2010.

Indeed, funding issues are further complicated by the tendency of voters to micro-manage spending through ballot initiatives and referendums, allocating moneys for favored popular projects while overlooking needs for more mundane activities. When sixteen business and civic leaders convened at the University of Denver's Colorado Economic Futures Panel to discuss solutions to the state's economic problems in 2009, they drew conclusions that could be equally applied to economic problems in Colorado Springs:

> *Central to the problem is the practice of making fiscal policy by public referendum through amendments to the Colorado Constitution. It is a haphazard approach where citizens are asked to make major fiscal decisions in isolation, based on one-sided "facts" provided by proponents and opponents. Making fiscal policy by referendum is a process where over-simplification and under-analysis are the established norms; where conflicting policies and unintended consequences are the logical outcomes.*[17]

But money has not been the only problem. Other conditions have undermined the legacy of the parks. The balkanization of the Colorado Springs community resulting from geographical sprawl and the establishment of special district neighborhoods has worked against a unified vision for the city and its parks system. As the city expanded, political leaders failed to connect the economic and social well-being of the community with the health of a vigorous park system; they failed to provide a vision of an inclusive and democratic system that could and would advance the public good. And as citizens lost faith in their representational government, reactionary politics and poor leadership created a vacuum in which the parks suffered.

Beautiful urban lower gardens were once the pride of Colorado Springs.

Other behaviors compounded problems. City leaders and residents alike failed to appreciate, respect, and support the experienced, knowledgeable, and professional park staff necessary to manage and grow a large park system. This led to further reductions in staff and incapacitated the abilities of those remaining. As the staff suffered from attrition, an unsustainable and excessive reliance on volunteers created the illusion of a solution while the reality was further deterioration within. Further widespread acquisition of open space and new parks and resources nonetheless continued—without sufficient funds to provide maintenance—and individuals' natural tendencies to support favored parks, programs, and policies over a more generalized vision of the public good chipped away at the overall system.

Each difficulty augmented the next, and eventually the system stalled.

NEW WAYS OF THINKING

Forum members agreed that the ways of thinking that created a problem will not be the thinking that will solve the problem. The organization, strategies, interests, and politics that brought the parks to their present dilemma will not be the processes that will resolve the crises. The parks of Colorado Springs offer enormous possibilities for community revitalization, civic pleasure, inspiring beauty, liberating play, and economic prosperity, but for this to happen, new leadership and forward thinking need to emerge. The people of Colorado Springs must conceptualize and act in startling new ways—just as so many have done in the past—to re-imagine and rebuild their parks.

What are the considerations? What are the possibilities?

WATER IN THE HIGH DESERT — AN INTEGRATED SOLUTION?

Any viable park system in the twenty-first century western United States will have to address the questions of water—questions about use, conservation, management, distribution, and planning. Indeed, water will be to the twenty-first century as oil has been to the twentieth. It is our most valuable—and limited—resource. A healthful and vibrant parks system (and community) requires water—mindfully and prudently used.

Native plants, trees, grasses and flowers both preserve resources and establish regional identity. Colorado Springs Utilities xeriscape garden, 2010.

Certainly the high costs of water have been an impediment to sound budgeting for the Colorado Springs Parks Department, and the lack of irrigation due to water's expense has caused severe financial losses in turf, gardens, and the urban forest. Only one or two years of neglect have severely affected the urban forest. Hundreds of trees—trees that had been nurtured for decades by the Parks Forestry Division and that represent an enormous investment of maintenance, energy, and money—are now lost. New solutions could prevent recurrent attrition.

"It bothers me to think that we will just continue the way we always have. We've got to find a way to not use so much water. Xeriscape. New irrigation methods."

Judith Rice-Jones, Forum Participant, September, 2010.

Careful attention to water is not a new idea; indeed, past successful city administrators have kept water considerations uppermost in their minds. In 1901, the city's founders included an explanation of their 100-Year Water Plan in *The Century Chest,* a collection of letters to be read in 2001 by future citizens. In his letter, "The Present Water Supply of Colorado Springs," Civil Engineer Edwin A. Sawyer described in detail "the sources from which we procure the water, the amount needed for domestic use and irrigation, the cost of our waterworks, and some of the plans now under discussion for the increase of our water supply in the future."[18] Subsequent city leaders, administrators, and managers have managed water, planned and built delivery systems, projected future needs, and procured resources with remarkable skill and thoughtfulness. Yet their resourcefulness has not always transferred to other departments effectively. The wisdom—the accumulated savvy of how to anticipate and meet critical needs—cannot stay compartmentalized within individual departments. The Parks Department could benefit from new ways of approaching these issues—as could the city in general.

For example, innovative use of storm water is one important possibility. Colorado Springs could learn from cities such as Denver, Longmont, and Fort Collins, where significant advances in storm water redirection and rainwater redirection have protected established communities and benefitted their parks. Partnerships between the Parks, Engineering, and Street Departments could result in using rainwater where it falls, thereby minimizing the need to upgrade the storm water system as well as reducing water costs to the Parks Department and insuring adequate irrigation. Rainwater falling on parking lots in parks could be directed to the landscape rather than to storm water systems; curbs could be cut on medians and tree lawns to allow rainfall to drench planting areas with only the excess flowing into storm drains.

Water considerations lead to many other possibilities. There are so many agencies whose essential interests are tied to water. The City of Colorado Springs Engineering Department; the Colorado Springs Utilities; the Fountain Creek Watershed, Flood Control, and Greenway District; the Pikes Peak Regional Water Authority; and the City and County Parks all have significant water needs and problems. In imagining a newly configured parks and recreation system, park advocates could search for available opportunities to develop an integrated water use solution that meets the needs of all these stakeholders within given constraints.[19] An innovative, collaborative inter-agency response to water acquisition, management, and distribution could solve many of the parks'—and city's—problems.

The city could also choose to invest in sustainable designs of parks, parkways, roads, and buildings that advance conservation efforts; it could endorse prudent landscaping using native plants, trees, and grasses that both preserve resources and establish regional identity. A reasoned and enlightened approach to the acquisition, management, and use of available water resources—and the strategies associated with this approach—should inform any new vision for the parks system.

NEW DEMOGRAPHICS AND SOCIAL CONSIDERATIONS

Forum participants emphasized the importance of anticipating future needs. Parks are for people—all the people—and park planning for the future must seriously consider changing demographics. In fifteen to twenty years, the city's population will include many more people from a diversity of cultural backgrounds, with different habits, interests, and traditions. A relatively smaller percentage of park users will likely value current interests—hiking and backpacking to seek solitude in the wilderness, for example. As demographics change, so do the physical capacities, languages, ethnicities, lifestyles, needs, and aspirations of those the parks serve.[20] Park planners need to plan to accommodate these changes, looking at who the audiences will be in future parks and making everyone welcome.

This perspective applies to the youthful generation as well. People in all disciplines are concerned about American youth sitting indoors, playing video games, texting, using their computers, and not venturing outside.[21] But critics need to tread lightly. This is a generational phenomenon brought about by the availability and promotion of inexpensive technological products and the encouragement of parents and teachers (and marketers) who have put kids on this path. Park advocates need to recognize this behavior as the stimulation it is—one that encourages cognitive growth—and consider how to help youth balance this aspect of their lives with the discovery that lies out-of-doors.

People should encourage kids to get outside for the sake of outdoor enjoyment—not simply to get them away from the computer—and introduce them to parks where they find a balance of stimulating fun physical activities and natural enjoyment that complements their other interests. Kids could be provided opportunities to enjoy guided hikes, perhaps learning about Global Positioning Systems (GPS) or wildlife conservation systems. They could participate with their families in programs such as the American Hiking Society's "Volunteer Vacation" program or their new initiative "Families on Foot." They could engage in meaningful volunteer and service-learning activities, and benefit from the friendship and mentoring of interesting naturalist guides. They could discover the joy of parks.[22]

"Any program has a life cycle. You need it for a while and then things change and then you don't need it. And when you don't need something anymore, it should go away. What can't go away are the places for people."

Nancy Lewis, Forum Participant, September, 2010.

When youth are exposed to interpretive and environmental education, when they have the opportunity to freely play and discover, when they acquire important understanding and appreciation of the out-of-doors, they create memories and skills that help them develop into happy individuals, productive citizens and strong leaders—exactly the people who will be needed one day to carry on the legacy of the parks.

Similarly, parks provide an important place for citizens to thrive as they age. Examples abound of grandmothers in their seventies participating in tai chi exercises and evening walks, retirees walking in safety in public parks to keep their weight down and stay fit mentally as well as physically, elderly gentlemen enjoying outings with their children and grandchildren. When people move physically and enjoy the outdoors, they are better able to take care of themselves. As Paul Sherer of the *Trust for Public Land* notes: "One way to promote the health of all Americans is to put parks where people live."[23]

Parks designed with a commitment to embracing a diverse citizenry—to supporting people from a variety of backgrounds, a range of different means, and through all stages of their lives—play an important role in building a civil society. Any vision for a meaningful parks system needs to hold this awareness close and be committed to supporting everyone.

MAINTENANCE VERSUS LAND ACQUISITION

The constant acquisition and development of new properties without addressing the accumulating needs for ongoing maintenance has created a difficult dilemma for the parks and recreation system. Maintenance of properties is critical. For people to enjoy their parks, the parks must be clean and they must be safe. For people to relish a sense of pride and community identity, the parks must be attractive and welcoming. For people to play, recreate, and refresh, parks must offer the environments that support their needs and interests. This takes constant attention and daily recurring care.

Park advocates must find ways to garner the same level of strong public support for maintenance of the city's parklands as has existed for the acquisition of property. Most of the spectacular sites in the region have been acquired; well-organized and committed residents have seen to accomplishing those goals. But future residents and families may not have the same priorities for land acquisition as current voters; indeed, they may find more value in the availability of well-maintained neighborhood parks, athletic fields, and swimming pools. New land added now, solely to meet arbitrary standards of parkland ratios to population, creates additional drain on an overburdened system. Any further acquisition of land should be put on hold until the recent purchases (through TOPS) have been completely paid and, most importantly, the careful maintenance of the city's current holdings is assured. In keeping a balanced and healthy system in place, decision-makers must commit first and foremost to the maintenance of present resources to insure their continued quality.

EXPLORING MODELS

How does one achieve and sustain all of these goals? To imagine a viable and re-invented parks system requires an open-minded and collaborative effort. Forum participants embraced a variety of perspectives exploring what new approaches might be workable for the Colorado Springs parks system, subscribing to the admonition of the National Parks Commission that "solving these pressing problems will require that governmental bodies, educational institutions, businesses, and non-profit organizations work differently—and together."[24]

"What's ahead of us, I'm convinced, will not have any resemblance to what we've had."

Bill Ruskin, Forum Participant, September, 2010.

WHAT ARE THE POSSIBILITIES?

Forum participants brainstormed. Perhaps a revitalized Parks Department would not be an integrated department as it has been, but would include a range of organizations to provide services in four or five different ways. Perhaps a partial solution would be to utilize a series of special districts (similar to neighborhood associations) to maintain neighborhood parks, since neighborhood parks and recreation programs are what need help the most, and what residents require the most. Medians could become the responsibility of neighborhood special districts; Business Improvement Districts could maintain medians in other areas.

Recreational programs and downtown parks could be advanced through the Parks Department's collaboration with non-profits or corporate entities. To date, there has been an aversion to acknowledging and including the corporate world in publicly sponsored programs—when McDonald's noted their contribution to the Acacia Park playground with a small plaque some years ago, that action spurred an editorial backlash in a local newspaper—but business involvement is needed to support Colorado Springs' parks.

Not only could willing businesses offer promising financial support for park programs, but they could also provide a methodology that would effect sound and efficient administration. With a business-like approach to solving the complex challenges of a large city park and recreation system, people would be better able to see all the issues, establish important priorities, and set essential criteria—including standards for tradeoffs and measurements of affordability.[25] An enlightened, sustainably conscious business approach would enable park advocates to collaborate effectively with local government agencies, businesses, private donors, colleges, and community service projects.

Other successful parks across the nation have demonstrated the effectiveness of engaging in corporate partnerships. When the private sector became involved in downtown areas in Chicago, St. Louis, and Oklahoma City, for example, property values rose, programs flourished, and the local economy grew. Acacia and Antlers Park in downtown Colorado Springs are prime candidates for adoption and overhaul by the private sector. Monument Creek flowing directly through the downtown offers significant possibilities for a rejuvenated waterway; other waterways within the city also offer potential amenities that could be developed. The Downtown Action Plan conceived by a group of Colorado Springs citizens advocated for the completion of a park ring connecting existing parks around the seven core downtown sections through land acquisition and trail connection.[26] As a downtown project, this would be highly visible, benefit tourism, and offer opportunities for healthy recreation for downtown workers and residents. The opportunities to partner with local businesses for mutual benefit are plentiful.

"We always look for the silver bullet. We think there's one singular solution. But the solution for parks may be very different. It may be multidimensional."

Mike Anderson, Forum Participant, September, 2010.

Colorado Springs has three willing sectors to bring together: private, public, and non-profit. Creative and collaborative partnerships among the three could accomplish successes the city alone has failed to achieve. In the process, the city and the Parks Department could draw on the extensive resource of individual volunteers and volunteer groups who have unfailingly come to the rescue of the city parks time and time again. Throughout the parks' history, volunteers have worked hard, added value, and highlighted critical projects. They emphasized partnering, and they gained community support. The people of Colorado Springs love their parks, and they are extraordinarily generous with their time, energy, and effort. Future programs that embrace volunteers, integrating their talents and willingness into the system without exploiting or excessively relying upon them, will generate huge dividends.

VISIONARY LEADERSHIP

Such ideas lead naturally to questions of organization, authority, and funding. Should a re-imagined Parks Department be a part of city government? Should the City and County Parks Departments be merged into one agency, a different funding mechanism created, and a governance group elected to run it? What is an appropriate role for a Parks Advisory Board? How do the many Friends groups function best and how can the

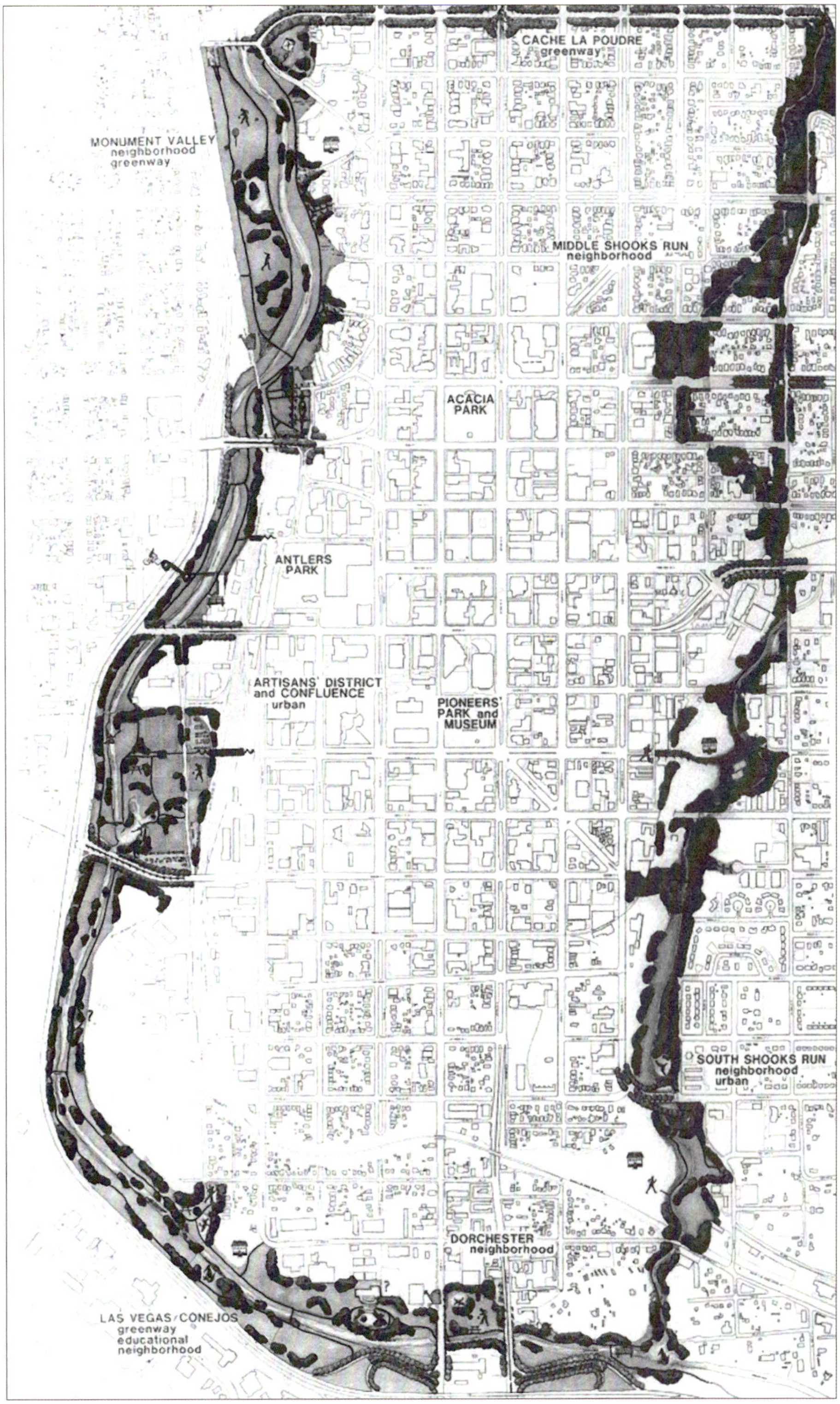

The Downtown Action Plan, formulated in 1992 and updated in 2005, advocates for a "ring of connected parks" surrounding the core downtown area, connecting Monument Valley Park, Middle Shooks Run, South Shooks Run, Dorchester Park, Confluence Park, and Antlers Park through developed greenways and districts. Acacia Park and Pioneers Park rest within the "string of pearls." The idea expanded on Elaine Freed's 1978 Park Center Proposal to redevelop Monument Valley Park as the keystone park in a core area called the Park Center, connecting Monument Valley with Shooks Run Park, Antlers Park, and Acacia Park.

"Some of these decisions need to have a business approach. People who love the parks will miss the affordability question."

Bill Ruskin speaking with Mike Anderson, Forum Participants, September, 2010.

department embrace volunteers in ways that tap their expertise and support their growth? Is there a role for conservancies? How can the city create new sources of funding revenue and fund-raising to support parks? How do park advocates bring business to the table and generate private park financing that is critical to getting parks off the ground and maintaining them into the future? Who will generate the next Parks, Recreation, and Cultural Services Master Plan—now absent in the overall system—that will provide an integrated and focused vision for the future of the parks?

These are not planning questions, but political questions. Not one of these important issues can be resolved without the emergence of robust leadership. In 1871, Colorado Springs was blessed with the clear-sighted vision and civic commitment of its founder, General Palmer. Through the years, generous, intelligent and open-minded city leaders have continued to forge the way to build a big-hearted and beautiful city. They have understood the legacy that has been passed down from generation to generation; they have respected and considered existing legal restraints and ramifications; they have imagined new possibilities and brought them to fruition. Such leaders could lead—not simply react. They inspired an informed citizenry to consider, respond, engage, and vote to preserve and advance the public good.

"The city was formerly governed by people whose interest was in the city as being a good place to live. . . . We've lost the identity that parks are an important element of the city because we don't have leadership saying that now. The answer will come from the younger people who will be our leaders."

Jim Colvin, Forum Participant, September, 2010.

The best public servants of Colorado Springs were people who identified with the city, who loved it as their home, who saw the big picture and embraced the whole community—not just one neighborhood, not just one interest, not just one aspect. The people who have made a difference could see the entire system—all the parks and parkland, all the open space and programs, all the neighborhoods, all the needs, and all the people and the relationships that lay within—and they placed the community's well-being above any other considerations.

Such leadership is what is needed today. A new generation of political leaders is necessary to advance innovative ideas, to forge collaboration between those with different interests, to achieve real and tangible results, to preserve the rich and bountiful legacy of the parks of Colorado Springs. Whatever the specific details of the next solutions may be, they cannot be arrived at without leadership from people who understand and value the Colorado Springs community—its history and its potential—and who can help imagine the solutions that fit with its unique individual identity.

THE RETURN OF AN ETHIC

If we understand and respect our history, we will be able to preserve and advance the best of our traditions. If we understand the source of our difficulties, we can learn to prioritize and develop new strategies. If we commit to a common vision, we can focus on our primary needs and serve the public good.

Our parks are a wonderful and life-enhancing legacy. They are available to us today as a remarkable and valuable resource. As we adapt to change, we should do so with wisdom and imagination, in ways that allow all people to continue to grow, to thrive, and to prosper—together. We need neighborhood parks. We need beauty in the streets. We need recreational opportunities so all citizens can live healthy and active lives. We need to be good stewards of the natural environment in which we live. We need to balance social needs and economic needs, personal needs, and public needs. We need places for people.

These were our roots. This was our ethic. It's up to us if we want it back.

Monument Creek approaching the Bijou Street bridge, south end of Monument Valley Park, 2010.

Endnotes

Chapter One: A City of Jewels

[1] Amanda Ellis. *The Colorado Springs Story.* The Dentan Printing Company. Colorado Springs, CO. 1954. p. 6.

[2] William Palmer. Letter cited in John Sterling Fisher, *A Builder of the West: The Life of General William Jackson Palmer.* The Caxton Printers. Caldwell, ID. 1939.

[3] Helen Hunt Jackson became best known for *A Century of Dishonor* and *Ramona,* writings inspired by her activism against the atrocities and injustices committed against Native Americans. Born in Amherst, Massachusetts, and educated in New York City, she was friend to both Emily Dickinson and Harriet Beecher Stowe. In 1875, she married William Jackson, banker and railroad executive, in Colorado Springs. She was buried at Helen Hunt Falls in Cheyenne Cañon; her remains were later removed to Evergreen Cemetery.

[4] Helen Hunt Jackson. *Bits of Travel at Home.* Roberts Brothers: Boston. 1878. p. 224.

[5] Marshall Sprague. *Newport in the Rockies.* Swallow Press/Ohio University Press. Athens, Ohio. 1961, 1987. p. 18.

[6] Judith Finley, ed. *"The Century Chest Letters of 1901: A Colorado Springs Legacy."* The Colorado College, Colorado Springs, Colorado. 2001. p. 63. Edward Ensign's letter was included in the Century Chest—a wonderful project whereby the leading citizens of Colorado Springs in 1901 wrote letters to the future that were opened in 2001. Ensign was one of the first state foresters in the Colorado Forestry Association.

[7] In his *Gazette Telegraph* article, "How Colorado Springs Got Its Water, Parks Told by Pioneer" former City Clerk H.C. McCreery recounts the transfer of the Antlers Park property from General Palmer to the city in 1892. Calling a special session of the Colorado Springs Council on a Monday morning, the General offered the property and the Council unanimously accepted. As McCreery explains: "In general conversation among the crowd it was remembered that a few days before this occurred, a party of surveyors had been seen running a line up the hill west of the town and out over the mesa toward the Garden of the Gods. Then the information leaked out that they were railroad men of the Denver and Fort Worth Company, and it was generally believed that had General Palmer not stopped the work as he did, they would have crossed what is now the [Antlers] park and built through the Garden and into Manitou." April 21, 1935.

[8] Finley. *The Century Chest Letters of 1901.* p. 62.

[9] Judith Rice-Jones. "William Jackson Palmer—Park Builder" in *Legends, Labors and Loves: William Jackson Palmer, 1836-1909.* Eds. T. Blevins et al. Pikes Peak Library District Publication. Colorado Springs, CO. 2009. References to France are quoted from Palmer's journals and letters in the collection of the Colorado Historical Society library.

[10] Frederick Law Olmsted, 1822-1903, is considered the originator of American landscape architecture; Calvert Vaux, 1824-1895, an English-born architect and landscape designer, collaborated with Olmsted on New York's Central Park.

[11] According to Marshall Sprague, "The late Springs millionaire, William Lennox, used to boast that his first Pikes Peak job was planting McAllister cottonwoods at 50 cents a tree for the first five blocks of Cascade Avenue." *Newport in the Rockies.* p. 316.

[12] William Jackson Palmer, personal letter for the Century Chest, August 1, 1901.

[13] *Report of the Park Commission.* Colorado Springs, CO. 1908. p. 11.

[14] In 1882, Colorado College President E.P. Tenny had purchased real estate in Cheyenne Cañon, hoping the speculation would bring additional funds to the college. The City of Colorado Springs purchased the 640 acres from the college with the city's first voter-approved bond issue. "Life and Times of the *Cañon.*" *The Cañon Companion: A Guide to North Cheyenne Cañon City Park.* p. 3.

[15] William Jackson Palmer, personal letter for the Century Chest, August 1, 1901.

[16] Charles W. Leavitt quoted in Robert Imlay, "The Gardens of Charles M. Schwab, Esq., Loretto, PA, Charles Wellford Leavitt, Landscape Engineer." *The Architectural Record*, Vol. 47, Number 5, May 1920. p. 388.

[17] In addition to his parkland gifts, General Palmer also donated twenty acres for Colorado College and five acres for the Deaf and Blind School in 1874, and the sites of Prospect Lake and Mesa Reservoir in 1890.

[18] Sprague. *Newport In The Rockies*, pp. 165, 332. The twenty-acre Stratton Park was divided into sixty housing lots. *The Cañon Companion.* p. 3.

[19] Donald McGilchrist. "The Gardens of Glen Eyrie" in *Legends, Labors and Loves: William Jackson Palmer, 1836-1909.* Eds. T. Blevins *et. al.* Pikes Peak Library District Publication. Colorado Springs, CO. 2009. pp. 227-228.

[20] Bruce Woodard. *The Garden of the Gods Story,* Pruett Press, Inc., Boulder, CO. 1955. p. 41. In 1892, Paul Goerke bought land southwest of the Garden of the Gods that included Steamboat Rock, Balanced Rock, and Mushroom Park. He and his son sold curios and photographed tourists on burros in front of Balanced Rock. In 1909, the Goerkes constructed a barricade across the road between Balanced Rock and Steamboat Rock, claiming it as their property, and a battle with Manitou Springs ensued. The legal dispute and bitter arguments continued until 1932, when the city of Colorado Springs acquired the property from the Goerkes and added it to the Garden. (*Take A Walk on the Wild Side. A Visitors Guide to the Garden of the Gods Park.* Published by Friends of the Garden of the Gods. Colorado Springs, CO. 2000. pp. 4-5.)

[21] Sprague. *Newport In The Rockies,* p. 137.

[22] *Report of the Park Commission.* Colorado Springs, CO. 1908. p. 8.

[23] "Extractions: Conditions placed in deeds of park lands by General Palmer and in effect today." From a report by City Manager Biery dated December 10, 1965. See Appendix.

[24] *Report of the Park Commission.* Colorado Springs, CO. 1908. p. 13.

[25] "Gift of More Than Million." *Colorado Springs Gazette.* May 7, 1907. p. 1.

[26] *Report of the Park Commission.* Colorado Springs, CO. 1908. p. 9.

Chapter Two: Sending Down Roots

[1] Cited by Edward Warren in "The Birds of Monument Valley Park, Colorado Springs, Colorado." *Bird-Lore. A Bi-Monthly Magazine Devoted to the Study & Protection of Birds.* p. 228.

[2] "Urges Public to Cooperate with Park Board: City's Possessions Described by Asa T. Jones." *Colorado Springs Gazette Telegraph.* May 25, 1916. 6:1.

[3] Members of the first Park Commission were Horace G. Lunt, President; Irving Howbert; F.F. Castello; J.F. Lily; D.V. Donaldson; and E.C. Van Diest, Secretary.

[4] "Springs Parks: Unexcelled in Entire Country." *Colorado Springs Gazette Annual Edition.* February 18, 1912. p. 1.

[5] "Urges Public to Cooperate with Park Board: City's Possessions Described by Asa T. Jones" *Colorado Springs Gazette Telegraph.* May 25, 1916. 6:1.

[6] "Unique Parks in a Country of Parks." *Colorado Springs Gazette Telegraph.* February 25, 1917. p. 13

[7] "City Park System Is Spacious and Beautiful and Famous the World Over." *Colorado Springs Gazette Telegraph.* February 24, 1918. Sec. A. p. 1.

[8] "Most Wonderful Park System in the World: Natural Beauty Spot Delight of Thousands." *Colorado Springs Gazette Telegraph.* March 27, 1921. Sec. 4.

[9] Quoted by Galen Cranz. *The Politics of Park Design.* MIT Press. Cambridge, MA. 1982. p. 15.

[10] *Report of the Park Commission.* Colorado Springs, CO, 1908. pp. 23-24.

[11] *Report of the Park Commission.* Colorado Springs, CO, 1908. p. 25.

[12] *Report of the Park Commission.* Colorado Springs, CO, 1908. p. 25. In Acacia Park, shuffleboard courts and a band shell had been installed at the turn of the century.

[13] See Cranz, *The Politics of Park Design,* page 8. By 1910, the national progressive movement resulted in a reformist zeal in park design and purpose that focused on improving the lives of the weak, the poor, and the disadvantaged. Parks came to be seen as a means to a democratic social end: assimilation of immigrants and improvement of civic life. The new emphasis on structure and organization that permeated park thinking nationwide resulted in the creation of municipal facilities for recreation—golf, swimming, beaches, tennis courts, picnic areas, and organized playgrounds. Parks were now to offer organized activities, particularly those promoting good citizenship. For example, games for children were considered an improvement over simply playing because they offered a context for teaching and learning social mores. Eventually play broadened to include a general range of activities for young and old, and parks became a place for activities—often organized and led—as well as for landscape beauty.

[14] The importance of the park system to the city was reflected in the Colorado Springs municipal flag, designed in 1912 by members of the Civic League. The symbolism of the flag was explained as follows: "White Field represents the cleanliness and health of the City, and the Blue Border our Blue Skies; the Shield carries the Sun, of which we are justly proud; the Mountain stands for Pikes Peak, and

on it are pictured the gold ingots of our mining industries; the Green Band about the Shield represents the park system surrounding the City."

[15] Superintendent Dunman, landscape gardener and former worker (as a youth) on the estate of King Edward VII, remained with the city until 1921, when he returned to Nebraska as landscape gardener for the University of Nebraska.

[16] George W. Thorne and Jessie R. Thorne, officers of the East Colorado City Land and Improvement Company, gave Thornedale Park—2.86 acres—to Colorado City on April 28, 1902. Anthony Bott deeded Bott Park—4.06 acres—to Colorado City on September 24, 1897.

[17] The *Gazette Telegraph* reported in 1917 that a "number of public-spirited women" raised a "private fund" to purchase a thirty-foot slide and two horizontal ladders for Dorchester and Boulder Park grounds to match those at Prospect Lake. ("Unique Parks in a Country of Parks." *Colorado Springs Gazette Telegraph*. February 25, 1917. p. 4.)

[18] "Prospect Lake formerly has been under the jurisdiction of the water department but recently has been transferred to the park commission. The greater part of this property is included in the lake, a storage reservoir. . . . The park commission is planning to lay out a modern camping ground here with every convenience possible. The site is ideal, being out of the main part of the city and commanding a magnificent view of the mountains. A municipal playground at the lake affords pleasure for the hundreds of children. A wide drive around the lake makes it a favorite for those seeking short drives." "Most Wonderful Park System in the World: Natural Beauty Spot Delight of Thousands." *Colorado Springs Gazette Telegraph*. March 27, 1921. Section 4.

[19] "Unique Parks in a Country of Parks." *Colorado Springs Gazette Telegraph*. February 25, 1917. p. 4.

[20] Ibid. p. 5.

[21] "City Park System Is Spacious and Beautiful and Famous the World Over." *Colorado Springs Gazette Telegraph*. February 24, 1918. Sec. A:1.

[22] Although the construction of buildings in the Garden of the Gods was a violation of the Perkins deed, the Hidden Inn was built and opened in June 1915 with the enthusiastic endorsement of the Colorado Springs Park Commissioners and the City Council. Indeed, in a *Gazette* article of the day, it was noted that "the park commissioners were felicitated upon their good taste in adding this new and novel attraction to the Garden of the Gods." ("New Hidden Inn Is Officially Opened." *Colorado Springs Gazette Telegraph*. June 29, 1915. p. 5.)

[23] According to *The Cañon Companion*, "In 1917, automobiles were allowed on the park's one-lane road, but regulations were strict: 'The time during which automobiles may drive up Cheyenne Cañon is between 5 and 7 o'clock in the evening. No car is permitted to descend from Bruin Inn until 7:30 o'clock, thus giving a car starting up at the last possible minute a full half hour to make the trip.' In 1919, park visitors complained that automobiles with their 'honk, weight and speed,' had an unfair advantage over pedestrians, and frequently forced foot travelers to leap into roadside snow banks. The city developed plans to build a foot trail away from the road." When a storm washed out the road in 1921, a larger venue allowed two-way vehicle traffic all the way to the Bruin Inn. The Bruin Inn remained a tourist attraction until it burned down in December 1957.

[24] "Money for Street Work." *Colorado Springs Gazette*. June 30, 1913.

[25] "Springs Parks: Unexcelled in Entire Country." *Colorado Springs Gazette*. February 18, 1912. p. 1.

[26] "Shakespearean Garden Will Be Planted Today." *Colorado Springs Gazette*. May 19, 1916. p. 5.

[27] "City Park System Is Spacious and Beautiful and Famous the World Over." *Colorado Springs Gazette*. February 24, 1918. A:1.

[28] Edward Warren. "The Birds of Monument Valley Park." *Colorado Springs Gazette*. May 28, 1915.

[29] "Rock Garden Once a Top Attraction." *Colorado Springs Gazette Telegraph*. July 20, 1985. F:33.

[30] "Palmer Park—Least Known, Most Fascinating, of City's Plots." *Colorado Springs Gazette Telegraph*. June 19, 1927.

[31] "Glorious Playground Season Opens in City's Parks Tomorrow Afternoon." *Colorado Springs Sunday Gazette and Telegraph*. June 15, 1930.

[32] The purchase of the Goerke property, including the famous Mushroom Rocks, Balanced Rock, and Steamboat Rock, was particularly gratifying to local residents who had been deliberately walled off from the tourist attraction by Paul Goerke and his son since 1892.

[33] "Name Clotworthy to Park Board." *Colorado Springs Gazette Telegraph*. January 24, 1934. 1:4.

[34] "75 Years Ago Today." *Colorado Springs Gazette*. 2008.

[35] "Kirkwood to Be at Head of Park System." *Colorado Springs Gazette Telegraph*. February 12, 1935. p. 1.

[36] "Memorial Day Recalled When Flood Caused Havoc." *The Free Press.* Colorado Springs, CO. March 12, 1963. p. 8.

[37] Stuart Dodge, a teenager at the time, recalled seeing an entire house carried along Monument Creek and smashed to pieces against the Bijou Street bridge. Dodge would later become a Colorado Springs Parks Advisory Board member and member of the State Historical Society. In 1998, he was active in the movement to revitalize Monument Valley Park. (Dru Wilson. "TRAIL OF HISTORY/ Monument Valley Park's Historic Gems Reveal Clues About the People Who Helped Shape Colorado Springs." *Colorado Springs Gazette.* June 25, 1998.)

[38] "Park System of Colorado Springs Is Unique." *Colorado Springs Gazette & Telegraph.* Tourist Ed., May 10, 1936. p.1.

[39] Ibid.

[40] "Improvements Add Beauty to City's System of Parks." *Colorado Springs Sunday Gazette and Telegraph.* April 28, 1936.

[41] Clarence Stewart. "City's Magnificent Park System Almost Entirely Given by Region Benefactors." *Colorado Springs Gazette Telegraph.* August 8, 1937. p. 8

[42] Clarence Stewart. "City's Far-Flung Park System Ready for Summer Season." *Colorado Springs Gazette Telegraph.* May 2, 1937. p. 2:1.

[43] The U.S. Army Camp Carson—later to become Fort Carson—opened in Colorado Springs in 1942.

[44] The North Cheyenne Cañon amphitheatre was built by Fort Carson troops, who used it as a classroom for teaching the 38th Regimental Combat Team the climbing techniques used in World War II. Climbing exhibitions continued until 1983. The amphitheatre was torn down in 1997.

[45] Stanley Payne. "Beautification and Recreation Keynotes of Park Development." *Colorado Springs Sunday Gazette & Telegraph.* March 25, 1945. Sec. 2.5:1.

[46] "When Segregation Ruled Baseball." *Colorado Matters.* Ryan Warner interview with Jessie Vaughan and Joe Morgan. KCFR Radio. July 21, 2009.

[47] Ibid.

[48] Quoted by Galen Cranz in *The Politics of Park Design*, p. 214.

[49] "When Will Boulder Park Be Finished?" *Colorado Springs Free Press.* February 15, 1947. p. 6. The day following the publication of this article, the Gazette Telegraph quoted Assistant Park Superintendent George Carlson as saying "Boulder Park will be a complete park by next fall."

[50] "Elmer W. Allen, Candidate for City Council Two-Year Term." *Colorado Springs Free Press.* March 26, 1947. 8:3.

[51] "Approval of Parks Proposal Scraps 40-Year-Old Board." *Colorado Springs Gazette Telegraph.* April 2, 1947. p. 1.

[52] Members of the new parks advisory commission were announced on July 9, 1947: Kathleen Marriage, Washington Pastorius, J.R. DeFries, E.S. Keithley, William Kice, Kenneth Brookhart, and Ray Ryerson.

[53] Director Russell, his wife and daughter lived in an apartment over the bathhouse at Prospect Lake when they first moved to Colorado Springs, later moving to the Cragmoor area. In the late 1950s, the director worked with nationally known agronomist Dr. John Montieth Jr. in mapping the roads of the new Air Force Academy. He also drew the landscaping specifications for the campus and worked on the Air Gardens, the area between two cadet dormitories close to Fairchild Hall.

[54] Cranz importantly argues that while there was a general increase in demand for parks, the disregard for articulating and arguing purpose implied a lack of philosophy: "Instead of giving careful attention to programming, park administrators now endeavored to expand the physical system. . . . Facts, not their meaning, would speak for themselves. . . . More and bigger were argument enough." *The Politics of Park Design.* p. 103.

[55] In July 1940, City Council approved the annexation of the "circus grounds" north of Prospect Lake and west of the Union Printers Home; the 120 acres were already city-owned, but had been outside the city limits. But it was not until 1953 that the legal annexation was accomplished. Prior to 1953, state law required annexation by a municipality to be initiated by residents of the proposed area. Since Memorial Park had no residents, the city had no legal way to accomplish this annexation—even though it owned the property—until the law was changed. ("Bill May Add Parks to City." *Colorado Springs Gazette Telegraph.* March 25, 1953. p. 1.)

[56] "Memorial Park Plans Make Hit But Cost Requires Study." *Colorado Springs Gazette Telegraph.* September 1, 1948. p. 1.

[57] "Council Approves Ordinance Rezoning Dorchester Park." *Colorado Springs Gazette Telegraph.* September 15, 1948. p. 15.

[58] However, some were not altogether delighted with this development in the management and purpose of parks, which was occurring nationwide. Harvey S. Crass, in his 1948 article "Parks—Now and 25 Years Hence," argued "The city park is gradually becoming functional in its character and, if some recreationalists had their way, would all consist of baseball fields, tennis courts, shuffleboard courts, and other specialized facilities that are hot by day and ablaze with floodlights at night. We must realize that beauty and congenial surroundings are an important adjunct to such planning and, let us not forget, that some of us require a place of peace and rest even before the grave." (*Parks and Recreation*. Vol. 31. December 1948. pp. 710-712. Quoted by Galen Cranz in *The Politics of Park Design*.)

[59] The Boulder Crescent playground was removed in the early 1980s, after it was vandalized, no longer met safety standards, and was a health and safety problem due to its use as a shelter by homeless people. Decades later, readers contributing to Linda Navarro's September 8, 2006 *Colorado Springs Gazette Telegraph* column, "Did You Ever Wonder," happily remembered the slide as a "large bright orange ladybug," "the pumpkin slide," a "buried dinosaur egg," a "whale," and the "little cheese house."

[60] "Park Board Asks $30,000 Hike in Proposed Budget." *Colorado Springs Gazette Telegraph*. August 27, 1953. 1:5.

[61] "District Setup or $2,778,700 Bond Issue for Parks Proposed." *Colorado Springs Gazette Telegraph*. August 22, 1958. p. 1.

[62] James Taylor, who had earned degrees in Horticulture and Landscape Architecture, also served as President of the National Parks Executives Association.

[63] The street address of the Parks and Recreation Building was later renamed as Recreation Way.

[64] "Taylor, City Park Chief Quits; Will Go to New Jersey." *Colorado Springs Gazette Telegraph*. September 5, 1963. 1:3.

[65] Ibid.

Chapter Three: Growing Pains

[1] Low population density has been a continuing problem for sprawling Colorado Springs. While larger in geographical area than Pittsburgh, St. Louis, and Denver, Colorado Springs has had a much smaller population base than these cities to support and finance its infrastructure needs.

[2] People were generally pleased with the department's activities. Indeed, the largest parks controversy seemed to be over the removal and subsequent replacement of the plaque in Boulder Crescent Park commemorating the slaying of local residents by Arapahoe Indians in 1868.

[3] In 1965, the American Institute of Park Executives changed its name to the National Recreation and Park Association, reflecting an ideological shift to the integration of physical park facilities with recreational programs. As Galen Cranz describes in *Politics of Urban Park Design:* "If the pleasure ground had been a pious patriarch, the reform park a social worker, the recreation facility a waitress or car mechanic, the new park was something of a performance artist." p. 138.

[4] "Park Experts Outline Needs to League of Women Voters." *Colorado Springs Free Press*. April 3, 1964. p. 6.

[5] The call for an ice rink at Memorial Park reflected the absence of resources for skaters. In 1963, ice skating availability was limited to flooded areas in Monument Valley Park, and Wasson and Palmer High Schools; hockey was allowed only on the rink at the Antlers Park; and no skating was allowed at Prospect Lake or Pikeview Reservoir—considered too dangerous due to thin ice.

[6] New parks from 1960–1969 included Twain, Wagner, Madison, Wilson, Wasson, Mountain View, Grant, Honeybear, Little Britches, Munchkin, Jackson, Trues Mill, Keller, Happy Hollow, Meadows, Monterey, and Ute Valley Parks.

[7] "Metropolitan Park Area Planning Urged by Taylor." *Colorado Springs Gazette Telegraph*. June 4, 1963. 1:7.

[8] Stu Richter, then Assistant Director, agreed with Taylor's proposal for a larger metropolitan parks district, arguing "[i]n some cases 50 per cent of people using the city's park and recreational facilities come from outside of the city limits, paying only a fee to keep their consciences clear." He proposed all who benefited from the parks should share equally in their support. Richter further pointed out that the per capita expenditure for parks in Colorado Springs was below the national average. ("Metropolitan Park Area Planning Urged by Taylor." *Colorado Springs Gazette Telegraph*. June 4, 1963. 1:7.) But the Colorado Springs Parks and Recreation Department would remain a city function well into the future. In 1973, a call for the consolidation of city and county parks departments into one district was defeated by the city vote, with only the county residents voting in favor; in 1978, both the city and county residents vetoed the merger of the two park departments. When the topic resurfaced in 1993, city and country administrators discussed a proposal to join their park resources, but the status quo remained in effect.

[9] The first parkland ordinance was adopted by City Council in 1951 to ensure adequate parkland as the city grew through development.

[10] "Richter Asks Community Help for Park System." *Colorado Springs Gazette Telegraph.* February 27, 1965. p. 1.

[11] "Horticultural Arts Society Here Plans to Extend Demonstration Garden in Monument Valley Location." *Colorado Springs Gazette Telegraph.* October 3, 1965. G:6.

[12] In 1968, the city purchased the remaining White House Ranch property adjacent to the Garden of the Gods from Egmont Vrooman, who had bought it following the death of L.L. Dent. A City Council Resolution set the intended use of the property as: "to make the White House Ranch a center where interested and concerned people can encounter the natural environment and perceive man's early relationship to it in a reserve which includes an early western ranch setting." (David Jones and Deborah Abele. *White House Ranch Master Plan: Final Report to the City of Colorado Springs Park and Recreation Department.* LRA: Land Resource Associates. March, 1990. p. 65.) Historically, the property had been known as Rock Ledge Ranch when it was built by the Chambers family in 1874. General Palmer bought the property when the Chambers retired in 1907, and had a residence—the Orchard House—built there for his sister-in-law and her husband. In 1940, the property was acquired by Mr. and Mrs. Dent, and they painted the Orchard House white; subsequently the property came to be known as the White House Ranch. In 1973, a reproduction of a small colonial-style chapel was donated to the White House Ranch by the local chapter of American Mothers, and in 1974 the Kappa Kappa Gamma Alumnae Association remodeled the Orchard House at the ranch. The city of Colorado Springs renamed the property Rock Ledge Ranch—the name given it by the Chambers—in 1995.

[13] Director Richter was quoted as saying the lack of opportunity was caused in part by the girls' birthright. "Girls have always been expected to dwell on household activities," he said, "while men have been expected to be more athletic." ("City Plays Catch-Up in Park Development." *Colorado Springs Gazette Telegraph.* October 9, 1970. B:1.)

[14] Ibid.

[15] "Richter Says Without Sales Tax Park Development Will Have to 'Wait Another Five Years or So'." *Colorado Springs Gazette Telegraph.* April 28, 1972. A:4-6.

[16] Local developer Tom Spear argued against what he considered an "unfair" ordinance, saying "When you tax one industry from 10 to 40 percent of its basic commodity, the tax becomes unfair, since its purpose is to alleviate a problem of the whole city. It would be just as unfair to tax the automobile industry heavily to pay for public transportation and street repairs." ("Land Dedication for Schools, Parks Gets Planners Okay." *Colorado Springs Gazette Telegraph.* July 17, 1973. A 9:3.)

[17] The legal Parkland Dedication Ordinance read as follows: 7.7.1203: DEDICATION OF LAND FOR PARKS:

It is hereby found and determined:

A. That a part of the public need for parks generated by the influx of new residents should be provided for by mandatory dedication of land or fees in lieu thereof as a condition of final plat approval.

B. That it is reasonable to require the dedication of land or payment of fees-in-lieu thereof to provide the following facilities: neighborhood park or community park, resulting in a total requirement of 7.5 acres per one thousand (1,000) persons.

C. That the 1970 Federal Census shows that, in the City, there are an average of 3.1 persons per owner-occupied dwelling and 2.2 persons per renter-occupied dwelling.

D. That the density of owner-occupied developments is usually eight (8) dwelling units per acre or less while the density of renter-occupied developments is usually greater than eight (8) dwelling units per acre.

E. That, for purposes of determining the park land dedication requirement, where the gross residential land density is greater than eight (8) dwelling units per acre, the population averages 2.2 persons per dwelling unit and where the gross residential land density is less than or equal to eight (8) dwelling units per acre, the population averages 3.1 persons per dwelling unit.

F. That the resulting requirements of land to be dedicated for parks and open space is 0.0165 acres (719 square feet) per dwelling unit for residential land densities in excess of eight (8) dwelling units per acre, and 0.02325 acres (1,013 square feet) per dwelling unit for residential land densities of eight (8) dwelling units per acre or less.

G. That the City's requirements for regional parks, open spaces and special facilities should be provided from sources other than those set forth in this part. (Ord. 96-44; Ord. 01-42)

[18] "Controversial Dedication Ordinance Okayed by City." *Colorado Springs Gazette Telegraph.* August 29, 1973. G 2:4.

[19] The 1996 *Colorado Springs Open Space Plan* points out original Parkland Dedication Ordinance requirements were for parks and did not include public open space. However, the Open Space Plan explained: "While the majority of dedicated land and fees are devoted to neighborhood parks. . . . The City may give a developer partial or full parkland dedication credit for private open space if the private open space meets certain criteria. In practice, this credit has also been extended to include public open space as well. Additions to Austin Bluffs, Garden of the Gods and Palmer Parks were obtained through dedications." (p. 22)

[20] Nina Bondarook. "Acquisitions of Parkland Set Record." *Colorado Springs Gazette Telegraph.* December 21, 1983. C:4.

[21] Ibid.

[22] "Welcome to Thin City." *CBS News.* October 25, 2009.

[23] New parks from 1970-1979 included: Carver, Van Diest, Fremont, Thorndale, Penrose, Gilberson, Henry, Discovery, Portal, Tomah, Villa Loma, Village Green, Wildflower, Otero, Prairie Grass, Flanagan, Centennial, Roswell, George Fellows, High Street, Keystone, Quail Lake, South Shooks Run, Broadview, North Shooks Run, Otis, Bristol, Erindale, Homestead, Pioneer, Blunt, Dublin, Roosevelt, Rudy, and Jenkins.

[24] "Park Department Operations Job, Avocation for Buerkle." *Colorado Springs Gazette Telegraph.* May 27, 1973. B:1.

[25] In 1974, boat rentals at Prospect Lake included eight paddleboats, two canoes, and four sailboats.

[26] As Galen Cranz notes in *Politics of Urban Park Design,* "This [school-park] plan coupling contributed to the development of the neighborhood theory, the idea that a given geographic unit and a given population cluster should have one each of a series of urban facilities. . . and more generally to the systematic urban planning that characterized the era." p. 120.

[27] *Beautification Plan for the City of Colorado Springs.* Prepared for the Park and Recreation Department, City of Colorado Springs, Colorado, by N.E.S., Inc. December, 1987. p. 41.

[28] Board members included Celia Rasor, Nancy Avila, Frank Parisi, Bill Ruskin, Juan Reid, David Feruzza, Judy Finley, Robert Loevy, and Bruce Shepard.

[29] "Open Space Advisors Appointed to Study Park Land Development." *Colorado Springs Gazette Telegraph.* January 10, 1975. C:1.

[30] "Park and Rec Has $2.6 Million in Capital Improvement Budget." *Colorado Springs Gazette Telegraph.* June 26, 1974. C 17:1.

[31] The Memorial Ice Rink was renamed the Mark "Pa" Sertich Ice Center in 1986 in honor of the caretaker of the ice rink. He was remembered by his son, Steve Sertich, assistant coach at Colorado College, as "a character of a man. He talked a funny way and he wore that funny hat. . . . He was a great listener and a friend to a lot of people." (Ralph Routon. "It's Papa's Rink." *Colorado Springs Gazette Telegraph.* November 1, 1986. D:1.)

[32] Email correspondence from Tim Boddington to Judith Rice-Jones on July 21, 2009. The Boddington Trust continues to donate an annual stipend for the upkeep of Boddington Field.

[33] While master plans offered opportunities to focus resources and increase efficiencies, they also led to systems thinking and bureaucratization. The disadvantages to this, as Galen Cranz argues in *The Politics of Park Design,* were a certain loss of idealism, authority, and prestige. Rather than creating a value standard, parks became responsive simply to public demand. She argues: "Development of planning studies was a preoccupation of park administrators during this period. . . .[T]his turned them into statisticians relying on quantitative studies. . . . Like all bureaucracies, the park department took on a life of its own and came to be committed first to its own maintenance and enhancement." (p. 109)

[34] The Garden of the Gods Master Plan, in the works from 1973-1975, included a complete renovation of its hiking and horse trail system in an effort to combat erosion. City Council approved $60,000 in 1978 to partially fund the project. In 1976, the White House Ranch Master Plan was completed as part of the Garden of the Gods plan. It recommended the ranch be a multi-use center for environmentally related programs: community-oriented educational programs; housing for small-scale workshops, conferences, and displays; nature trails and the reconstruction of the earlier reservoir for wildlife preservation; and a living history program.

[35] In October 1974, park planners had told City Council that the city currently had no developed plans at all for forty-two parks, and a total of sixty-seven required planning attention. ("More Than Half City Parks Have No Developing Plans." *Colorado Springs Gazette Telegraph.* October 10, 1974. B 18:3.)

[36] Specific 1976 Park Master Plan recommendations included the following: 1) An open space and park acquisition and development program to be continuously pursued through the community, conveniently distributed for populations served; 2) Neighborhood and community parks to be designed to accommodate a wide range of recreational activities, including both individual and organized activities, active and passive pursuits; 3) Cooperation between the Parks Department and school districts to be continued; 4) Park sites to be large enough to accommodate a number of uses and minimize maintenance problems of caring for many small parks; 5) Additional regional parks to be considered, which of necessity would be located at the fringes of the city; 6) A comprehensive trail system and appropriate open space parcels to be considered to connect park sites and focal points within the community. Select open spaces to preserve natural features and provide visual relief to the urban landscape; 7) A variety of implementation techniques to be used to develop the recommended open space system. Stated goals were to provide visual and psychological relief, to preserve and enhance natural and man-made features and amenities, to provide visual and physical continuity to the overall system, to provide a

viable alternative to "natural hazard" areas where development might be a danger, to provide recreational opportunities for all citizens and visitors, to provide a consistent and high level of maintenance, to increase public awareness of the benefits and opportunities of the parks and recreation system, to achieve an adequate degree of safety, and to develop an adequate level of financing.

[37] *Open Space, Park and Recreation Plan.* Colorado Springs Park and Recreation Department, prepared by THK Associates. Denver, CO. 1976. p. 139. In 1977, the William J. Palmer Parks Foundation was organized by Bill Ruskin and a core of dedicated park supporters. Support for capital improvements was the main intent of the original foundation, rather than land acquisition. However, over the years land acquisition was the direction the foundation took and more land was acquired through the foundation than money raised for capital improvements. One of the early accomplishments of the foundation was the acceptance of the donation of land east of the Navigators entrance, which included funds for the restoration of the John Blair bridge, part of the trails system today. After acquiring several properties adjacent to the Garden of the Gods, the foundation began conservation projects in the Black Forest and on Pikes Peak. As time passed the William Palmer Foundation drifted away from the Parks Department and its original purpose of fund-raising (which never became a significant factor) and focused entirely on land acquisition. Now known as The Palmer Land Trust, the trust advances conservation efforts throughout southeastern Colorado, managing conservation easements in ten Colorado counties.

[38] *Open Space, Park and Recreation Plan.* Colorado Springs Park and Recreation Department, prepared by THK Associates. Denver, CO. 1976. p. 139.

[39] "City Heirs Agreement Is Topic of Heated Debate." *Colorado Springs Gazette Telegraph.* August 25, 1970. B:1.

[40] Kyer et al. versus the City of Colorado Springs. Civil action suit # 66897, Division 2. Filed in District Court, El Paso County, September 21, 1971.

[41] "City Motion to Dismiss Denied by Judge Hinton." *Colorado Springs Gazette Telegraph.* January 11, 1972. D:12.

[42] Kyer et al. versus the City of Colorado Springs. Civil action suit # 66897, Division 2. Stipulation for Declaratory Judgment. Filed in District Court, El Paso County, February 19, 1974.

[43] "Council Okays Park Deal Over Protests of Citizens." *Colorado Springs Gazette Telegraph.* February 9, 1977. A:1.

[44] "Guarantee Asked on Palmer Lands." *Colorado Springs Gazette Telegraph.* February 23, 1977. D1:1.

[45] "Park and Rec Advisory Board 'Almost' Censures City Council." *Colorado Springs Gazette Telegraph.* April 5, 1974. B:1.

[46] The subsequent 1982 White House Ranch Master Plan focused upon the use of the site as a historical program that provided education about life in the Pikes Peak Region from 1860-1910.

[47] The Pioneers Museum drew 121,789 visitors from 1979-1981. The city provided 28 percent of the museum's $1.7 million budget over that period, with 9 percent coming from the sale of the old museum, and grants and donations totaled $1.09 million. A total of 961 artifacts were donated in 1980.

Chapter Four: The System Blossoms

[1] Dedications took place at Briargate Park, the UCCS/City of Colorado Springs Sports Complex, Roosevelt Park, Emerson Park, the Fountain Boulevard Median, Panorama Park, Bricker Park, Adams Park, the National Recreation Trails at the White House Ranch, Monument Valley and Memorial Park tennis courts, renovation of Monument Valley Pool, Mid-Shooks Run, Shooks Run Bikeway, Comstock Park, Erindale Park, Keystone Park, Sabin Park, and the renovation of Valley Hi Municipal Golf Course. All were financed either by the 1979 bond issue, the department's 1980 capital improvement fund, the Community Development Block Grants Fund, or a Department of Transportation Grant. (Debra Skodack. "Marathon Dedications Will Open 21 City Parks." *Colorado Springs Gazette Telegraph.* September 28, 1980. B:7.)

[2] Pat West, chairwoman of an Eastborough neighborhood group, noted, "The neighborhood is pretty proud of what it's done. . . . None of us really knew how to approach the City Council, but somehow we did get together and got a park here. It's so important to really get the people out there and get them interested." (Ibid.)

[3] Celebration events occurred at these new parks, some of which were already opened: Broadmoor Bluffs, Broadmoor Valley, Carver, Cottonwood Creek, Dorchester, Dublin, Fairfax, Frontier, Golden Hills, High Plains, Pinecliff, Thorndale, the Environmental Center at Sondermann, and Rudy.

[4] Janie Vonderlage, "No New Parks Likely in '81, Says Director." *Colorado Springs Gazette Telegraph.* October 17, 1980. B:4.

[5] Jordan Kenyon, "City Parks Outlook." *Colorado Springs Gazette Telegraph.* September 7, 1982. D 1:1.

[6] Ibid.

[7] "Protection of People, Property Called Impossible." *Colorado Springs Gazette Telegraph.* September 7, 1982. D 1:1.

[8] *Memorial Park Master Plan.* 1983. p. 4.

[9] In 1952, the Junior League had provided the funds for Conejos Park, which was ultimately dismantled in an urban renewal project.

[10] The Park Matching Fund was established with a $10,000 grant from the Junior League's Community Trust, from which other groups could apply for matching funds to purchase park improvements. The League's 1981 Parks Gift Catalog listed what items the formal gardens needed and what the prices were for them. Citizens and groups could select materials, equipment, landscaping items—concrete steps, zinnia edging, lighting, or park benches, for example—and apply for matching funds from the Junior League to purchase them for the project. (Dorothy Aldridge. "Gardens to Blossom With New Look." *Colorado Springs Gazette Telegraph.* April 24, 1982. D:14.)

[11] Ibid.

[12] Leslie Henderson. "Volunteers Give Love and Sweat to City's Flowers." *Colorado Springs Gazette Telegraph.* July 26, 1983. D:1.

[13] Linda DuVal. "Planted: Fuhlrodt Makes City Blocks Blooming Success." *Colorado Springs Gazette Telegraph.* August 14, 1982. D:25.

[14] Gail Randall, "Man Honored for Long Service to Civic Beauty." *Colorado Springs Gazette Telegraph.* December 4, 1989. B:1.

[15] Ken Conklin, "Beauty of Trees Will Stay Forever, City Vows." *Colorado Springs Gazette Telegraph.* March 16, 1986. G:1.

[16] The Park and Recreation Department initiated a program to plan for ongoing beautification of Colorado Springs in 1987. Under the direction of Bill Ruskin and Gene Fuhlrodt, NES, Inc., a land planning and landscape architectural firm, provided research and design services. A sub-committee of volunteers included members from the Partnership for Community Design (an outgrowth of the 1987 Community Design Forum) and Citizens' Goals, Project 2000. Despite the range of ideas generated, the plan was never implemented.

[17] Citizens voiced particular concerns that "Palmer Park is in a serious state of deterioration (i.e., erosion, abuse and beetle kill). . . . The Park is in desperate need of preventive maintenance and substantial improvements based on heavy use." (*Palmer Park Master Plan.* 1984. p.5.) The 1982 White House Ranch Master Plan determined the primary importance of the facility was historical and recommended continuation and expansion of the historic programs. It recommended a phased relocation of non-historic programs to other parks or locations within the White House Ranch boundaries. It also proposed a new Visitors Center that would serve the Garden of the Gods and the White House Ranch, as well as provide non-historic uses currently housed at the ranch. (*1990 White House Ranch Master Plan.* pp. 67-68.)

[18] Marilyn Billings, president of El Paso County Horseman's Council, while arguing for recreational nature trails, noted her club included 2,500 members and that horsemen contributed about $7 million annually to the city tax base. (Debra Skodack. "Parks, Trails Suggested at Springs Public Hearing." *Colorado Springs Gazette Telegraph.* March 11, 1981. B 2:4.)

[19] Dru Wilson. "City Board OK's Park Master Plan." *Colorado Springs Gazette Telegraph.* November 24, 1981. D:1.

[20] Adopted by Parks and Recreation Advisory Board and by City Council (Ord. 81-110), the 1981 Multi-use Trail Plan identified over 120 miles of designated trail corridor. The task force also oversaw the production of a trail plan for Monument Valley Park and recommended seven critical trail links to be acquired. City Council amended the City Subdivision Ordinance at this time to allow developers to dedicate land for trails within the adopted corridors as well as land for parks.

[21] Rebecca Cantwell. "Plans For Park Unveiled." *Colorado Springs Gazette Telegraph.* March 15, 1985. 1.1.

[22] Silent Rain, Pring Ranch, Oak Valley, High Plains, Mountain Shadows, Stetson Hills, Woodland Hills, Rockrimmon, Beacon Hill, Cheyenne Meadows, and Neal Ranch were all acquired in the 1980s.

[23] Rich Laden. "New Neighborhood Parks Slashed from Tight City Budget." *Colorado Springs Gazette Telegraph.* October 8, 1987.

[24] Rebecca Cantwell. "Dreams of Seniors' Center Realized." *Colorado Springs Gazette Telegraph.* January 13, 1985. B:1.

[25] Ibid.

[26] Ibid.

[27] Dr. Richard Beidleman had been a long-time parks and environmental advocate in Colorado Springs. Professor of biology (and environmental researcher) at Colorado College, he had worked tirelessly for parkland preservation, including advancing such projects as the Aiken Canyon preserve (south of Colorado Springs), preservation of the Garden of the Gods, restoration of Monument Valley Park, advancement of the Palmer Land Trust, and other environmental causes.

[28] Upton Gardens Nursery had been founded in 1916 by Kathleen Marriage and her husband George Marriage, who operated it until 1943. A woman before her time, Mrs. Marriage pioneered the art of landscape design and gardening in the Pikes Peak region. Born in Kildare County, Ireland, a student of landscape design in England, she designed gardens in Maine, Rhode Island, and Chicago as well as Colorado Springs. She was sought internationally for horticultural advice, introduced new varieties of plants to Colorado, and was the first to argue for xeriscape gardening—selecting plants for their suitability to a dry, arid environment and grouping them according to their watering needs. In her honor, the Kathleen Marriage Garden in Sondermann Park was designed and dedicated on July 7, 2000, a cottage garden reminiscent of England, but emphasizing native, drought tolerant plants and alpine flowers.

[29] *Colorado Springs Open Space, Park and Recreation Master Plan Update: 1988.* Prepared by the Colorado Springs Park and Recreation Department. Colorado Springs, CO: The Department; 1988. 6-4.

[30] The Beidleman Environmental Center received the 1990 Governor's Celebrate Colorado Environmental Award for its significant contribution to safeguard and improve Colorado's environment, presented in May, 1991.

[31] According to the *1986 Colorado Springs Multi-Use Trails Master Plan,* sixty miles of trails within or close to the city were available to city residents in 1986, though many of these were located within city parks.

[32] The Multi-Use Trails Task Force produced a 1981 plan identifying over 120 miles of designated trail corridors; it was adopted by the Parks and Recreation Board and City Council (Ord. 81-110). The Task Force also oversaw the production of a trail plan for Monument Valley and recommended critical trail links. As a result of their work, City Council permitted dedication of land for trails within the adopted corridors as meeting the Parkland Dedication Ordinance requirements. (CH. 15-3-1297-A-3).

[33] To succeed, authors of the 1986 Multi-Use Trails Master Plan called for four things: 1) A champion—an individual, or group of individuals, committed to realizing the vision; 2) Public support of the effort at the highest level; 3) A realizable, credible plan that offers real benefits to the public; 4) A workable phasing process, continuous with in-the-ground results each year. *Colorado Springs Multi-Use Trail Master Plan.* 1986. pp. 52-53.

[34] Some planners prioritized developing trail systems through the Monument Valley corridor, from Monument Valley to Bear Creek Canyon, and connecting south Douglas Creek with the Garden of the Gods; others promoted more ambitious goals, hoping to develop over one hundred miles of trails within the city.

[35] Progress would be real but gradual. As pointed out in the 1997 Colorado Springs Open Space Plan: "Regional trails are planned and coordinated through the cooperative efforts of the involved jurisdictions, partially through the Bicycle and Pedestrian Advisory Committee of the Pikes Peak Area Council of Governments. . . . [O]f the approximately 159 [in 1996] planned trails, over 50 miles had been completed by mid-summer 1996."

[36] See the Trails and Open Space Coalition website. www.trailsandopenspaces.org/history.html.

[37] In 1988, the Patty Jewett Golf Course offered a twenty-seven-hole regulation course, a driving range, concession area, and several multi-purpose rooms on 237 acres in the center of Colorado Springs. Valley Hi Golf Course in south Colorado Springs provided an eighteen-hole regulation course, outdoor swimming pool, concession area, and four multi-use rooms on 181 acres.

[38] Rich Laden. "Parks Veteran Gets Top Job/New Director Has Worked for Department 22 Years." *Colorado Springs Gazette Telegraph.* June 4, 1988. B:1.

[39] After the ski area's return to the Broadmoor Hotel, Vail Associates made an unsuccessful attempt to keep it in operation. When that proved untenable, the idea of running it as a potentially profitable skiing facility was abandoned.

[40] Phil Frederickson. "Nancy Lewis Director, Colorado Springs Park and Recreation Department." *Colorado Springs Gazette Telegraph.* October 23, 1988. C:5.

[41] Lottery-funded park programs ranged from $450,000 for Memorial Park to $9,200 to renovate Acacia Park shuffleboards. Other projects included lighting and bleachers for the North Nevada Four Diamonds complex, fencing and restrooms at Valley Hi Golf Course, and improvements to Palmer Park, Old Farm, Deerfield, North Cheyenne Cañon, Garden Ranch, Carver, Jackson, the Garden of the Gods, and Tuckerman Parks. Another $20,000 was allocated to begin the planning and design of the community park in Norwood. (Nina Bonderook. "29 Springs Park Projects Allotted Lottery Money." *Colorado Springs Gazette Telegraph.* November 17, 1983. B:10.)

[42] Rich Laden. "Parkland Lies Fallow While Major Projects Pursued, Critics Say." *Colorado Springs Gazette Telegraph.* October 17, 1988. A:2.

[43] The Gallagher Amendment, passed by Colorado voters in 1982, also affected city receipts. The amendment stated that residential property owners should never pay more than 45 percent of the total property taxes in the state. Commercial property owners carried the remainder of the burden. As residences grew faster than businesses in the state, the ratio of per individual tax burden increasingly favored the resident over the business operator. The increased tax burden on business meant the business community could rely

neither on a perpetually low tax burden nor a city with great services, depressing business growth. (J. Adrian Stanley. "Tabor Tyranny: Or Why Our City Will Never Really Recover from an Economic Downturn." *Colorado Springs Independent.* April 9, 2009.) The negative economic impact on business growth would ripple through the Colorado Springs economy for the next several decades, impacting the city's ability to fund its parks, as well as other services.

[44] Rich Laden, "Council Reverses Decision to Earmark Tax for Parks. 5-4 Vote Kills Plan to Spend $1.26 Million." *Colorado Springs Gazette Telegraph.* August 10, 1988. CITY/STATE Section. 1.

[45] Ibid.

[46] Private funds also supported the Pioneers Museum renovation. The Friends of the Pioneers Museum donated $20,000 to pay for a fountain, the Broadmoor Garden Club donated $10,000 for flower beds and planters around the fountain and the museum's west entrance, and twelve parks benches, at a cost of $775 each, were donated by individuals and businesses.

[47] Projects included in the city's proposed 1989 $17.5 million dollar capital improvements budget included $260,000 for the Mountain Shadows Park; $270,000 for the five-acre Cheyenne Meadows park; $175,000 for the 3.2 acre Penstemon Park; $225,000 for the 5.7 acre Piñon Valley Park; and $80,000 for the completion of the five-acre Golden Hills Park. The list also included $400,000 for the development of multi-use trails and $200,000 for the restoration of Monument Valley Park. Improvements were funded by the city's one-half percent sales tax, lottery revenues, and federal community development block grant funds. General fund money was not allocated for capital improvements that year.

[48] *Colorado Springs Open Space, Park and Recreation Master Plan Update: 1988.* Prepared by the Colorado Springs Park and Recreation Department. Colorado Springs, CO: The Department; 1988. 5-3.

[49] With population increases and inflation, higher costs for maintenance and operations were inevitable. Trail and open space maintenance included such activities as trash and litter pickup, trail grading and sweeping, erosion control, tree trimming and removal, weed mowing, facility cleaning and repair, road repair, and vandalism repair. The urban park maintenance was even higher, including fertilizer, water, and labor for turf grass and athletic field maintenance, in addition to general maintenance.

[50] Over 324 projects were listed in the 1988 Master Plan update. At that point, twelve neighborhood parks remained undeveloped. Over 1,700 acres were needed for new community parks. There were also 600 acres of undeveloped regional parklands and 25 miles of undeveloped trail corridors owned by the city. Based on population growth projections, the city would need another 866 acres of new parkland by 1995 to maintain the average of 25 acres per 1,000 population. It was also noted the city did not have sufficient tennis courts, sports fields, swimming pools, recreational facilities, and golf courses, again according to NRPA standards. (Dru Wilson. "Alternate Funding Sought for Development of Parks. Master Plan Sees Little Budget Growth." *Colorado Springs Gazette Telegraph.* January 23, 1989. B:1.)

[51] In addition to city funding for land acquisitions, possible alternative funding methods were suggested: developers actually building parks; cooperative programs between the developer, city, and neighborhood including volunteer labor, in-kind services, and donations; and/or establishment of neighborhood park development fees for new neighborhoods. Possibilities for private/public lease-development, management agreements, bond programs, and fund-raising through private foundations were noted. (*Colorado Springs Open Space, Park and Recreation Master Plan Update: 1988.* Prepared by the Colorado Springs Park and Recreation Department. Colorado Springs, CO: The Department; 1988. 8-4.)

[52] The Master Plan Update also proposed the organization of "improvement districts for development of new neighborhood parks or the redevelopment of existing neighborhood parks. . . . The district would dissolve when the specified revenue need for the park development or redevelopment had been generated." Suggested possibilities included a citywide Park Maintenance District, temporary Park Maintenance Districts in newly developed areas of city, or permanent landscape districts to fund maintenance of medians, streetscapes, and other non-park developments. (*Colorado Springs Open Space, Park and Recreation Master Plan Update: 1988.* Prepared by the Colorado Springs Parks and Recreation Department. Colorado Springs, CO: The Department; 1988. 8-4.)

Chapter Five: Purpose, Preservation and Growth

[1] The movement for TABOR was initiated in Colorado Springs in 1991 and passed as law in the city. A similar law was later adopted statewide. Consequently, Colorado Springs is the only Colorado city to have to comply with TABOR as both a city and a state law.

[2] As J. Adrian Stanley points out, "TABOR does require the city keep an emergency fund—but for the city to tap it, the declared emergency cannot be economic in nature." ("Tabor Tyranny: Or Why Our City Will Never Really Recover from an Economic Downturn." *Colorado Springs Independent.* April 9, 2009. p. 3)

[3] Stanley notes that "Bell Policy Center of Denver, a think-tank that conducted a ten-year study of TABOR in 2003, calls it 'the most restrictive limitation in the country for how it has suppressed government spending and lowered property taxes, making it simultaneously the most loved, hated and feared law of the land.'" When Fred Crowley, economist and associate research professor at the University of Colorado at Colorado Springs, modeled the city budget from 1998-2003, he "found that it *had dropped* about 20 percent in *inflation-adjusted* dollars" due to TABOR. (Ibid. pp. 1-2.)

[4] Ibid. p. 2.

[5] Ibid. p. 4.

[6] Many problems existed with special districts. With the formation of a special district, developers could set the mill levy rate to pay off bonds before residents arrived, thereby avoiding a tax election that would otherwise be required by TABOR. Oftentimes, new residents were unaware of the existence and/or implications of special district governance when they moved into their new homes. When a district's independent board of directors was being elected, voters were often uninformed about when elections were held, where to vote, or even what issues were present on the ballot, though 2009 state legislation tried to create more transparency with Senate Bill 87. The bill strengthens requirements for special districts to post public notices in newspapers and official buildings, and requires disclosure of special district taxes to potential homebuyers.

[7] Homeowners, too, created special districts to fund community improvements. In 2005, Colorado Springs developers began to add a mill levy to residents' property tax bills to actually fund the building and maintenance of parks and recreation centers, enabling homeowners to skip standing in the backlog line of city park development. While city officials had to approve the design of these parks, and the parks had to be open to all members of the public, parks actually were owned and run by the metro districts, creating a potential for conflict.

[8] In 2009, J. Adrian Stanley points out taxes in special districts can be as much as ten times more than the current city rate. "So in a hypothetical case, for an average home in Colorado Springs (market value of $267,000), the homeowner would pay the city $105 in property tax, but that could rise to $1000 in a highly taxed special district." ("Tabor Tyranny: Or Why Our City Will Never Really Recover from an Economic Downturn." *Colorado Springs Independent.* April 9, 2009. p. 3.)

[9] Barry Noreen. "The View from Here." *Colorado Springs Gazette.* July 16, 2009.

[10] In April 1990, Governor Romer had appointed the Great Outdoors Citizens Committee to put together a proposal for an Outdoors Trust. The committee found that the demand for trail, watchable wildlife facilities, state and local park facilities, and other outdoor amenities was not being met by the state, that opportunities for land acquisition were being lost, and that preserving and promoting outdoor amenities was vital to state tourism, the second-largest segment of Colorado's economy. The proposal to create a permanent Great Outdoors Trust was introduced in the legislature in 1991, with bipartisan leaders proposing a temporary sales tax or personal income tax to fund the proposition. However, the bill to place a tax-funded Great Outdoors Colorado amendment on the 1992 ballot was killed in a Senate committee. The 1992 voter-driven referendum to re-direct lottery funds resolved the question.

[11] In 1992, net lottery proceeds were distributed as follows: $48.5 million to the state capital construction fund—mostly for prisons; $5.6 million to state parks; and $22.2 million to the Conservation Trust Fund, which distributed grants to cities, towns, and park districts.

[12] Projects included Mountain Shadows, Cheyenne Meadows, Penstemon, Valley, and Golden Hills Parks.

[13] New neighborhood parks in 1991 included Heathercrest, Meadowlark, Deerfield Hills, and Dublin.

[14] The White House Master Plan also proposed relocating and expanding the Rocky Mountain Arboretum to provide "an outdoor area for the display of native and drought-tolerant plants suitable for use in the Pikes Peak region." Managed by volunteers from the Horticultural Arts Society, the 13.7 acre arboretum displayed exhibits by botanical zones: riparian, plains, foothills, montane, subalpine, and alpine.

[15] The house was built by James Starsmore's father, using rocks taken from the banks of Cheyenne Creek, on the corner of South Nevada Avenue and Cheyenne Road. James later owned the Ivywild Evergreen Nursery across Cheyenne Road. After he died in 1978, his wife, Mary, sold the nursery property to Safeway in the 1980s and the homestead property to McDonald's in 1989, and the city acquired the stone house for use as a visitors center in North Cheyenne Cañon. The twelve-hour move on April 3, 1990 followed Cheyenne Road west, turned north on Cascade Avenue, and then went west on Cheyenne Boulevard to the park entrance. The roadway was closed three blocks ahead and two blocks behind the house for crews to move and replace electrical, telephone, and cable lines as the house, supported by sixty-four wheels, inched along its route. Fred Mais, of the Parks and Recreation Design and Development division, oversaw the unique transportation of the building.

[16] The Boy Scout Troop #256 and the Colorado Disc Sports Association "adopted" Cottonwood Creek Park and helped park staff keep it clean for all users.

[17] Homeowners were provided a $110 certificate toward purchase of a tree, good for two years.

[18] Warhole, Debbie. "Tree Program Under Review by the City." *Colorado Springs Gazette Telegraph.* August 9, 1992. G:16.

[19] Interestingly, this purchase scuttled attempts by other railroads to purchase the line and use it for hauling freight through the center of the city, an outcome similar to General Palmer's motivation for acquiring and donating the Antlers Park to the city in 1892.

[20] These included the Rock Island Trail, linking Academy Boulevard and North Shooks Run, the Academy Boulevard section of the Homestead/Villa Loma Trail from Maizeland Boulevard to Constitution Avenue, and the Palmer Mesa Trail, between Fillmore and Uintah Streets.

[21] Barry Noreen. "Front Range Corridor Is Years Away. Obstacles to Linking Parks Studied." *Colorado Springs Gazette Telegraph.* January 26, 1991. B:1.

[22] "Donated Land to Link Up Trail/Company Gives 35 Acres to Connect City with Park." *Colorado Springs Gazette Telegraph.* April 5, 1995. B:1.

[23] Teresa Owen-Cooper. "Lottery Cash to Extend Trail/Greenway Receives $2 Million Grant." *Colorado Springs Gazette Telegraph.* October 24, 1996. A:8.

[24] Some of the groups involved included the Pikes Peak Area Trails Coalition, a confederation of outdoor groups called Section 16 Intact, and the Trails, Open Space, and Parks (TOPS) group.

[25] According to the 1997 *Colorado Springs Open Space Plan,* in 1996, City Council adopted this goal: "The City recognizes that the preservation and acquisition of open space is critical in maintaining the quality of life in this community. In 1996, the City should evaluate and pursue alternative means of providing for open space. An open space plan should be completed during 1996."

[26] Jeff Thomas. "Open Space '90s Battle Cry/Preservation Efforts Galvanize Over Section 16." *Colorado Springs Gazette Telegraph.* July 31, 1995. B:4.

[27] Ibid.

[28] *Ute Valley Park Master Development Plan and Program.* p. 3.

[29] Similar in acreage to community parks, the sports complex focused on developed sports facilities with only limited acreage devoted to un-programmed use.

[30] The acreage was bordered by Fillmore Street to the south, the Denver and Rio Grande tracks to the west, Douglas Creek to the north, and Monument Creek and residential areas to the east. Some of it was privately owned, and some was part of the RTC (Resolution Trust Corporation) holdings resulting from the federal savings and loan bailout. The RTC portion was bought for back taxes owed, about $265,000.

[31] The Banning-Lewis Ranch was owned by developer Frank Aries in 1988 and then acquired by a Phoenix savings and loan. When that institution failed, the federal government's Resolution Trust Corporation took over the property, eventually selling it to Saudi investors, whose management company deeded the site to the city according to the original annexation agreement.

[32] The Chuckwagon Pavilion had been built in 1938 to provide a permanent home to the Colorado Springs Jaycees, who had started the first of their annual Chuckwagon dinners in 1935 to entertain visitors and promote the Colorado Springs area. In the 1950s, Jaycees would feed and entertain groups of 700 on Monday, Wednesday, and Friday nights from June to Labor Day. The events were discontinued in the 1970s.

[33] Studies included evaluation of environmental and historical features of the park, and assessment of the vegetation, wildlife, aesthetics, geology, archeology, history, soil, hydrography, and gradients. Analyses of traffic, user and community surveys, and inquiries into user conflicts were also completed.

[34] *Garden of the Gods Master Plan.* City of Colorado Springs Parks and Recreation Department. 1994. p. 13.

[35] Number 4 of the obligatory conditions of the Perkins' deed stated: "No building or structure shall be erected on the premises for purposes other than may be necessary to properly care for, protect and maintain the same as a public park, nor upon any road or highway, through or upon the said premises." See Appendix.

[36] Barry Noreen. "Garden of the Gods Work Gets a Lofty Boost from Trust Fund." *Colorado Springs Gazette Telegraph.* March 22, 1995. B:6.

[37] Lou Oiler. "Trail Fixers on the Job at Park/Group to Continue Project Today." *Colorado Springs Gazette Telegraph.* June 4, 1995. B:2.

[38] The realignment was estimated to cost about $490,000, an amount Hill loaned to the city.

[39] Barry Noreen. "Private Visitors Center OK'd for Garden of the Gods/Council's Vote Unanimous." December 15, 1993. B:4.

[40] Barry Noreen. "Deal Urged for Center in Garden of the Gods/Private Money for Building Linked to Realigning Street." *Colorado Springs Gazette Telegraph.* October 1, 1993. A:3.

[41] Ibid.

[42] Two separate lawsuits—later combined into one—claimed that the city's plan to build the visitors center violated portions of the city charter and the proposed development violated the rights of local American Indians, some of whom viewed the park as sacred ground. In August 1994 the parties reached an agreement in which the city promised that all would have free access to the visitors center's parking lot, the tram would operate only on existing park roads, and the city would retain the option of taking over the tram should Hill give up the operation. The city also agreed the center would be consistent with the 1994 Garden of the Gods Master Plan. While the litigants were satisfied the amendments provided protection that had not existed, city officials maintained the agreement did little to change the deal, but spelled out provisions in more detail.

[43] Bill Vogrin. "Visitors Center Wins Rave Reviews." *Colorado Springs Gazette Telegraph.* May 16, 1995. A:6.

[44] Ibid.

[45] All profits from the Garden of the Gods Visitors Center have been directed into the Foundation, which exists to support the park. In 1995, Nancy Lewis, former Colorado Springs Parks Director, was selected out of retirement to direct the Foundation, which distributes grants to the city for projects in the Garden of the Gods.

[46] Dave Philipps. "A Century of Preservation." *Colorado Springs Gazette Telegraph.* February 8, 2009. A:1.

[47] In the 1990s, Master Plans were completed for the White House Ranch, Ute Valley Park, the Garden of the Gods, Palmer Park, Acacia Park, North Cheyenne Cañon, the Pikes Peak Greenway, Patty Jewett Golf Course, and Valley Hi Golf Course, among others.

[48] The Parks and Recreation Department took steps to find a suitable location to build a park for skateboarders, asking for public input on the idea in 1996 with the intention to include it as a project in their 1997 budget.

[49] In an effort to resolve differences between mountain bikers and other trail users, the Parks Department developed a 1995 Rules of the Trail policy. Highlights of the policy were that Parks and Recreation would designate areas and trails where mountain biking would be allowed; it would consider erosion, natural drainage patterns, and wildlife habitats; and etiquette education programs for trail users would be implemented. Advisory signs would be placed at trailheads with information about the length, description, levels of difficulty, directions, and safety precautions, and brochures outlining responsible bicycle practices for both on- and off-road bicycling would be attached to new bicycles sold within Colorado Springs.

[50] The sports complex was named in honor of "Goose" Gossage, Wasson High School graduate and a major league pitcher for twenty-two years. Gossage was voted into the Baseball Hall of Fame in 2008.

[51] Tim Bergsten. "New Gossage Youth Complex Is Recreation Jewel/City Park Facilities in Growing Demand by Kids and Adults." *Colorado Springs Gazette Telegraph.* February 25, 1996. PROGRESS:12.

[52] The Parks Department was recognized as an "outstanding organization" by the Colorado Special Olympics in 1996 for its programs.

[53] Marty Grantz. "Growth Challenges the Springs' Parks and Recreation Department." *Colorado Springs Gazette Telegraph.* February 23, 1997. PROGRESS:4.

[54] Gene DeLoux. "Smooth Sliding. After a Generation of Splintery Playground Equipment, Kids Are Flipping Over the Return of Metal Apparatus." *Colorado Springs Gazette Telegraph.* April 7, 1995. B:1.

[55] The department proposed that first a value be set for services provided and then determinations made regarding who should pay for them. Those programs that provided a broad "public good"—parks, trails, playground equipment, restrooms, and open space, for example—would be paid for by taxpayers and not entail a specific user fee (though nominal fees would be charged for tennis courts, shuffleboard courts, or nature classes). Programs that fell into the category of "merit good"—swimming lessons, CPR classes, and rehabilitative programs, youth team sports, youth day camps and senior fitness training, as examples—would be financed through a mixture of fees and tax subsidies. Those that seemed to be primarily "private good"—examples being adult team sports, rental of private facilities, leisure classes, and cemetery services—would require user fees to cover most or all of the costs.

[56] Rich Laden. "Open-Space Tax Is an Idea Whose Time Has Come." *Colorado Springs Gazette Telegraph.* April 3, 1997. A:4.

[57] *Colorado Springs Open Space Plan: A Plan for the Conservation of Natural Areas and Greenways.* 1997. p. 13.

[58] The Open Space Plan explained the usefulness of the land trust: "Land trusts are private, non-profit groups established to administer conservation easements or otherwise arrange open space conservation. The William J. Palmer Parks Foundation Inc. (informally

known as the Palmer Foundation) is a local land trust that holds conservation easements on a number of properties in the city, including public open space areas purchased with Greater Outdoors Colorado (GOCO) funds. The Palmer Foundation has been instrumental in the preservation of approximately 2,400 acres within El Paso and Teller counties. The Foundation also acts as the holder of conservation easements in public acquisitions made with GOCO grant funds, such as Sinton Pond and parts of the Pikes Peak Greenway." (Ibid. p. 23)

59 In 1999, Terry Putman, Parks and Recreation Planning Manager, was appointed the city's TOPS coordinator. Chris Lieber would hold this position from 2006 to 2010.

60 Initial TOPS Working Committee members were Ken Andrew, Doug Carter, Randle Case II, Theresa Cavalier, Stephen Harris, Patti Margrave, Lee Milner, Ann Oatman-Gardner, and Frogard Ryan.

61 Pam Zubeck. "Springs Takes Possession of Open Space/300 Acres Purchased from Stratton Trust." *Colorado Springs Gazette Telegraph.* July 9, 1998. CITY/STATE:8.

62 Ibid.

63 One of the many advantages of TOPS money was the ability it gave the city to leverage other grants and partner with other organizations. The 1,680 acre J.L. Ranch in southeast Colorado Springs would become a state park, funded by a state GOCO grant as well as city TOPS receipts. The acreage to complete the Monument Creek trail—thirty acres roughly between Woodmen Valley Road and the Air Force Academy—received additional support from a GOCO grant and city general funds transferred from the Sand Creek Community Park; Sand Creek's city funds were replaced when excess acreage at the Gossage Sports Complex was sold. The additional University Park (formerly known as the Houck property) open space was funded with TOPS funds and a city GOCO grant, and would connect with existing trails in Austin Bluffs and Pulpit Rock Park, linking those two open spaces in the north-central part of the city. Open space advocates found this gratifying, having lost an earlier campaign to prevent the University Park development from happening at all. City Council had rejected the seventy-four-acre parcel purchase in 1998, but was convinced to reconsider by the TOPS Working Committee. The University Park developers—who had fought bitterly to retain their development options—had earlier transferred 187 acres of open space to the city, as required by the Parkland Dedication Ordinance.

64 Pam Zubeck. "City Invites Masses to the Decision Table." *Colorado Springs Gazette Telegraph.* September 21, 1997. A:9.

65 *Springs Community Improvements Program Executive Summary.* Executive Summary p. 1.

66 Pam Zubeck. "Developers Dominate Panels/Council Defends Appointments." *Colorado Springs Gazette Telegraph.* January 25, 1998. CITY/STATE:5.

67 Key projects to receive funding from the 1997 tax retention included the Colorado Springs Youth Sports Complex, as well as the animal shelter and drainage and traffic proposals. Retention of the 1998 taxes would allow for construction of two community centers, one on the northeast side and one on the southeast. The bond approval would enable the completion of the other SCIP priorities.

68 Improvements to Sertich Ice Center included $600,000 for the refrigeration plant, $150,000 for boards and glass, $50,000 for ADA accessibility, and $25,000 for the lobby remodel, in addition to architectural and engineering fees.

69 Bill Vogrin. "Side Streets: Money for Parks, Rec Centers Seems Like a Fairy Tale." *Colorado Springs Gazette.* May 26, 2010.

70 Nancy Lewis Park was located on the grounds of the old turf farm southwest of Fillmore and Union. The money raised from the Legacy of Trees program would benefit hospice, a program to care for terminally ill people, by supporting patients who could not afford to pay. For a complete list of the trees in the Nancy Lewis Park arboretum, see Appendix.

71 Rich Laden. "Pupils' Pennies Make Park Possible/Steele Community Fully Funds Project." *Colorado Springs Gazette.* January 21, 1997. CITY/STATE:3.

72 The Taylor Park project was paid for with a $25,000 grant from El Pomar, $25,000 each from the Gates Foundation, Colorado Springs District 11 and the city of Colorado Springs, and a $75,000 GOCO grant.

73 Dedicated entirely to youth activities, the El Pomar Youth Sports Complex was located in a lower-income area, where thirty thousand neighborhood households had a median income of less than $30,000.

74 In 2005, a $200,000 GOCO grant provided for construction of an artificial-turf soccer field, which allowed for extended playing seasons and reduced water consumption and maintenance costs at El Pomar Sports Complex.

Chapter Six: From Bloom to Bust

[1] Overall strategic plans and the prioritization of capital improvement projects had been directed by the city's Capital Improvement Program Office from 1990-1996; the 2000 Parks and Recreation Master Plan picked up where the Capital Improvement Program Office had left off.

[2] *Colorado Springs Parks, Recreation and Trails 2000-2010 Master Plan.* p. 93.

[3] Other sources from which Parks and Recreation had received grants included the State Trails Program and the Transportation Equity Act for the Twenty-First Century (TEA 21), successor to the Intermodal Surface Transportation Act (ISTEA). Grant funding, however, was unpredictable. Conservative estimates were used for financial planning. (*See Colorado Springs Parks, Recreation and Trails 2000-2010 Master Plan.* p. 89.)

[4] Nancy Lewis also served as co-chair of SCIP.

[5] Pam Zubeck. "$250 Million for Projects/Citizens Panel May Recommend Half-Cent Sales Tax Hike." *Colorado Springs Gazette.* October 4, 2000. A:1.

[6] Ed Sealover. "SCIP It, Voters Tell City/Sales Tax Increase Suffers a Big Defeat." *Colorado Springs Gazette.* April 4, 2001. A:1.

[7] Ed Sealover. "Vote Shifts Projects' Pace. Springs Timetable Ranges from Slowly to Not At All." *Colorado Springs Gazette.* November 8, 2001. METRO:7.

[8] The reservoir itself would remain in the hands of a private irrigation company. To help with the Big Johnson purchase, the city also received a $275,000 GOCO grant in 2001. Later, the city refinanced its purchase of Big Johnson, lowering its annual payment, to enable it to access more TOPS funds immediately for additional open space purchases. The Big Johnson Open Space would be paid off in July 2006.

[9] According to the Palmer Land Trust website, Bluestem Prairie (Big Johnson) "is dominated by a mixed grass prairie composed of grasses including blue grama, buffalograss, sideoats grama, big bluestem, little bluestem, sleepygrass, and green needlegrass. Other plant species include wavyleaf thistle, silver sage, prickly poppy, scarlet gillia, Easter daisy, sagebrush, yucca, and rabbitbrush. It is worth noting that big bluestem is a rare and imperiled grass species; Bluestem Prairie Open Space provides a safe haven for this elusive species." http://www.palmerlandtrust.org/protected-lands/ublic-properties/bluestem-prairie.

[10] Bill McKeown. "Deal Preserves Reservoir Land." *Colorado Springs Gazette.* September 29, 2000. METRO:1.

[11] Ed Sealover. "Away from It All, But Not Far/650-Acre Open Space in Colorado Springs Offers Views of the Past." *Colorado Springs Gazette.* December 2, 2002. METRO:2.

[12] Blodgett Peak was purchased for $2 million, and High Chaparral for $1.2 million. Of High Chaparral, the city purchased fifty-four acres and another nineteen were deeded by the current landowner for possible extension of any east-west corridors. (Ed Sealover. "A Boost for Parks, Open Space/Ruling Allows TOPS to Continue Through 2025." *Colorado Springs Gazette.* February 28, 2006. A:1).

[13] Total TOPS open space purchases to this point included Stratton Open Space, $4.5 million; University Park, $1.3 million; J.L. Ranch, $6.2 million; Big Johnson, $8.9 million; Blodgett Peak, $2 million; and High Chaparral, $1.2 million.

[14] Ed Sealover. "Open Land Proximity Debated/Some Want Space Saved in Inner City." *Colorado Springs Gazette.* November 18, 2001. METRO:2.

[15] The Pikes Peak Greenway Trail was all but finished when a flood destroyed large sections of the trail in 1991. Restored by 2002, a continuous pathway connected the New Santa Fe Regional Trail, the Greenway, and the Fountain Creek Regional Trail. New footbridges on several portions of the Greenway were completed by then.

[16] Importantly, the 2003 TOPS extension included a clause that stipulated 6 percent of annual TOPS revenues would be spent on stewardship of TOPS-funded properties—guaranteed maintenance money.

[17] Not everyone supported new open space acquisitions. A longtime local tax opponent sued the city to prevent the 2003 TOPS extension from going into effect. Arguing that the extension was a "tax increase" that violated TABOR restrictions and was therefore illegal, the plaintiff had his position upheld by the district court. But when the matter was appealed to the Colorado Supreme Court, justices reversed the lower court's decision, saying the extension suggested a continuation of the status quo, not an increase in tax. The decision meant the TOPS tax would continue until December 2025, as the voters had decided.

[18] Journalist Ruth Obee describes the almost 300-million-year-old formations: "Geologically speaking, the rose-gold and salmon-pink monoliths, dunes, towers, steeples, pinnacles and mushrooms are not only breathtakingly beautiful, they are unique—nothing quite like them exists anywhere else on earth." ("Red Rock Canyon, The Secret Garden of the Gods." *The Colorado Springs Independent.* June 21, 2001.)

[19] Ibid.

[20] To avoid having to obtain voter approval for the debt as would be required by TABOR, the city used a financing tool called certificates of participation, or COPS, which are sold much like bonds, to finance the deal. A city-controlled non-profit company assumed the debt and leased the property back to the city at a cost of about $1.4 million annually, the same amount required to pay off the debt it had assumed.

[21] This GOCO grant, the largest the city had yet received, was also significant in that it awarded the money despite the complications of the city's use of certificates of participation to purchase the property. The COPS strategy meant the city would not actually own the property for another fifteen years. Should the city default, certificate holders would take the land in defaults. That GOCO officials granted funds despite this sticking point was "a huge leap of faith," according to Parks Director Paul Butcher. (Ed Sealover. "Springs Lands Outdoors Grant." *Colorado Springs Gazette.* December 9, 2003. METRO:11.)

[22] Ovetta Sampson. "Keeping Parks Safe, Clean a Labor of Love for Gieck," *Colorado Springs Gazette.* April 29, 2002. LIFE:6.

[23] From 1997–2002, new parks (in addition to those described earlier) included Leon Young South Sports Complex, Ford Frick Park, Fred McKown Park, Remington Park, LuLu Pollard Park, Creekside Open Space, Broadmoor Glen, Judge Lunt Park, Northgate Open Space, Marshall Sprague Park, Kathleen Marriage Garden, Explorer Park, Roy Benavidez Park, John Stone Park, Frank Castello Park, Sky View Adult Sports Complex, Wilson Ranch, Pring Ranch Park, and Springs Ranch Park.

[24] Ed Sealover. "More Parks Stretching Staff Too Thin, Department Says." *Colorado Springs Gazette.* April 15, 2002. A:1.

[25] Colorado Springs' employee to parkland acreage ratio of 1:22 compared poorly to that of other Colorado cities: Denver: 1:13; Fort Collins: 1:12; Westminster: 1:11; and Lakewood: 1:13.

[26] Ed Sealover. "Resources Stretched Thin for Embattled Parks Staff." *Colorado Springs Gazette.* October 5, 2003. METRO:22.

[27] Ed Sealover. "City Will Cut Back on Water/Springs Plans to Reduce Usage by 10 Percent." *Colorado Springs Gazette.* April 12, 2002. METRO:6.

[28] Council members Larry Small and Jerry Heimlicher spearheaded the move to recruit volunteers to manage median plantings. Heimlicher justified his position: "Our whole issue is we didn't have any money to do it, so it was either this or dirt." (Ed Sealover. "Volunteer Flower Beds Criticized by Parks Board." *Colorado Springs Gazette.* July 9, 2004. METRO:19.) The only flowerbeds to continue to receive professional care were those funded by special districts such as the Business Improvement District downtown.

[29] Ed Sealover. "Volunteer Gardeners Don't Dig Their Jobs." *Colorado Springs Gazette.* September 10, 2004. METRO:19.

[30] In 2007, the city honored Springs in Bloom gardeners with these awards: Individual Award: Penrose Hospital and North Cascade neighbors for the Cascade Avenue and Madison Street bed; Business Award: Women's Associates PC for the Rockrimmon Boulevard and Dawson Drive bed; Service Group Award: Centennial No. 58 Order of the Easter Star for the Cascade Avenue and Willamette Avenue bed; Individual Design Award: Bill and Thea Vander Wel for the Flintridge Drive and El Canto Drive bed; and Overall Bed Award: Colorado College on Cascade Avenue at Colorado College.

[31] The eighty-two-year-old City Auditorium needed $1.7 million of repairs, including the installation of air-conditioning and modernization of its plumbing.

[32] In 2004, fifteen small neighborhood parks were in the queue to be built, as well as five athletic complexes and one regional park. Besides these, the Banning-Lewis Ranch development project, which was in the planning stages, was expected to bring on another one hundred parks. Despite the backlog of new parks awaiting construction, the city-wide budget crunch induced city leaders to use lottery funds to sustain existing parks by covering expenses the city itself had been funding—a legal move other cities were also taking, though not what had been intended by the original lottery bill. In the 2004 budget reduction, Colorado Springs officials shifted $400,000 of lottery funds toward park maintenance, and simultaneously cut the Parks Department general fund budget by $1.1 million. They also slated lottery receipts to cover the budgeted salaries for the Parks Design Division, formerly funded through the general budget. The following year, an additional $400,000 in lottery money was used for general parks maintenance, and none for new park and ball field construction. In 2006, the Design and Development Division budget was moved back into the general fund, and the lottery funds were redirected to park improvements.

[33] Ed Sealover. "Odds Against New Parks." *Colorado Springs Gazette.* December 19, 2004. A:1.

[34] In the Springs Ranch neighborhood, only ten acres of parks existed to serve 3,800 families. (Ed Sealover. "Tight Budgets Prompt Park Partnerships." Colorado Springs Gazette. March 1, 2004. METRO:16.)

[35] Seventy percent of the voters were in favor of repairing the lake, including a majority in all but four precincts within the entire city.

[36] Ed Sealover. "A Part of History Won't Run Dry." *Colorado Springs Gazette*. April 10, 2004.

[37] In 2008, Lyda Hill, developer of the Garden of the Gods Visitors Center, was awarded the Palmer Land Trust's Stuart P. Dodge Award for conservation leadership in honor of her efforts to protect and preserve the Garden.

[38] Capital improvement funds came from all four major funding sources for the department: grants, state lottery, the city general fund, and the TOPS tax. New parks were scheduled for Springs Ranch, University Park, and Stetson Ridge South. Van Diest Park was scheduled for renovation and Memorial Park's south side was scheduled for $100,000 of improvements. Venezia Park, 110 acres slated for development at Union Boulevard and Briargate Parkway, was still on hold.

[39] 2007 TOPS money was directed toward the second phase of Wildflower and Stetson Ridge parks, construction of Prairie Grass and Copper Creek, and completion of Stetson Ridge Northview Park. Three more maintenance technicians were hired, and $1 million put aside for trails development.

[40] Ed Sealover. "Fund Plans Aims to Build Parks." *Colorado Springs Gazette.* July 15, 2005.

[41] The first Garden of the Gods Race was held in 1976. In 2007, more than 1,300 runners from 33 states and international sites participated in the run.

[42] The annual Fourth of July festival in Memorial Park continued until 2008, when it was canceled for lack of funds.

[43] John Venezia Park's Master Plan called for an open "pasture," a "homestead" area with a playground, spray ground and picnic shelter, and the "range" including four soccer fields, two basketball courts, two in-line hockey courts, and four tennis courts. Eighty acres would remain undeveloped, due to the habitation of the Prebles Meadow Jumping Mouse. While the build-out date remained uncertain, residents were delighted with the plans for development of the longstanding area into a new neighborhood resource. In 2010, financing had been approved for John Venezia Park and Certificates of Participation were ready to be sold. But the city's concerns over finding funding for ongoing maintenance delayed the project indefinitely.

[44] The professionally designed skate park was funded with a $120,000 grant from Phil Long Community Fund and Denver Bronco Charities; a $200,000 GOCO grant; $385,000 from TOPS; and $460,000 from park land funds. The Skate Friends of Colorado Springs contributed $20,000 toward the park's construction.

[45] Colorado State Parks received $843,612 from GOCO to purchase part of the Cheyenne Mountain summit; Colorado Springs TOPS money was used for the rest. GOCO also granted the city $1 million toward the purchase of Section 16—short of the estimated $3.2 million price—when the city's lease of the land was up in 2010.

[46] El Paso County had intended to purchase Corral Bluffs for a motorcycle park, a plan that was dropped when surveys of the area disclosed ancient archaeological and paleontological sites, as well as golden eagle and prairie falcon nests.

[47] The purchase from the Colorado Springs and Eastern Railroad Company was made for $2.5 million, TOPS money, which the city would use to buy the property in five segments over five years.

[48] Funds for the project were $662,270 from GOCO, $557,000 from the city, and $11,000 from the county.

[49] Bill Vogrin. "An Investment in the City's Future." *Colorado Springs Gazette.* January 1, 2008.

[50] The Parks Department budget went from $7,413,828 in 2008 to $5,000,748 in 2009—a 22 percent reduction.

[51] Daniel Chacon. "CITY BUDGET: City Parks Department Leans Heavily on the Lottery." *Colorado Springs Gazette.* October 12, 2009.

[52] Volunteers were asked to perform routine maintenance at least twice a month: removing trash, eliminating weeds, replacing scattered wood chips, reporting vandalism and damage.

[53] Daniel Chacon. "Give Money to Parks, Not Pools." *Colorado Springs Gazette.* June 22, 2009.

[54] From 2002 to 2008, the city's population had increased by 2.5 percent and consumer prices rose 13 percent. While the city's general fund had grown during that time period, it had not kept pace at the same rate. The city had $664 to spend per resident in 2002 and only $624 in 2008. Nearly half of that amount was allocated to public safety services: police and fire. That figure was to drop even further in the next two years.

[55] According to John Weiss, publisher of the *Colorado Springs Independent,* the effects of the tax increase would be: "For the first year, the owner of a Colorado Springs home valued at $262,000 would pay an additional $126, or less than $2.50 a week. Over the following four years, property taxes will increase about 37 cents a week per year. By 2015, a typical home's property tax will be $210 higher than today. That's just $4 more each week, a small price to pay for maintaining city services at current levels." It was anticipated with the increased property tax the city could avoid the elimination of nearly 250 positions, the closing of community centers, pools, and the Pioneers Museum, and the loss of more than 60,000 hours of bus service in 2010. (Weiss, John and Steven Pope. "Yes on 2C, No on 300." *Colorado Springs Independent.* September 10, 2009.)

[56] Daniel Chacon. "Crushing Defeat Delivers a Message: Shrink Government." *Colorado Springs Gazette.* November 3, 2009.

[57] With the reorganization, the Parks Department was first assigned to report to the Chief of the Fire Department and subsequently to the Assistant City Manager.

[58] In January 2010, the city's budget deficit for 2011 was projected to be $27 million, for 2012 $12 million, and for 2013 $11 million, according to the Parks and Recreation Advisory Board January 2010 minutes.

[59] In addition to the Adopt-A-Park program, the Parks Department initiated an Adopt-A-Trashcan program, appealing to citizens to help provide services the department could no longer manage. By April, a total of eighty-three cans in thirty-seven parks were adopted. (Colorado Springs Parks Advisory Board Minutes. April 8, 2010.)

[60] The Kathy Loo Conservation Fund donated $30,000 to help with the Sustainable Parks Initiative, including volunteerism.

[61] Leslie Eaton. "Strapped City Cuts and Cuts and Cuts." *The Wall Street Journal.* Economy: April 13, 2010.

[62] Under the new private operation, admission to the outdoor pools increased from $7 to $8 for adults and from $4 to $6 for youth. At the Memorial Park Aquatics Center, prices went from $7 to $12 for adults and doubled from $4 to $8 for youth and seniors.

[63] Prior to 2009, the Aquatics Program provided thousands of hours of swim lessons, public swimming, and water fitness classes to over 200,000 youth, seniors, adults, and individuals with disabilities. This included over 7,000 swim lesson participants annually, primarily youth. The program certified, employed, and mentored hundreds of lifeguards, water safety instructors, and cashiers, being one of the largest employers of teenagers in the city. Including ten full-time staff, operating expenses were approximately $1million annually between 2007-2009, of which the city funded 50 percent.

[64] Leslie Eaton. "Strapped City Cuts and Cuts and Cuts." *The Wall Street Journal.* Economy: April 13, 2010.

[65] J. Adrian Stanley. "What We'll Lose: If Colorado Springs Community Centers Close, The Fallout Could Be Immeasurable." *Colorado Springs Independent.* February 18, 2010.

[66] The Colorado Springs Housing Authority, located at 831 South Nevada Avenue, administers public housing programs for the city and coordinates senior community services programs.

[67] "The intent of the Housing Authority is to operate the Senior Center with the current staff and programs but with the added support of the Housing Authority in order to continue to provide services to the seniors in the community. The Housing Authority is considering opening a market at the Human Services Complex as in the past. Also, they will work with Silver Key regarding transportation from senior housing, which they operate, to the Senior Center." (*Colorado Springs Park Advisory Board Minutes.* September 9, 2010.)

[68] John Hazelhurst. "Coloradans Big on Volunteerism of All Types." *Colorado Springs Business Journal.* March 5, 2010.

[69] Water rates had increased 56.9 percent from 2008-2010, and were forecast to increase 10-12 percent annually for the next 8 to 10 years.

[70] Debbie Kelly. "Downtown Jewel Loses Shimmer as Water Disappears." *Colorado Springs Independent.* August 5, 2010.

[71] "Did You Ever Wonder: Monument Valley Ponds." *The Gazette.* October 15, 2010.

[72] Paul Butcher interview. May 5, 2010.

[73] The City Manager, Penelope Culbreath-Graft, also tendered her resignation to City Council in Spring 2010.

[74] The Police Department, Fire Department, Airport, Financial and Administrative Services, and Community, Infrastructure, and Development Team were organized to report directly to Interim City Manager Steve Cox.

[75] As part of the city's reorganization, Pikes Peak—America's Mountain became a part of the Parks, Recreation, and Cultural Services Department. Pikes Peak Highway is an Enterprise Operation that encompasses the North Slope Recreation Area, and works closely with the U.S. Forest Service. The Administration, Cultural Services, Recreation Services, Golf and Cemetery Enterprises, Human Services Complex, and Pikes Peak—America's Mountain were to report to King; Park Maintenance, Design, Development, and TOPS, Regional Parks, Open Space, and Trails and Forestry were assigned to Schroeder.

[76] A local contractor contributed a decorative fence for the project. A Colorado Garden Show Grant and Care and Share provided $7,000, Laura and Tim Spear provided $1,000 through Forest Edge Garden, the *Colorado Springs Independent* donation campaign provided $6,250, and private donors contributed $500 for the Dorchester Park Urban Garden. Pikes Peak Urban Gardens supported the project's water and other expenses. Partners included Care and Share, Springs Rescue Mission, Catholic Charities, Marian House, Urban Peak, Designer Columns and Piers, LLC, and Downtown Chipotle Restaurant.

[77] The playground resulted from a partnership between the Parks TOPS program, the Swing High Project (a local non-profit), and Olympic medal-winning gymnast Michelle Dusserre-Farrell. The universally accessible playground provides extensive ramping and

rubber play surfacing, harnessed swings, elevated sand tables, and other features designed specifically to meet the needs of children with disabilities. The project was funded by TOPS, GOCO grants, PLDO fees, the Phil Long Community Fund, the Gates Family Foundation, King Soopers, Aerials Gymnastics, and donors to the Swing High Project.

[78] The Corral Bluffs Alliance (CoBA), in partnership with the Parks Department, had been providing guided hikes to the public and taken responsibility for cleaning up the open space.

[79] The saga of acquiring Section 16 was explained at the Colorado Springs Parks Advisory Board meeting in September 2010. According to the Board's posted minutes: "Manitou Section 16 was owned by the Colorado State Land Board. El Paso County leased Section 16 from the State Land Board from 1972 to July 2004. The lease first expired in 1994 and the County chose not to renew stating it could not afford the maintenance and the $640 a year lease payment. The County changed its position and tried to renegotiate the lease, but the State Land Board chose to entertain development offers. Citizen groups emerged to advocate for the purchase of Section 16. At that time, the County submitted a grant application to GOCO to acquire the property but it was denied because there were no matching funds. One group, Section 16 Intact, worked with then Representative Marcy Morrison to preserve the property by amending the constitutional mission of the State Land Board. This work was eventually approved by the voters as Amendment 16, which created the Stewardship Trust. In 1995, the State Land Board extended the lease with El Paso County and urged the County to develop a strategy for acquiring the property. In 1997, El Paso County set aside $640,000 for the acquisition. In July 2004, the State Land Board reassigned the lease to Colorado Springs for one year with the understanding that the City would acquire the property. The lease increased from $640 in 1994 to $9,600 in 2004 to $40,000 in 2005. The lease was funded by GOCO from 2005-2010. The lease will expire on December 31, 2010. In 2007, GOCO awarded $1 million toward acquisition. In 2009, GOCO extended the project deadline for one year." (*Colorado Springs Parks and Recreation Advisory Board Minutes.* September 9, 2010.)

[80] The anticipated city budget deficit for 2011 was adjusted in September when Lisa Bigelow, Budget Manager, provided City Council an update on the budget outlook. Essentially, the $27 million 2011 budget deficit projected earlier in the year had reduced to $25.4 million, most notably due to improved sales and use tax revenue collections, and improvements in other areas (i.e., city reorganization, police and fire pension plan changes, city benefit program changes, implementation of second Voluntary Attrition Retirement Program, savings from the Pikes Peak Highway paving project, methodology for calculating PILT as a one-time expenditure, etc.). A non-profit group, the Community Partnership Project, had formed to explore taking over the operation of the community centers. The non-profit Friends of Aquatics, supporting city aquatics programs since 1999, was challenged to keep the Cottonwood Creek Recreation Center open in 2011, the only remaining community pool with the only indoor wave pool in southern Colorado. Their hopes were to support CCRC to a level of self-sufficiency by 2013, possibly finding a means to reopen another outdoor pool or Prospect Lake by 2013. (*Colorado Springs Parks and Recreation Advisory Board Minutes.* November and December, 2010.)

[81] Daniel Chacon. "TOPS Question Leaves Parks Backers Torn." *Colorado Springs Gazette.* September 13, 2010. A:1.

Chapter Seven: A Future of Possibilities

[1] Denis Galvin, National Park Commissioner and Former Deputy Director of the National Park Service, quoted in *Advancing the National Park Idea: National Parks Second Century Commission Report.* 2010. p. 23.

[2] Patrick Arden, "The High Cost of Free Parks." *Next American City Magazine.* Summer, 2010.

[3] In Stamford, Connecticut, the Mill River Collaborative, a nonprofit private-public group, is working in 2010 to fund a $60 million rebuilding of Mill River Park with a combination of methods: a tax-increment financing district, federal and local government resources, and $20 million raised through private donations. They are following the example of Hartford, Connecticut, where a restored downtown riverwalk connecting four revitalized parks was funded with more than $60 million raised from private and public sources. Hartford's renewed riverfront is said to have attracted more than $1 billion worth of investment. In 2010, offering a heavy schedule of events and festivals, it drew more than 960,000 visitors. (Elizabeth Kim, "Can Stamford Build the Next Great Urban Park?" *The Stamford Advocate.* December 21, 2010.)

[4] Rudolph Bush, "Dallas 'Love Your Parks' Summit Woos Volunteers, Funding." *The Dallas Morning News.* November 7, 2010.

[5] Peter Harnik. *Urban Green.* p. 8.

[6] In October 2001, the Trust for Public Land (TPL) convened a multidisciplinary group of urban and park experts for a two-day meeting to explore what elements contribute to an excellent city park system. Their conclusions from the Houston meeting delineated the following important activities, requirements and considerations to plan and execute an excellent park system: 1) the use of Mission Statements and updates; 2) ongoing planning and community development; 3) sufficient resources to meet system's goals; 4) equitable access; 5) user satisfaction; 6) safety from physical hazards and crime; and 7) external benefits to the city.

[7] St. Louis' Citygarden, west of the famed Gateway Arch, includes trees, sculpture, a 180-foot rectangular basin with a six-foot waterfall, a child-pleasing "spray-plaza," an LED video wall displaying art and movies, plus a popular café overlooking the combined attractions. Locally quarried limestone walls match the curves of the nearby Mississippi and Missouri Rivers; a series of terraces represents the high cliffs of river bluffs. Manhattan's High Line Park provides a sliver of green space for people to stroll, chat, picnic, and catch stunning views of the city, while Discovery Green, on the east side of downtown Houston, features 100-year-old oak trees, native gardens with indigenous plants, birds and butterflies, a model boat basin, fountains, lawns, and major people-watching. Houston's public-private venture laid a LEED-certified carpet of green over two former surface parking lots, transforming 12.5 acres into an amenities-laden park that generated nearby development. Varied, different, and appealing, these newly designed parks have become major "must-see" tourist attractions.

[8] Katie Thomas, "Revival of a River Alters a City's Course in Sports." *The New York Times.* April 22, 2008.

[9] Tim Wohlgenant, "Investing in Parks Pays Off." *The Denver Post.* August 12, 2010. Wohlgenant writes: "Denver's many parks, natural areas and recreation centers are dearly loved. Every weekend, thousands of people are drawn to paths along the South Platte River and Cherry Creek to bike, skate, or stroll along the water. Families flock to Confluence Park where Cherry Creek merges with the South Platte River, to bask in the sun near the rapids. Parks across the city pulse with sports, picnics, dog-walkers, and sunbathers. And our unique inventory of mountain parks draws many of us to the foothills and Denver's surrounding areas."

[10] As a result of the greenway, Boulder residents commute by bike twenty times the national average, and nearly one person in ten walks to work. Ryan Donahue. ("Moving Traffic to the Trail: Boulder's Multipurpose Greenway." *City Parks Blog.* December 8, 2010.)

[11] Galen Cranz had earlier described ideological stages of park design: from pastoral in the late nineteenth century to reformist in the early 1900s, to recreational in the mid-twentieth century, to open space interests and emphases in the late 1900s. See *Politics of Urban Park Design,* 1982.

[12] Galen Cranz and Michael Boland. "The Ecological Park as an Emerging Type. [Research and Debate]." *Places.* July 1, 2003.

[13] This ideal of sustainably designed "ecological parks" is supported and advanced by the Sustainable Sites Initiative, a formal national initiative for ecologically developed and maintained parks. Organized as an inter-disciplinary effort by the American Society of Landscape Architects, the Lady Bird Johnson Wildflower Center at the University of Texas at Austin, and the United States Botanic Garden, the site offers voluntary national guidelines and performance benchmarks for sustainable land design, construction, and maintenance practices. See http://www.sustainablesites.org/.

[14] As J. Adrian Stanley argues, "Sales tax is a lousy way to fund government services. More than half the city's general fund is collected from a 2 percent sales and use tax. . . . Total revenue from property tax (a stable source of funding not dependent on shopping sprees) makes up 10 percent of general fund. In 2008, per capita property tax in Colorado Springs was about $55. . . . But [others] may be paying extremely high property tax—to little [special] taxing districts. So, when the city wants to raise property taxes to pay for things like police and fire, [they're] thinking taxes are already high enough." ("Tabor Tyranny." *Colorado Springs Independent.* April 9, 2009. pp. 2-3.)

[15] In addition to sales-tax revenue problems, Colorado Springs' commitment to fund city pensions for those police and firefighters who served the city increased 94 percent from 2006 to 2008, further hampering city funding of other functions, and will continue to rise. While "new hires" in police and fire will be covered by the state police and fire pension plan in the future, the city will still need to meet its present commitments for pensions for the next thirty to forty years, reducing its ability to invest in other services.

[16] As Mike Anderson, former Deputy City Manager explained, the debt per capita in Colorado Springs is very low—approximately $100—while $850 per person is average for a city of the same size.

[17] The Colorado Economic Futures Panel's final report recommended putting lawmaking back in the hands of lawmakers, bringing property tax back in a meaningful way, and greatly increasing governmental transparency as feasible solutions to Colorado's economic problems. (J. Adrian Stanley. "Tabor Tyranny." *Colorado Springs Independent.* April 9, 2009. p. 4.)

[18] Edwin A. Sawyer. "The Present Water Supply of Colorado Springs." Handwritten letter for *The Century Chest.* August 2, 1901.

[19] Possible constraints to an innovative integrated solution regarding water use include the November 2010 phase-out of Stormwater Enterprise and PILT funding to the City General Fund; the recent drop in City and County tax collections; the loss of City sales tax to increased retail growth outside city limits; the increased regulatory enforcement of the Clean Water Act (stormwater) by the federal Environmental Protection Agency and the State Health Department; and the TABOR requirement for voter approval of any new taxes.

[20] This point was also argued in *Advancing the National Park Idea: National Parks Second Century Commission Report,* cautioning that "Changing demographics test the very idea of a shared . . . culture, or common . . . ideals." 2010. pp. 15-16.

[21] Many programs have been initiated to counteract what has been labeled "outdoor deprivation disorder," including President Obama's "America's Great Outdoors Initiative"; Michelle Obama's "Let's Move" and "Let's Move Outdoors" campaigns; physicians' advocacy for outdoor program activities, including volunteer health guides in parks; health insurers supporting programs like the "Kids in the Parks Initiative" in North Carolina; and the National Wildlife Federation's "Be Out There" public-education campaign advocating daily outdoors unstructured playtime for children. Parks provide the necessary environment for these activities. (Jane Brody, "Head Out for a Daily Dose of Green Space." *The New York Times.* Personal Health. November 29, 2010.)

[22] Parks are a primary resource to counter what some are terming the "play deficit," the lack of opportunity for children to engage in unstructured, imaginative, stimulating, self-directed playtime. In fall 2010, a coalition called Play for Tomorrow organized a giant play date in Central Park to demonstrate to families the learning, fun, growth, and excitement that come from unstructured play. Games like I Spy and Capture the Flag, mounds of Play-Doh, sidewalk chalk, building blocks, puzzles, and more engaged more than 50,000 players. The US Play Coalition, a group of doctors, educators, and parks and recreation officials, strongly advocates for the importance of outdoor play. And KaBOOM, a non-profit organization advocating for free play for children, has built 1,900 playgrounds across the country, most in low-income neighborhoods, and in September helped organize Play Days in 1,600 communities, incorporating community park areas.

[23] Paul Sherer. "A Healthier America? It's a Walk in the Park." *The Trust for Public Land.* http://www.tpl.org/tier3_cd/cfm?content_item_id=14589&folder_id=2606. Retrieved December 30, 2010.

[24] *Advancing the National Park Idea: National Parks Second Century Commission Report.* 2010. p. 16.

[25] A business-like approach, looking at the costs associated with the system and determining how to get the lowest possible costs for services rendered, would promote fiscal responsibility. A process that looked inward to see how to save costs within the system, and looked outward to compare costs with desired results and outcome, performed in a non-emotional sense, could help achieve the greatest good for the lowest possible cost. The decision-makers should not let their enthusiasm for the parks limit their ability to see the appropriate level for expansion and development. A strong strategic evaluation must be done on every planned future park acquisition.

[26] The Colorado Springs Downtown Action Plan was formally adopted in 1992. In 2005, an updated strategic plan was initiated, a two-year initiative known as "Imagine Downtown," which was subsequently incorporated into the city's land use master plan in 2007.

APPENDIX 1

Colorado Springs Parks: Chronology of Acquisition

Decade	Date*	Park, Trail, Open Space, Natural Area	Classification
1870	1871	Acacia Park,115 E. Platte Ave.	Special purpose park
	1875	Evergreen Cemetery, 1005 S. Hancock Ave.	Cemetery
1880	1882	Antlers Park, 31 W. Pikes Peak Ave.	Special purpose park
	1885	North Cheyenne Cañon, 2110 N. Cheyenne Cañon Rd.	Natural area
	1888	Bott Park, 815 S. 26th St.	Neighborhood park
1890	1892	Dorchester Park, 1130 S. Nevada Ave.	Neighborhood park
	1893	Boulder Crescent Park, 290 N. Cascade Ave.	Mini park
	1896	Fairview Cemetery, 1000 S. 26th St.	Cemetery
	1897	Vermijo Park, 2601 W. Vermijo Ave.	Neighborhood park
1900	1900	Stratton Park, Cheyenne Rd., property sold in 1928.	Community park
	1902	Thorndale Park, 2310 W. Uintah St.	Neighborhood park
	1907	Monument Valley Park, 170 W. Cache la Poudre St.	Community park
	1907	Palmer Park, 3650 Maizeland Rd.	Natural area
	1907	Westend, Westend Ave. & S. 26th St.	Special resource area
	1909	Garden of Gods Park, 3130 N. 30th St.	Natural area
	1909	Boulder Park, 1210 E. Boulder St.	Neighborhood park
1910	1912	Prospect Lake, 1605 E. Pikes Peak Ave.	Community park
	1915	Bear Creek Cañon Park, 501 Bear Creek Rd.	Natural area
	1919	Patty Jewett Golf Course, 900 E. Espanola St.	Golf course
1920	1923	Fountain Park, 901 E. Fountain Blvd.	Neighborhood park
	1926	Bancroft Park, 2408 W. Colorado Ave.	Special purpose park
1930	1939	Cucharras Park, 1121 W. Cucharras St.	Mini park
1940	1940	North Cheyenne Cañon Visitor Center, 2110 N. Cheyenne Cañon Rd.	Visitor center
	1944	Conejos Playground, 314-318 Conejos St.; in 1952 became a park; removed in urban renewal project in 1980s.	Mini park
	1948	Memorial Park, 1605 E. Pikes Peak Ave.	Community park
	1949	Lunar Park, 2112 E. Uintah St.	Neighborhood park
1950	1950	Bonforte Park, 2323 N. Wahsatch Ave.	Neighborhood park
	1952	Conejos Park, 314-318 Conejos St., removed in urban renewal project in 1980s	Neighborhood park
	1952	Winfield Scott [Stratton] Park, 2506 Sycamore St.	Special resource area
	1955	Jefferson Park, 2580 Lelaray St.	Neighborhood park
	1955	Pike Park, 2610 N. Chestnut St.	Neighborhood park
	1955	Audubon Park, 2460 N. Circle Dr.	Neighborhood park
	1958	Westmoor Park, 3315 Water St.	Neighborhood park
	1959	Douglas Creek, 1319 Holland Park Blvd.	Open space
1960	1960	Twain Park, 3320 E. San Miguel St.	Neighborhood park

	1961	Garden Ranch, South off Flintridge Dr. by N. Union Blvd.	Special resource area
	1962	Wagner Park, 3637 E. Bijou St.	Neighborhood park
	1963	Madison Park, 2122 N. Murray Blvd.	Neighborhood park
	1964	Wilson Park, 4501 Palmer Park Blvd.	Neighborhood park
	1966	Wasson Park, 1910 N. Circle Dr.	Neighborhood park
	1967	Mountain View Playground, 206 Longfellow Dr.	Mini park
	1967	Grant Park, 2821 Shadowglen Dr.	Neighborhood park
	1967	Honeybear Playground, 226 Longfellow Dr.	Mini park
	1967	Little Britches Playground, 4105 Channing Pl.	Mini park
	1967	Munchkin Playground, 4319 Vehr Dr.	Mini park
	1968	Jackson Park, 1111 Holland Park Blvd.	Neighborhood park
	1968	Trues Mill Park, 305 Longfellow Dr.	Mini park
	1968	Keller Park, 4950 Meadowland Blvd.	Neighborhood park
	1968	Happy Hollow Playground, 218 Milton Dr.	Mini park
	1968	Meadows Park, 1990 S. El Paso Ave.	Neighborhood park
	1968	Monterey Park, 2225 Monterey Rd.	Neighborhood park
	1969	Ute Valley Park, 1705 Vindicator Dr.	Natural area
1970	1970	Carver Park, 4242 N. Carefree Cir.	Neighborhood park
	1971	Van Diest Park, 1520 S. Chelton Rd.	Neighborhood park
	1972	Danville Park, 1147 Mountview Ln.	Neighborhood park
	1972	Fremont Park, 5080 El Camino Dr.	Neighborhood park
	1972	Penrose Park, 4295 S. Nonchalant Cir.	Neighborhood park
	1972	Giberson Park, 2890 Ferber Dr.	Neighborhood park
	1972	Henry Park, 1404 Lehmberg Blvd.	Neighborhood park
	1972	Discovery Park, 155 Buckeye Dr.	Neighborhood park
	1972	Portal Park, 3535 N. Hancock Ave.	Neighborhood park
	1972	Tomah Park, 5285 Tomah Dr.	Neighborhood park
	1972	Villa Loma Park, 5055 Escapardo Way	Neighborhood park
	1972	Village Green Park, 3590 N. Carefree Cir.	Neighborhood park
	1972	Wildflower Park, 980 W. Nolte Dr.	Neighborhood park
	1973	Otero Park, 4630 Iron Horse Trail.	Neighborhood park
	1973	Alamo Square Park, 215 S. Tejon St.	Special purpose park
	1973	Memorial Ice Rink (renamed Sertich in 1986), 1605 E. Pikes Peak Ave.	Sports complex
	1973	Memorial Municipool, 1605 E. Pikes Peak Avenue. (Renovated as Aquatics and Fitness Center in 2001.)	Recreation center
	1973	Prairie Grass Park, 710 Chapman Dr.	Neighborhood park
	1973	Flanagan Park, 3132 N. Prospect St.	Neighborhood park
	1973	Centennial Park, 3480 El Morro Rd.	Neighborhood park
	1973	Roswell Park, 515 Polk St.	Neighborhood park
	1974	George Fellows Park, 5711 Tuckerman Dr.	Neighborhood park
	1974	Sunset Mesa, 5685 Flintridge Dr.	Open space

	1974	High Street Park renamed John Prairie Dog O'Byrne in 2009, 505 E. Bijou St.	Mini park
	1974	Keystone Park, 6050 Sapporo Dr.	Neighborhood park
	1974	Quail Lake Park, 915 E. Cheyenne Mountain Blvd.	Community park
	1974	South Shooks Run Park, 402 E. Fountain Blvd.	Neighborhood park
	1975	Deerfield Hills Community Center, 4290 Deerfield Hills Rd.	Community center
	1975	Broadview, Mesa Rd., north of Sondermann Park.	Open space
	1975	Mesa Open Space, 1402 Manitou Blvd.	Open space
	1975	Valley Hi Golf Course, 610 S. Chelton Rd.	Golf course
	1976	Austin Bluffs Open Space, 1910 Rimwood Dr.	Open space
	1976	Mid Shooks Run Park, 631 E. St. Vrain St.	Neighborhood park
	1976	North Shooks Run Park, 706 N. Franklin St.	Neighborhood park
	1976	Otis Park, 731 N. Iowa Ave.	Neighborhood park
	1977	Bristol Park, 910 N. Walnut St.	Neighborhood park
	1977	Otis Park Community Center, 731 N. Iowa Ave.	Community center
	1977	Erindale Park, 1705 Twin Oaks Dr.	Neighborhood park
	1977	Homestead Park, 5300 S. Carefree Cir.	Neighborhood park
	1977	Iron Horse, 4350 Iron Horse Trail.	Special resource area
	1977	Pioneer Park, 1101 Cenotaph Cir.	Neighborhood park
	1978	Blunt Park, 2329 W. Vermijo Ave.	Neighborhood park
	1978	Dublin Park, 2450 Roundtop Dr.	Neighborhood park
	1979	Roosevelt Park, 219 Byron Dr.	Neighborhood park
	1979	Rudy Park, 5360 Cracker Barrel Cir.	Neighborhood park
	1979	Jenkins Park, 1019 S. Skyway Blvd.	Neighborhood park
1980	1980	Blair Bridge, 4001 N. 30th St.	Open space
	1980	Old Farm Park, 4585 W. Old Farm Cir.	Neighborhood park
	1980	Foothills Park, 853 Allegheny Dr.	Neighborhood park
	1980	Oak Valley Ranch, White Buffalo Rd.	Open space
	1981	Deerfield Park, 4290 Deerfield Hills Rd.	Neighborhood park
	1981	Golden Hills Park, 6155 Delmonico Dr.	Neighborhood park
	1981	Promontory Point, Limit St. & W. Bijou St.	Open space
	1981	Silent Rain, 2169 Silent Rain Dr.	Open space
	1981	Heathercrest Park, 1975 Heathercrest Dr.	Neighborhood park
	1982	Sondermann Park, 740 W. Caramillo St.	Open space
	1982	Franklin Park, 2951 E. Dale St.	Neighborhood park
	1982	Meadows Community Center, 1939 S. El Paso Ave.	Community center
	1983	Sagebrush Park, 651 Crestline Dr.	Neighborhood park
	1983	Meadowlark Park, 2709 Dickens Dr.	Neighborhood park
	1983	Piñon Valley Park, 5585 Mule Deer Dr.	Neighborhood park
	1983	City Auditorium, 221 E. Kowa St.	Special center

	1984	Garden Ranch Park, 2220 W. Montebello Dr	Neighborhood park
	1984	Rampart Park, 8270 Lexington Dr.	Community park
	1984	Penstemon Park, 1375 Jet Wing Cir.	Neighborhood park
	1984	Golf Acres Senior Center, 1434 N. Hancock	Community center
	1984	High Plains, south of Mirage Dr.	Open space
	1984	Pinecliff Park, 855 Popes Valley Dr.	Neighborhood park
	1984	Frontier Park, 3725 Meadow Ridge Dr.	Neighborhood park
	1985	Betty Krouse Park, 2415 E. Cache la Poudre St.	Neighborhood park
	1985	Fairfax Park, 8175 Chancellor Dr.	Neighborhood park
	1985	Adams Park, 851 Boggs Pl.	Neighborhood park
	1985	Cottonwood Creek Park, 7040 Rangewood Dr,	Community park
	1985	Woodstone Park, 1315 Carlson Dr.	Neighborhood park
	1985	Rampart Recreation Center, 8250 Lexington Dr.	Recreation center
	1985	Roy Benavidez Park, 3395 Afternoon Cir.	Neighborhood park
	1986	Sierra Park, 2150 Jet Wing Dr.	Neighborhood park
	1986	Panorama Park, 4540 Fenton Rd.	Neighborhood park
	1986	Sandstone Park, 4650 Pring Ranch Rd.	Neighborhood park
	1986	Mountain Shadows, 2440 Brogans Bluff Dr.	Special resource area
	1986	Mountain Shadows Park, 5151 Flying W. Ranch Rd.	Neighborhood park
	1986	Stetson Hills, Charlotte Pkwy & Barnes Rd.	Special resource area
	1986	Woodland Hills, south side of Beechwood Ct.	Special resource area
	1986	Pring Ranch, Pring Ranch Rd. & Barnes Rd.	Special resource area
	1986	Leon Young Youth Ball Field, 1335 S. Chelton Rd.	Sports complex
	1986	Bricker Park, 4850 Dover Dr.	Neighborhood park
	1986	Senior Center, Golf Acres. Transferred to Housing Authority in 2010.	Community center
	1987	Broadmoor Valley Park, 3750 Broadmoor Valley Rd.	Neighborhood park
	1987	Rockrimmon, Tamarron Dr. & Saddle Mountain Rd.	Open space
	1987	Beidleman Environmental Center, 740 W. Caramillo St.	Visitor center
	1987	Panorama Recreation Center, 2145 S. Chelton Rd.	Recreation center
	1988	Wedgewood Park, 2830 Parliament Dr.	Neighborhood park
	1988	Beacon Hill, 750 Beacon Ridge Dr.	Special resource area
	1988	Broadmoor Bluffs Park, 5315 Farthing Dr.	Neighborhood park
	1988	Cheyenne Meadows Park, 3868 Glenmeadow Dr.	Neighborhood park
	1988	Woodland Hills Park, 3617 Woodland Hills Dr.	Neighborhood park
	1988	Explorer Park, 4260 Bardot Dr.	Neighborhood park
	1988	Glen Oaks Park, 5445 Broadmoor Bluffs Dr.	Neighborhood park
	1989	Cheyenne Meadows, Cheyenne Meadows Rd. & Bayfield Dr.	Open space
	1989	Neal Ranch, 5085 Neal Ranch Rd.	Special resource area
	1989	Oak Meadow Park, 4960 Farthing Dr.	Neighborhood park
	1989	Hillside Community Center, 925 S. Institute St.	Community center

1990	1990	Frank Waters Park, 501 E. Platte Ave.	Mini park
	1990	Sky View Adult Softball Complex, 2890 Resnik Dr.	Sports complex
	1991	Nancy Lewis Park, 2615 Logan Ave.	Neighborhood park
	1991	Candleflower Park, 7690 Contrails Dr.	Neighborhood park
	1992	Gossage Youth Sports Complex, 3225-3950 Mark Dabling Blvd.	Sports complex
	1992	North Slope Recreation Area, Pikes Peak Hwy.	Natural area
	1992	Starsmore Discovery Center opens, 2120 South Cheyenne Cañon Rd.	Visitor/special center
	1993	Woodmen Valley Park, 2525 W. Woodmen Rd.	Neighborhood park
	1993	Marshall Sprague Park, 3492 Woodmen Rd.	Neighborhood park
	1993	[Jimmy Camp Creek Park] Banning Lewis Ranch, Hwy 24 at Constitution	Natural area
	1993	Briargate, various locations within Briargate	Special resource area
	1994	Vindicator Knob, NE corner Vindicator Dr. & Centennial Blvd.	Special resource area
	1994	Peregrine, east & west of Sawback Tr..	Special resource area
	1994	Oak Valley Ranch Park, 2325 Silent Rain Dr.	Neighborhood park
	1994	Mesa Valley, Mesa Rd. behind Holmes Middle School	Open space
	1994	Kathleen O'Neill Marriage Park, 2320 Amberwood Ln.	Neighborhood park
	1995	Norman Coleman Park, 6300 Barnes Rd.	Community park
	1995	Meadowridge Park, 8320 Boxelder Dr.	Neighborhood park
	1995	Southface, east of Grey Wolf Ct.	Open space
	1995	Woodmen Valley, 2526 W. Woodmen Rd.	Open space
	1995	Garden of the Gods Visitors Center, 1805 N. 30th St.	Visitors center
	1996	Ford Frick Park, 8025 N. Union Blvd.	Neighborhood park
	1996	Harlan-Wolfe Park, 905 W. Cheyenne Rd.	Special resource area
	1996	Remington Park, 2750 Pony Tracks Dr.	Neighborhood park
	1996	Lulu Pollard Park, 2550 Dynamic Dr.	Neighborhood park
	1996	Broadmoor Glen, 4035 Danceglen Dr.	Neighborhood park
	1996	Frontier Park, 3725 Meadow Ridge Dr.	Neighborhood park
	1996	Sinton Pond, Sinton Rd.	Open space
	1996	Skyway Park, south of North Star Dr. & Milky Way.	Neighborhood park
	1996	Wickes Park, south of Wickes Dr. & Moorfield Ave.	Neighborhood park
	1997	Buckskin Charlie Park, 7665 Scarborough Dr.	Neighborhood park
	1997	Wilson Ranch Park, 2335 Allegheny Dr.	Community park
	1997	Frank Castello Park, 7640 Potomac Dr.	Neighborhood park
	1997	Fred McKown Park, 5155 Balsam St.	Neighborhood park
	1997	Judge Lunt Park, 4870 Seton Pl.	Neighborhood park
	1997	Creekside, Amberwood Ln. north of Kathleen Marriage Park	Special resource area
	1997	Cresta, east of Cresta Rd.	Special resource area
	1997	University Park Entryway, Rockhurst Blvd.	Special resource area
	1998	North Gate, various open space areas	Open space

	1998	Stratton, 1789 La Veta Way.	Open space
	1999	John Stone Park, 4017 Family Pl.	Neighborhood park
	1999	El Pomar Youth Sports Complex, 2230 Executive Cir.	Sports complex
	1999	Springs Ranch Park, 2990 Pony Tracks Dr.	Neighborhood park
	1999	Laura Gilpin Park, 7415 Kettle Drum St.	Neighborhood park
2000	2000	City Hall Park, 107 N. Nevada Ave.	Special purpose park
	2000	Eugene McCleary Park, 5214 Pioneer Mesa Dr.	Neighborhood park
	2000	Cheyenne Mountain State Park Backdrop, S. Hwy. 115 & Pine Oaks Rd.	Open space area
	2000	Frank M. Houck Park, 2002 Collegiate Dr.	Neighborhood park
	2000	Bluestem Prairie, S. Powers Blvd. & Drennan Rd.	Open space
	2000	Gold Camp Park, 1536 Gold Spike Ter.	Neighborhood park
	2000	Tutt Park, 3125 Tutt Blvd.	Sports complex
	2001	Cottonwood Creek Recreation Center, 3920 Dublin Blvd.	Recreation center
	2001	Stetson Park, 4870 Jedediah Smith Rd.	Neighborhood park
	2001	Blodgett Peak, 3898 W. Woodmen Rd.	Open space
	2001	Jack Templeton Park, 5347 Rose Ridge Ln.	Neighborhood park
	2001	Pring Ranch Park, 5264 Prairie Grass Ln.	Neighborhood park
	2001	Stratton Forest, east & west of Stratton Woods View	Natural resource area
	2001	High Chaparral, 5002 N. Powers Blvd.	Open space
	2002	Horace Shelby Park, 6442 Summit Peak Dr.	Neighborhood park
	2002	Jared Jensen Park, 6724 Windom Peak Blvd.	Neighborhood park
	2002	Ivywild Park, 1645 Dorchester St.	Mini park
	2002	Snowy River Park, 6152 Snowy River Dr.	Neighborhood park
	2002	Soaring Eagles Park, 3196 Spotted Tail Dr.	Neighborhood park
	2003	America the Beautiful (formerly Confluence Park), 126 Cimino Dr. (formerly Conejos St.)	Community park
	2003	Red Rock Canyon, 3615 W. High St.	Open space
	2003	Lawrence Ochs Sports Complex, 11000 N. Powers Blvd.	Sports complex
	2003	Mary M. Kyer Park, 1101 Middle Creek Pky.	Neighborhood park
	2003	High Meadows Park, 4216 Ashby Field Dr.	Neighborhood park
	2004	James H. Smith Sr. Park, 2205 Spring Blossom Dr.	Neighborhood park
	2004	Union Meadows, N. Union Blvd & Austin Bluffs Pkwy.	Open space
	2005	Fairfax Station, Scarborough Dr. & Manston Dr.	Open space
	2005	Ken Jordan Park, 5914 High Noon Ave.	Neighborhood park
	2005	Manitou Section 16 leased by city.	Open space
	2005	Sky View Park, 5100 Silver Hawk Ave,	Community park
	2005	West Creek Park, 8542 Winding Passage Dr.	Neighborhood park
	2006	John Venezia Park, 9330 N. Union Blvd.	Community park
	2006	Grey Hawk Park, 968 Spectrum Loop.	Neighborhood park
	2007	Founders Park, 755 S. Weber St.	Mini park

	2008	Corral Bluffs, Corral Valley Rd.	Open space
	2009	White Acres, S. 26th St. & Lower Gold Camp Rd.	Open space
	2009	West Community Center, 1620 W. Bijou St.	Community center
2010	2010	Manitou Section 16 acquired	Open space

* The date listed is the acquisition date for the site. Development may have occurred years later, occurred over a multiple year period, or the site may not yet have been developed. For many sites, especially those open spaces areas preserved in a natural state. the only development may be signage and a parking area. Dates also reflect date of responsibility to the Parks Department. For example, the City Auditorium was built in the early years of the twentieth century but became a responsibility of Parks in 1983. The West Intergenerational Center was located at West Middle School and is now, since 2009, located at the former Buena Vista School.

APPENDIX 2

"EXTRACTIONS: _______ CONDITIONS PLACED IN DEEDS OF PARK LANDS BY GENERAL PALMER AND IN EFFECT TODAY. – FROM A REPORT BY CITY MANAGER BIERY DATED DECEMBER 10, 1965."

MONUMENT VALLEY PARK

Deed #192-A – That intoxicating liquors shall never be manufactured, sold, or otherwise disposed of as a beverage in any place of public resort in or upon the premises hereby granted. Also that premises shall be held, maintained, carried on and forever kept as a park system solely for outdoor recreation enjoyment and use of the people of the City of Colorado Springs. A park fund was provided for by an act of Legislature of the State of Colorado approved April 10, 1905, from William J. Palmer agreeing to pay quarterly in advance to the City as an addition to the amount necessary to be raised by taxation for the purpose of the maintenance of such parks, boulevards, and driveways. Mr. Palmer also expresses his desire and conditions for the control and management of said properties including methods of electing officers of Park Commission. It is his desire and intention that Monument Valley Park shall be kept as a public path, with walks and grounds free from dangers of horses, vehicles of any kind, except such conveyances as invalid chairs, baby carriages, and bicycles propelled by human beings. It is an express limitation and condition of this conveyance that no roads or streets shall hereafter be opened either lengthwise or across Monument Valley Park, that no buildings or structures shall be erected except 1 or 2 buildings for buffets or restaurants with moderate provisions for sale of curios and such structures for shelter and for lavatories, music and dancing, as the Park Commission may think this desirable. It is further expressed that in any case of the limitation or conditions of this deed are broken by granter herein, then this deed shall become null and void, and all right and title and interest of, in and to the premises, and all thereof, hereby conveyed, shall revert to grantor and heirs.

NOTE: Special permission has been granted on various occasions from the Palmer heirs, to build parking areas and streets in Monument Valley Park.

PALMER PARK

II. It being my express desire that the said land herein conveyed shall be kept and maintained as a park, so far as possible in the condition on which nature has fashioned it, and in order that its natural conditions shall not be marred or destroyed, no buildings or constructions other than as stated in Clause A, or destruction of any kind, which may detract from the natural beauty of the land or its fitness for the controlling purpose of the outdoor recreation of the people, shall ever be permitted upon the land herein conveyed. All questions in regard to such detraction in case any such buildings or construction, other than in Clause A, or any destruction, should at any time be contemplated, shall first be determined solely by 3 (three) experts of conspicuous ability, selected by the grantees herein or their successors; and in case such landscape experts, or a majority of them, shall determine that such construction or destruction may constitute an injury to the park, it shall not be undertaken, and if undertaken without such references, or in face of an adverse determination, the land herein conveyed shall revert to me and my heirs.

CLAUSE A: There shall be exempt from this provision one or two buildings to be used as restaurants or buffets, and such constructions for shelter of man, beast and vehicle, and for lavatories, music and dancing as the Trustees may think desirable.

No railways of any kind shall be permitted to be constructed upon or through any portion of the premises herein granted for a park, and if the said Trustees ever grant such permission then the land herein conveyed shall revert to me and my heirs.

Until horseless carriages shall be improved so that they are as noiseless and odorless as horse-drawn vehicles, horseless carriages shall not be permitted to enter or travel over or through any portion of the said property herein conveyed for the purpose of a park.

PASEO ROAD

But the right of way herein conveyed for Palmer Park, Paseo and Boulevard is upon the express condition, limitation and reservation that all heavy traffic shall be kept off and debarred from use thereof; and also that automobiles and autocycles shall not be permitted to use the same, or any part thereof, except by the unanimous consent of the Park Commission.

NORTH CHEYENNE CANYON HIGH DRIVE

It is being understood and agreed that the strip of land hereinabove described is specifically granted for the use and purpose of a roadway, and in the event that the same shall hereafter cease to be used for that purpose, it shall then revert to and again become the property of the party of the first part hereto, his heirs and assigns.

ALL PARKS

That intoxicating liquors shall never be manufactured, sold or otherwise disposed of as a beverage in any place of public resort in or upon the premises hereby granted, or any part thereof, and it is herein and hereby reserved by me that in case any of the above conditions concerning intoxicating liquors are broken by the grantee herein, its successors or assigns, then this deed shall become null and void, and all the right, title and interest of, in and to the premises hereby conveyed shall revert to me and my heirs; and the said grantee herein by accepting this deed for itself and its successors and assigns, consents and agrees to the reservations and conditions aforesaid.

It is my desire, in conveying this property to the City of Colorado Springs for the benefit of the inhabitants thereof, that the property shall be so maintained that the greatest benefit and enjoyment thereof may be obtained by all the people of the said City, and to that end, and in order that the control and management of the property shall be removed as far as possible from partisan and political strife, and that it may be conducted upon strict and economical business principles for the most beneficial administration of the public parks, this conveyance is made upon the express condition that the power to manage and control the parks, boulevards and driveways of the City of Colorado Springs shall be, either by special charter or by an Act of the Legislature of Colorado, continued and maintained in a Board of Park Commissioners or Trustees, who, after appointment by the Mayor of the City of Colorado Springs, shall have the right to elect their successors and fill the vacancies arising in such Board, as at present provided for by an Act of the Legislature of the State of Colorado, approved April 10, 1905. But if, after ten years experience from and after the assumption by the City of Colorado Springs of any expense or maintenance of the parks, boulevards, driveways and roads hereby conveyed, the method for electing commissioners and filling the vacancies arising in the Board of Park Commissioners as now provided for by an Act of the Legislature of the State of Colorado, and if the people of Colorado Springs desire to avail themselves of any such change or amendment of the Act of April 10th, 1905,and by a majority vote of the citizens legally authorized to vote at any general election, adopt and use such change in the method of electing.

APPENDIX 3

"EXTRACTIONS: ______ OBLIGATORY CONDITIONS PLACED IN PERKINS' DEED CONVEYING THE GARDEN OF THE GODS TO THE CITY OF COLORADO SPRINGS, 1910."

Said obligatory conditions are as follows:

1. Intoxicating liquors shall never be manufactured, sold or otherwise disposed of as a beverage upon the premises hereby granted, and conveyed, or upon any part thereof, or upon any road or highway, through or upon the said premises.

2. The Granters herein reserve to themselves the right to erect at a place which they may select, a suitable tablet or inscription stating in substance by whom and for what purpose the land is given, which tablet or inscription after its original placing by granters shall be preserved by said city.

3. Said premises shall be continuously and forever known and designated as the "Garden of the Gods" and shall be used by the general public as a public park forever, and maintained as such by the City of Colorado Springs, its successors or assigns, for the benefit and advantage of the inhabitants of the City of Colorado Springs.

4. No building or structure shall be erected on the premises for purposes other than may be necessary to properly care for, protect and maintain the same as a public park, nor upon any road or highway, through or upon the said premises.

5. In case any of the limitations or conditions herein declared obligatory are broken by said City of Colorado Springs, its successors or assigns, then the said conveyance to said City shall become null and void and all the right, title and interest in and to the said premises by said instrument conveyed, shall at once revert to Robert F. Perkins, Alice Perkins Hooper, Edith Perkins Cunningham, Margaret Perkins Rice, Mary Russell Perkins and Charles E. Perkins, their heirs and assigns.

APPENDIX 4

HISTORICAL REFLECTIONS: COLORADO SPRINGS CITY GREENHOUSE

Compiled by Bill Brandenburg, with assistance from Price Oden, December 1983.

1907—a great year for the Park Department and Colorado Springs. Monument Valley Park was completed and General Palmer donated a greenhouse from his home in Glen Eyrie to the City of Colorado Springs. That first greenhouse is still operational and is known as the West House. During the operation of this single greenhouse, the idea of beautifying the City with flower beds became a reality. At this time, the annual flower beds were limited to Monument Valley Park. The greenhouse was located next to General Palmer's construction office in Monument Valley Park. The office is now the residence for the park caretaker.

Perennial plants were started in the new greenhouse in 1919 at the same time perennial flower beds were being prepared in Monument Valley Park. The caretaker for these beds was Charlie Senning. To enhance these flower beds, a rock garden was added in 1925. This work was done by Ted Borgars and Llewellyn Davis. The rocks came from Palmer Park. This area, located just north of Bijou and east of the railroad tracks, is now called the Formal Gardens.

There have been only three greenhouse foremen in the history of the Colorado Springs greenhouse. Early history is rather obscure as to who the first foreman was. However, in 1919 Tom Puckett became the foreman. He served in this position for 42 years until his retirement in 1961. Following Puckett is the current greenhouse foreman, Price Oden, who started with the greenhouse in 1941.

In 1935, immediately following the great flood in Colorado Springs, the W.P.A., as one of its projects, built a second greenhouse. This is now referred to as the Middle House. With the addition of a second greenhouse, more flower beds were added throughout the City. Tom Puckett, the greenhouse foreman at that time, met with Dell Doty, a designer for the Parks Department, and designs were created for all the flower beds.

Prior to this time, the greenhouse crew had the responsibility for planning the planting of the flower beds. The tradition of having a designer create designs for the flower beds is still being carried on. Following Dell Doty, Ben Frallin assumed this task and was followed by Art Garrett. Gene Fuhlrodt, who is currently doing the designing, assumed these duties, among others, from Art. Over the years, the sophistication of designs and the utilization of various types of flowers have steadily improved to the point where our flower beds have received national acclaim.

With the addition of the second greenhouse in 1935, the greenhouse took on added significance. The Park Superintendent, T.C. Kirkwood, who maintained an office in City Hall, met with the park crews every morning at the greenhouse. This lasted from 1939 to 1952.

Also in 1935, immediately after the flood, the home which the Park Superintendent lived in, located on Uintah between Mesa Road and Cascade Avenue (where there are presently tennis courts), had to be torn down because the flood eroded the banks and undermined its foundation. The garage was moved to the greenhouse. Gustav Hennenhofer, the Superintendent at that time, kept his 1932 Ford in it. It is currently being used for storage.

Transportation for the greenhouse prior to 1925 is also rather obscure. It is believed that flowers were transported to the flower beds by a horse-drawn wagon. It is known that a Model T Ford pickup was used from 1925 to 1929. In 1929, the Park Department purchased a new Model A Ford pickup which was used for the next 20 years. In 1949, a new Chevy pickup was purchased. The greenhouse fleet has grown from only one vehicle to the five vehicles currently being used during the summer months.

In 1975, a third greenhouse was built (some 40 years after the Middle House) which is now referred to as the Upper House. This addition allowed more flower beds to be added throughout the City.

Since its inception, the responsibility for the greenhouse was under the Park Department's General Foreman. In 1982, a change was made, and the greenhouse is now the responsibility of the City Forester, who is currently Ron Morrow.

From an obscure beginning, the role of the greenhouse has steadily grown to the point where more than 190 individual flower beds are designed, prepared, planted, and maintained annually. This is accomplished through the cooperative efforts of five permanent and up to eight seasonal employees, plus assistance from the Urban Forestry Division.

The greenhouse raises more than 115,000 flowers (from cuttings and seed) annually to accomplish its commitment to make Colorado Springs "The City Beautiful." Visitors from all over the world refer to our city as "The City of Flowers," which has resulted in several local and state awards (SpABA, HAS, Colorado Springs Design Alliance). Because of this, we are proud, and we strive to make each year a little better. With the cooperation of the weather, we feel confident that our goals will be achieved.

APPENDIX 5
NANCY LEWIS PARK ARBORETUM

Common Name	**Botanical Name**
Centurion Crabapple	*Malus* 'Centurion'
Indian Summer Crabapple	*Malus* 'Indian Summer'
Spring Snow Crabapple	*Malus* 'Spring Snow'
Bechtel Crabapple	*Malus* 'Bechtel'
Profusion Crabapple	*Malus* 'Profusion'
Robinson Crabapple	*Malus* 'Robinson'
Ohio Buckeye	*Aesculus glabra*
Toba Hawthorn	*Crataegus Laewgata* 'Toba'
Mayday Tree	*Prunus padus*
Princess Kay Plum	*Prunus nigra* 'Princess Kay'
Brandon Elm	*Ulmus americana* 'Brandon'
Wafer Ash	*Ptelea trifoliate*
Colorado Blue Spruce	*Picea pungens* 'Glauca'
Amur Corktree	*Phellodendron amurense*
Colorado Green Spruce	*Picea pungens*
Ponderosa Pine	*Pinus ponderosa*
Golden Raintree	*Koelreuteria paniculata*
Sunburst Honeylocust	*Gleditsia triachantos* 'Sunburst'
Kentucky Coffeetree	*Gymnocladus dioica*
Eastern Redbird	*Cercis Canadensis*
Littleleaf Linden	*Tilia cordata*
English Hawthorn	*Crataecus laevigata*
European Mountain Ash	Sorbus aucuparia
Stone Hill Pear	*Pyrus calleryana* 'Stone Hill'
Canadian Red Cherry	*Prunus virgeniana*
Austrian Pine	*Pinus nigra*
Norway Spruce	*Picea aries*
Northern Red Oak	*Quercus rubra*
Black Walnut	*Juglans nigra*
Turkish Filbert	*Corylus colurna*
Cockspur Hawthorn	*Crateous crusoalli*
River Birch	*Betula nigra*
Imperial Honeylocust	*Gleditsia triachantos* 'Imperial'
Western Larch	*Larex occidentalis*

Common Name	**Botanical Name**
Black Hills Spruce	*Picea glauca densata*
Golden Weeping Willow	*Salix alba Trustus*
Royal Red Norway Maple	*Acer platanoides* 'Royal Red'
Fairview Norway Maple	*Acer platanoides* 'Fairview'
Deborah Norway Maple	*Acer platanoides* 'Deborah'
Sugar Maple	*Acer saccharum*
Amur Maple	*Acer ginnala*
Tatarian Maple	*Acer tataricum*
Ginkgo	*Ginkgo biloba*
Bristlecone Pine	*Pinus aristata*
Piñon Pine	*Pinuse edulis*
Common Hackberry	*Celtis occidentalis*
Gray Dogwood	*Cornus racemosa*
White Mulberry	*Morus alba*
Catalpa	*Catalpa speciosa*
Eastern Red Cedar	*Juniperus virginiana*
Colorado Red Cedar	*Juniperus scopulorum* 'Wichita Blue'
Chinese Juniper	*Juniperus chinensis* 'Robusta Green'
Eastern Arborvitae	*Thuja occidentalis* 'Techny'
Bur Oak	*Quercus macrocarpa*
English Oak	*Quercus robur*
Autumn Purple Ash	*Fraxinus americana* 'Autumn Purple'
Fallgold Black Ash	*Fraxinus nigra* 'Fallgold'
Manchurian Ash	*Fraxinus manoshurica*
Cimarron Ash	*Fraxinus pennsylvanica* 'Cimarron'
Japanese Tree Lilac	*Syringa reinculata*
Seedless Green Ash	*Fraxinus pennsylvanica*
Lodgepole Pine	*Pinus contorta*
Japanese Zelcova	*Zelkova serrata*
Althena Lacebark Elm	*Ulmus parvifoija* 'Althena'
Homestead Elm	*Ulmus pumila* 'Homestead'
Camperdown Elm	*Ulmus glabra* 'Camperdown'

BIBLIOGRAPHY

Books

Cranz, Galen. *The Politics of Park Design.* Cambridge, MA: MIT Press, 1982.

Ellis, Amanda M. *The Colorado Springs Story.* Colorado Springs, CO: The Dentan Printing Company, 1954.

Finley, Judith Reid, ed. *The Century Chest Letters of 1901: A Colorado Springs Legacy.* Colorado Springs, CO: The Colorado College, 2001.

Fisher, John Sterling. *A Builder of the West: The Life of General William Jackson Palmer.* Caldwell, ID: The Caxton Printers, 1939.

Harnik, Peter. "The Excellent City Park System: What Makes It Great and How to Get There." *In The Human Metropolis: People and Nature in the 21st Century City.* Edited by Rutherford H. Platt. Cambridge, MA: University of Massachusetts Press in association with Lincoln Institute of Land Policy, 2006.

———. *Urban Green: Innovative Parks for Resurgent Cities.* Washington, DC: Island Press, 2010.

Jackson, Helen Hunt. *Bits of Travel at Home.*: Boston, MA: Roberts Brothers, 1878.

McGilchrist, Donald. "The Gardens of Glen Eyrie." In *Legends, Labors and Loves: William Jackson Palmer, 1836-1909.* Edited by. T. Blevins, D. Daily, C. Nicholl, C. P. Otto, K. S. Sturdevant. Colorado Springs, CO: Pikes Peak Library District Publication, 2009.

Public Treasures: Outdoor Sculpture in the Pikes Peak Region. Colorado Springs, CO: City of Colorado Springs Parks and Recreation Department, 1995.

Rice-Jones, Judith. "William Jackson Palmer—Park Builder." In *Legends, Labors and Loves: William Jackson Palmer, 1836-1909.* Edited by. T. Blevins, D. Daily, C. Nicholl, C. P. Otto, K. S. Sturdevant. Colorado Springs, CO: Pikes Peak Library District Publication, 2009.

Sprague, Marshall. *Colorado: A History.* Nashville. TN: W. W. Norton & Co., 1976, 1984.

———. *Newport in the Rockies.* Athens, OH: Swallow Press/Ohio University Press, 1961, 1987.

Swint, Sharon. *Historic Photos of Colorado Springs.* Nashville, TN: Turner Publishing Company, 2009.

Government and Legal Documents

A Proposal for Acacia Park. Colorado Springs, CO: Colorado Springs Parks and Recreation Department, Planning Division, December 6, 1973.

Advancing the National Park Idea: National Parks Second Century Commission Report. 2010.

Baldwin Planning and Geoplan Inc. *Open Space, Park and Recreation Plan Update, 1982-1986.* Colorado Springs, CO: Colorado Springs Parks and Recreation Department, November 1981.

Biery, James. "Extractions: _____Conditions Placed in Deeds of Park Lands by General Palmer and in Effect Today." Colorado Springs, CO: December 10, 1965.

Budget in Brief: Citizen's Guide to the 2003 General Fund Budget. Colorado Springs, CO: Office of Budget and Financial Analysis. May 2003.

Colorado Springs Multi-Use Trails Master Plan. Colorado Springs, CO: Colorado Springs Parks and Recreation Department and Colorado Springs Public Works Department, May 1986.

Colorado Springs Open Space Plan: A Plan for the Conservation of Natural Areas and Greenways. Colorado Springs, CO: 1997.

Colorado Springs Open Space, Park and Recreation Master Plan Update: 1988. Colorado Springs, CO: Colorado Springs Parks and Recreation Department, 1988.

Colorado Springs Parks, Recreation and Cultural Services Budget. Colorado Springs, CO: 2006.

Colorado Springs Parks, Recreation and Trails 2000-2010 Master Plan. Colorado Springs, CO: January 2000.

Downtown Action Plan: A Plan for the Future of Colorado Springs. Colorado Springs, CO: Downtown Action Plan Advisory Committee. [s.n.]: 1992.

Garden of the Gods Master Plan. Colorado Springs, CO: Colorado Springs Parks and Recreation Department. 1994.

Jones, David and Deborah Abele. *White House Ranch Master Plan: Final Report to the City of Colorado Springs Park and Recreation Department.* LRA: Land Resource Associates. March 1990.

Kyer et al. v. the City of Colorado Springs. Civil action suit # 66897, Division 2. El Paso County District Court. February 19, 1974.

Memorial Park Master Plan. Colorado Springs Parks and Recreation Department. William Wenk, Landscape Architect. Denver, CO. 1983.

National Register of Historic Places Registration Form: North Cheyenne Cañon Park, provided by Missye Bonds (and Michael Paglia). Friends of Cheyenne Cañon. May 18, 2008.

N.E.S., Inc. *Beautification Plan for the City of Colorado Springs.* Colorado Springs, CO: Colorado Springs Parks and Recreation Department, December 1987.

Palmer Park Master Plan. Colorado Springs, CO: Colorado Springs Parks and Recreation Department, 1984.

Palmer Park Master Plan. Colorado Springs, CO: Colorado Springs Parks and Recreation Department, 1997.

Parks and Recreation Department: 1991 Goals and Objectives: Year-End Status Report. Colorado Springs, CO: City of Colorado Springs.

Report of the Park Commission. Colorado Springs, CO: 1908

Robinson, Charles Mulford. *A General Plan for the Improvement of Colorado Springs.* Submitted to the Department of Public Works and Property. Colorado Springs, CO: May 1912.

Special Districts White Paper. Colorado Springs, CO: City of Colorado Springs Economic Development Department, Comprehensive Planning Division, June 2009.

Springs Community Improvements Program (SCIP) Executive Summary. Colorado Springs, CO: July 27, 1998.

THK Associates. *Open Space, Park and Recreation Plan.* Colorado Springs, CO: Colorado Springs Parks and Recreation Department, 1976.

Thomas and Thomas, Inc. *Acacia Park Master Plan.* Colorado Springs, CO: Colorado Springs Parks and Recreation Department, September 28, 1994.

Ute Valley Park: Master Development Plan and Program. Colorado Springs Parks and Recreation Department: December 1991.

Newspaper Articles

Acord, Deb. "City's Plans Designed to Improve Parks." *Colorado Springs Gazette Telegraph,* August 27, 1998. C:5.

———. "Open Wide: Everything You Need to Know about Some of El Paso County's Wildest Natural Treasures." *Colorado Springs Independent,* April 19, 2007. http://www.csindy.com/gyrobase/open-wide/Content?oid+1138139&mode=print.

———. "Ready. Set. Hike! Miles of Trails Beckon for your Memorial Day Weekend." *Colorado Springs Gazette,* May 23, 2002. OUT THERE:3.

Aldridge, Dorothy. "Gardens to Blossom with New Look." *Colorado Springs Gazette Telegraph,* April 24, 1982. D:14.

———. "Rock Garden Once a Top Attraction." *Colorado Springs Gazette Telegraph,* July 20, 1985. F:33.

Allegar, William. "Community Leaders Urge Funding of Parks." *Colorado Springs Gazette Telegraph,* October 21, 1987. B:1.

———. "Parks Official's Firing Upheld in Ski Broadmoor Overspending." *Colorado Springs Gazette Telegraph,* March 26, 1988. B:8.

Anderson, Malcolm. "District Setup or $2,778,700 Bond Issue for Parks Proposed." *Colorado Springs Gazette Telegraph,* August 22, 1958. 1.

———. "Seabees Fast Reviving Dorchester Park." *Colorado Springs Free Press,* June 7, 1949. 15.

Anton, Genevieve. "Camera Obscura May Be Scuttled." *Colorado Springs Gazette Telegraph,* September 18, 1992. B:1.

Associated Press. "Amendments May Conflict, Analysts Say." *Colorado Springs Gazette Telegraph,* November 15, 1992. B:3.

———. "Outdoors Ballot Issue Introduced: Trust Fund Draws Bipartisan Support." *Colorado Springs Gazette Telegraph,* March 6, 1991. B:1.

Baker, Fred. "Your City in Wartime." *Colorado Springs Gazette & Telegraph,* February 20, 1944. 12.

Bell, Tanya. "Parks Budget Proposal Could End Adult Sports." *Colorado Springs Gazette Telegraph,* July 5, 1997. B:2.

———. "Hospice Benefits from Trees Purchased for New Park." *Colorado Springs Gazette Telegraph,* February 27, 1996. CITY/STATE:6.

Bergsten, Tim. "New Gossage Youth Complex is Recreation Jewel: City Park Facilities in Growing Demand by Kids and Adults." *Colorado Springs Gazette Telegraph,* February 25, 1996. PROGRESS:12.

Blond, Becca. "Springs Ready for Summer Fun as Prospect Lake Beach Opens." *Colorado Springs Gazette,* May 25, 2001. METRO:6.

Bondarook, Nina. "Acquisitions of Parkland Set Record." *Colorado Springs Gazette Telegraph,* December 21, 1983. C:4.

———. "29 Springs Park Projects Allotted Lottery Money." *Colorado Springs Gazette Telegraph,* November 17, 1983. B:10.

Brody, Jane. "Head Out for a Daily Dose of Green Space." *The New York Times,* November 29, 2010. Personal Health. D:7.

Brown, Andrea. "Skate Park Opens to Big Crowds." *Colorado Springs Gazette,* December 13, 2008. http://www.gazette.com/common/printer/view.php?db=colgazette&id=44827.

Bush, Rudolph. "Dallas 'Love Your Parks' Summit Woos Volunteers, Funding." *The Dallas Morning News,* November 7, 2010.

Buynak, Jim. "Voters: Put Lottery Money in Parks, Wildlife." *Colorado Springs Gazette Telegraph,* November 4, 1992. B:3:2.

Cantwell, Rebecca. "Dreams of Seniors' Center Realized." *Colorado Springs Gazette Telegraph,* January 13, 1985. B:1.

———. "Plans for Park Unveiled." *Colorado Springs Gazette Telegraph,* March 15, 1985. 1:1.

Chacon, Daniel. "City Parks Department Leans Heavily on the Lottery." *Colorado Springs Gazette,* October 12, 2009. http://www.gazette.com/common/printer/view.php?db=colgazette&id=63674.

———. "City to Close Two Pools, Prospect Lake Swim Areas; Three Pools Survive." *Colorado Springs Gazette,* April 22, 2010. http://www.gazette.com/common/printer/view.php?db=colgazette&id=97531.

———. "Community Centers, Pools May Get Reprieve." *Colorado Springs Gazette,* March 23, 2010. http://www,gazette.com/common/printer/view.php?db=colgazette&id=96052.

———. "Council Votes 6–3 to Buy Open Space in County." *Colorado Springs Gazette,* October 22, 2010. A:3.

———. "Crushing Defeat Delivers a Message: Shrink Government." *Colorado Springs Gazette,* November 3, 2009. http://www.gazette.com/common/printer/view.php?db=colgazette&id=65031.

———. "Give Money to Parks, Not Pools." *Colorado Springs Gazette,* June 22, 2009. http://www.gazette.com/common/printer/view.php?db=colgazette&id=57083.

———. "The Only Pool City Funded in 2010 Now Faces Closure." *Colorado Springs Gazette,* September 25, 2010. Local News:3.

———. "Springs City Council Votes to Save Pioneers Museum." *Colorado Springs Gazette,* December 8, 2009. http://www.gazette.com/common/printer/view.php?db=colgazette&id=90485.

———. "TOPS Question Leaves Parks Backers Torn." *Colorado Springs Gazette,* September 13, 2010. A:1.

———. "USOC, Governing Bodies Give Boost to City's Sports, Rec." *Colorado Springs Gazette,* April 6, 2010. A:1.

Colorado Springs Free Press. "City to Open Rink in Monument Valley Park." December 19, 1963. 22.

———. "Elmer W. Allen, Candidate for City Council Two-Year Term." March 26, 1947. 8:3.

———. "Park Experts Outline Needs to League of Women Voters." April 3, 1964. 6.

———. "When Will Boulder Park Be Finished?" February 15, 1947. 6.

Colorado Springs Gazette. "City Park System is Spacious and Beautiful and Famous the World Over." February 24, 1918. A:1.

———. "City Park System to Be Popularized." May 21, 1935. 1.

———. "Monument Valley Ponds," Did You Ever Wonder. October 15. 2010.

———. "Director's Cuts Would Play Like A Horror Film." September 14, 2009. Local News:3.

———. "Ed Programs Will Continue at Park." March 6, 2010. LOCAL:9.

———. "Gift of More Than Million." May 7, 1907. 1.

———. "Money for Street Work," June 30, 1913.

———. "Name Clotworthy to Park Board." January 24, 1934. 1:4.

———. "New Hidden Inn Is Officially Opened." June 29, 1915. 5.

———. "Park Plan Continues to Evolve." August 10, 2003. Special Section:7:7.

———. "Shakespearean Garden will be Planted Today." May 19, 1916. 5.

———. "Sustainable Volunteering." April 14, 2010. http://www.gazette.com/common/printer/view.php?db=colgazette&id=97110.

———. "Unique Parks in a Country of Parks." Annual Edition, Feb 25, 1917. B:13.

Colorado Springs Gazette Annual Edition. "Springs Parks: Unexcelled in Entire Country." February 18, 1912. 1.

Colorado Springs Gazette Telegraph, "$12 Million Freeway Opened with Ceremony." July 2, 1960. A:1.

———. "75 City Parks Provide Recreational Variety." May 22, 1975. A:5:1.

———. "$200,000 Approved For Parks." May 23, 1972. B:1:4.

———. " 'Angel' Said Needed to Develop Park Near Steam Plant." October 23, 1951. 11.

———. "Approval of Parks Proposal Scraps 40-Year-Old Board." April 2, 1947. 1.

———. "Bill May Add Parks to City." March 25, 1963. 1

———. "City Busy Beautifying Once Unsightly Dorchester Park." April 8, 1951. A:3.

———. "City Council's Next Task is Setting up Park Department." May 28, 1947. 1.

———. "City Gains 7 Acres for Northeast Park." July 18, 1985. B:9.

———. "City Motion to Dismiss Denied by Judge Hinton." January 11, 1972. D:12.

———. "City Plays Catch-Up in Park Development." October 9, 1970. B:1.

———. "City Voters Narrowly Pass SCIP Proposal." April 7, 1999. A:6.

———. "Civic Groups and Park Department Talk Over Conejos Park Plans." July 3, 1952. 11:4.

———. "Council Accepts Title to Park Site: Jimmy Camp Creek Tract to be Springs' 3rd Largest." October 13, 1993. B:1.

———. "Council Acts to Put Parks Under Advisory Commission." July 1, 1947. 1

———. "Council and Park Board to Discuss New Park Plans." November 17, 1953. 1:6.

———. "Council Appoints Seven to Advisory Park Commission." July 9, 1947. 1.

———. "Council Approves Ordinance Rezoning Dorchester Park." September 15, 1948. 15.

———. "Council Okays Annexing Circus Ground and Lake." July 24, 1940. 7:1.

———. "Council Wants Action to Prevent Ruin of Parks." September 9, 1980. C:1.

———. "Dedication Ceremonies Slated for Three Parks." September 28, 1993. B:3.

———. "Donated Land to Link up Trail: Company Gives 35 Acres to Connect City with Park." April 5, 1995. B:1.

———. "Drainage Solution for Lake will Replace Sealing Plan." September 8, 1953. 1:4.

———. "Dunman Resigns Superintendency of Park System." Feburary 15, 1921. 1.

———. "El Pomar Gift Depends on Stratton Land Buy." March 12, 1998. CITY/STATE:4.

———. "Electorate to Decide Controversial Tax Question." May 28, 1972. B:1.

———. "Ex-Mayor's 'Gift' May Become Soccer Field." November 21, 1976. A:6.

———. “G. Hennenhofer Superintendent of City’s Parks.” February 19, 1921. 21.

———. “Golf and Museum Boards Abolished in New Park Plan.” June 5, 1947. 1:3.

———. “Guarantee Asked on Palmer Lands.” February 23, 1977. D:1:1.

———. “Horticultural Arts Society Here Plans to Extend Demonstration Garden in Monument Valley Location.” October 3, 1965. G:6.

———. “Install Playground in Antlers Park Now.” July 16, 1931. 1:3.

———. “Kirkwood to be at Head of Park System.” February 12, 1935. 1.

———. “Land Dedication for Schools, Parks Gets Planners Okay.” July 17, 1973. A:9:3.

———. “Lottery Funds to Finance Park Projects.” January 12, 1995. B:1.

———. “Make Way! Historic Stone House is Coming Through.” April 3, 1990. B:1.

———. “Memorial Park Designated Name for Prospect Area.” May 26, 1948. 11:7.

———. “Memorial Park Development Mixup Causes Council Uproar.” February 17, 1949. 1.

———. “Memorial Park Plan.” April 10, 1962. 13:1.

———. “Memorial Park Plans Make Hit but Cost Requires Study.” September 1, 1948. 1.

———. “Metropolitan Park Area Planning Urged by Taylor.” June 4, 1963. 1:7.

———. “More Than Half City Parks have no Developing Plans.” October 10, 1974. B:18:3.

———. “Most Wonderful Park System in the World: Natural Beauty Spot Delight of Thousands.” March 27, 1921. Section 4.

———. “New Boulder Park Recreational Area to be Ready in ’47.” February 16, 1947. 1.

———. “No Vote Given in Palmer’s Heirs Agreement.” September 9, 1970.

———. “Officials to Dedicate 14 Parks.” August 25, 1987. B:2.

———. “Open Space Advisors Appointed to Study Park Land Development.” January 10, 1975. C:1.

———. “Palmer Park—Least Known, Most Fascinating, of City’s Plots.” June 19, 1927. 5.

———. “Park and Rec Advisory Board ‘Almost’ Censures City Council.” April 5, 1974. B:1.

———. “Park and Rec Has $2.6 Million in Capital Improvement Budget.” June 26, 1974. C:17:1.

———. “Parks and Recreation Department Publishes List of 1974 Activities.” February 2, 1975. E:10:5.

———. “Park Board Asks $30,000 Hike in Proposed Budget.” August 27, 1953. 1:5.

———. “Park Board Issue Would Raise Property Taxes.” December 10, 1974. B:1:1.

———. “Park Board Outlines Ideas on Expansion and Programs.” June 9, 1951. 1.

———. “Park Board Recommends $2 Million in Purchases.” August 3, 1973. A:2.

———. “Park Board Sets Six-Year Program Cost at $1,582,700.” July 14, 1953. 13:4.

———. “Park Department Employees Kept Busy in 1975.” March 28, 1976. A:20:4.

———. “Park of the Month—Cottonwood Creek.” April 4, 1995. B:4.

———. “Pocketbook Issues Clobber Candidates, Bonds.” April 2, 1975. 1.

———. “Projects Outlined for City Parks When Spring Arrives.” December 10, 1950. D:8:4.

———. “Protection of People, Property Called Impossible.” September 7, 1982. D:1:1.

———. “Railroad’s Land Donation may be Park, Bikeway.” March 18, 1977. C:7.

———. “Recreation Plans Group to Confer with Council.” August 14, 1946. 8:5.

———. "Richter Asks Community Help for Park System." February 27, 1965. A:1.

———. "Richter Says without Sales Tax Park Development will have to 'Wait Another Five Years or So'." April 28, 1972. A:4:6.

———. "Slim Margin for Tax." June 7, 1972. A:1.

———. "Springs Lottery Share Shrinking: Projects Safe, Officials Say." July 27, 1989. B:1.

———. "Springs Recreational Facilities Are Improved." May 21, 1950. B:1:1.

———. "Stuart Richter Named New Parks Director." September 28, 1963. 1:7.

———. "Taylor, City Park Chief Quits; Will go to New Jersey." September 5, 1963. 1:3.

———. "Trail of History: Monument Valley Park's Historic Gems Reveal Clues about the People who Helped Shape Colorado Springs." June 25, 1998. OUT THERE:5.

———. "Urges Public to Cooperate with Park Board: City's Possessions Described by Asa T. Jones." May 25, 1916. 6:1.

Colorado Springs Gazette & Telegraph. "Park Board Spent All but One Cent." January 28, 1928. 1:5, 2:7.

———. "Park System of Colorado Springs Is Unique." May 10, 1936, Tourist edition. 1.

———. "Self-Perpetuating Board of Six over City Parks." October 27, 1946. 3.

———. "Visitors Find Ideal Playgrounds in Chain of Parks Here." 1925, Annual Edition. B:16.

Colorado Springs Sunday Gazette and Telegraph. "Glorious Playground Season Opens in City's Parks Tomorrow Afternoon," June 15, 1930. 10.

———. "Improvements Add Beauty to City's System of Parks." April 28, 1936. 7.

Conklin, Ken. "Beauty of Trees will Stay Forever, City Vows." *Colorado Springs Gazette Telegraph,* March 16, 1986. G:1.

Correll, Deedee. "Lottery Helps Fund Corridor." *Colorado Springs Gazette,* December 6, 2005. METRO:12.

Curtin, Dave. "Water Festival Helps Return Park to People: Prospect Lake Spruced Up." *Colorado Springs Gazette Telegraph,* June 19, 1989. B:1.

DeLoux, Gene. "Smooth Sliding: After A Generation of Splintery Playground Equipment, Kids Are Flipping over the Return of Metal Apparatus." *Colorado Springs Gazette Telegraph,* April 7, 1995. B:1.

Dire, Angela. "Region Receives Funds for Outdoor Projects." *Colorado Springs Gazette Telegraph,* December 6, 1996. B:3.

Dudley, C.S. "Palmer Park, Least Known, Most Fascinating of City's Plots." *Sunday Gazette and Telegraph,* June 19, 1927. 5.

DuVal, Linda. "City Park Master Plan is Already Completed—and Being Implemented." *Colorado Springs Gazette Telegraph,* February 23, 1977. D:1:1.

———. "Planted: Fuhlrodt Makes City Blocks Blooming Success." *Colorado Springs Gazette Telegraph,* August 14, 1982. D:25.

———. "Park Department Operations Job, Avocation for Buerkle." *Colorado Springs Gazette Telegraph,* May 27, 1973. B:1.

Eaton, Leslie. "Strapped City Cuts and Cuts and Cuts." *The Wall Street Journal,* April 13, 2010. Economy.

Flack, Ray. "Lottery Sales Boom Good News for Backers of Amendment Drive." *Colorado Springs Gazette Telegraph,* June 24, 1992. B:3:1.

Foster, Dick. "City Council OKs $60,000 for Garden of Gods Trails." *Colorado Springs Gazette Telegraph,* March 1, 1978. B:1.

Frederickson, Phil. "Nancy Lewis Director, Colorado Springs Parks and Recreation Department." *Colorado Springs Gazette Telegraph,* October 23, 1988. C:5.

The Free Press. "Memorial Day Recalled When Flood Caused Havoc." March 12, 1963. 8.

Gazette Telegraph. "Naval Reserves Act to Save Dorchester Park for City." May 25, 1949. 24.

Gomez, Brian. "Velodrome Still One of Sport's Finest." *Colorado Springs Gazette,* July 1, 2007. Sports:32.

Grantz, Marty. "Growth Challenges the Springs' Parks and Recreation Department." *Colorado Springs Gazette Telegraph,* February 23, 1997. PROGRESS:4.

Greco, JoAnn. "Cities Go for the Green." *The Washington Post,* August 1, 2010. F:5.

Griswold, Lester. "History of Colorado Springs Parks." *Colorado Springs Free Press,* March 23, 1949. 4:1.

Hazlehurst, John. "Coloradans Big on Volunteerism of All Types." *Colorado Springs Business Journal,* March 5, 2010. http://csbj.com/wpcontent/plugins/dmc_sociable_toolbar/wp=print.php?p=25797.

Heilman, Wayne. "Open Space for Sale: 174 Acres of Houck Land Available for $5 Million." *Colorado Springs Gazette,* April 8, 1998. A:6.

Henderson, Leslie. "Volunteers Give Love and Sweat to City's Flowers." *Colorado Springs Gazette Telegraph,* July 26, 1983. D:1.

Huspeni, Dennis. "Groups Want Park on Historic List." *Colorado Springs Gazette,* April 18, 2004. METRO:2:9.

———. "Volunteers Swinging into Action to Build Palmer Park Playground." *Colorado Springs Gazette Telegraph,* October 4, 1997. B:1.

Kelley, Debbie. "Downtown Jewel Loses Shimmer as Water Disappears." *Colorado Springs Independent,* August 5, 2010. http://www.csindy.com/gyrobase/monument-t-austerity/Content?oid=1800733.

Kenyon, Jordan. "City Parks Outlook." *Colorado Springs Gazette Telegraph,* September 7, 1982. D:1:1.

Kim, Elizabeth. "Can Stamford Build the Next Great Urban Park?" *The Stamford Advocate,* December 21, 2010. http://www.stamfordadvocate.com/default/article/Originally-in-the-Sunday-paper-Can-Stamford-913010.php.

Laden, Rich. "City Council Votes to Create Second Group That'll go after Financing for Open Space: Isaac Says 'Hysteria' Breaking out over Issue." *Colorado Springs Gazette Telegraph,* June 28, 1995. B:4.

———. "Council OKs Proposal for Railroad-Bed Park but Company Fighting to Keep Tracks." *Colorado Springs Gazette Telegraph,* March 1, 1989. B:1.

———. "Council to Consider Acquisition of Rail Line for Park, Trail System. Deal Would Stymie Plans to Use Tracks." *Colorado Springs Gazette Telegraph,* February 21, 1989. B:1.

———. "Council Reverses Decision to Earmark Tax for Parks. 5–4 Vote Kills Plan to Spend $1.26 Million." *Colorado Springs Gazette Telegraph,* August 10, 1988. CITY/STATE:1.

———. "Improvement Plan Includes Four Additional City Parks." *Colorado Springs Gazette Telegraph,* August 25, 1988. B:1.

———. "New Neighborhood Parks Slashed from Tight City Budget." *Colorado Springs Gazette Telegraph,* October 8, 1987. B:3.

———. "Open-Space Tax Is an Idea Whose Time Has Come." *Colorado Springs Gazette Telegraph,* April 3, 1997. A:4.

———. "Parkland Lies Fallow while Major Projects Pursued, Critics Say." *Colorado Springs Gazette Telegraph,* October 17, 1988. A:2.

———. "Parks Veteran Gets Top Job: New Director has Worked for Department 22 Years." *Colorado Springs Gazette Telegraph,* June 4, 1988. B:1.

———. "Proposed Sports Complex would be Springs' Largest." *Colorado Springs Gazette Telegraph,* August 12, 1992. B:1.

———. "Pupils' Pennies Make Park Possible: Steele Community Fully Funds Project." *Colorado Springs Gazette,* January 21, 1997. CITY/STATE:3.

———. "Recreation Fees Likely to Rise as Park Policy Shifts." *Colorado Springs Gazette Telegraph,* September 7, 1995. A:6.

———. "Springs Settles Lawsuit with Schenk." *Colorado Springs Gazette Telegraph,* September 10, 1992. A:1:1.

———. "Visitors Center Popular." *Colorado Springs Gazette Telegraph,* February 25, 1996. PROGRESS:12.

McCreery, H. C. "How Colorado Springs Got its Water, Parks Told by Pioneer." *Colorado Springs Gazette Telegraph,* April 21, 1935. 2:1:6.

McGlasson,W. J. "Council Okays Park Deal over Protests of Citizens." *Colorado Springs Gazette Telegraph,* February 9, 1977. A:1.

———. "Park, Rec. Operation Termed 'Free Wheeling'." *Colorado Springs Gazette Telegraph,* February 21, 1975. A:1.

McKeown, Bill. "Deal Preserves Reservoir Land." *Colorado Springs Gazette,* September 29, 2000. METRO:1.

———. "Disc-A-Palooza: Cottonwood Creek Park Features Sport." *Colorado Springs Gazette,* May 13, 2007. METRO:22.

———. "Public Has Grand Plans for City Park." *Colorado Springs Gazette,* April 13, 2007. METRO. 1:1.

Meier, Patty. "History under the Stars: the Pikes Peak Region's Colorful Past Comes Alive in Song at Garden of the Gods." *Colorado Springs Gazette Telegraph,* August 25, 1995. D:6.

Navarro, Linda. "Boulder Crescent Park Slide Remembered by Families," Did You Ever Wonder? *Colorado Springs Gazette Telegraph,* September 8, 2006.

Nipps, Emily. "City Gardeners Coax Beauty into Bloom in 119 Flower Beds." *Colorado Springs Gazette,* June 9, 1998. CITY/STATE:2.

Noreen, Barry. "Accord May Clear Way for New Visitors Center at Garden of the Gods," The View from Here. *Colorado Springs Gazette Telegraph,* August 24, 1994. B:2.

———. "Appeal Filed to Block Park's Visitors Center: Garden of the Gods Project Delayed," The View from Here. *Colorado Springs Gazette Telegraph,* January 21, 1994. A:8.

———. "Board Goes Looking for Outdoorsy Uses of Lottery Funds—and Hears Plenty," The View from Here. *Colorado Springs Gazette Telegraph,* November 12, 1993. B:1.

———. "Deal Urged for Center in Garden of the Gods: Private Money for Building Linked to Realigning Street," The View from Here. *Colorado Springs Gazette Telegraph,* October 1, 1993. A:3.

———. "Defending Area's Beauty Merits Snaps," The View from Here. *Colorado Springs Gazette Telegraph,* June 21, 2009. B:19.

———. "Fifteen Years Later, it's Time to Shove TABOR out the Door," The View from Here. *Colorado Springs Gazette Telegraph,* October 24, 2007. http://www.gazette.com/common/printer/view.php?db=colgazette&if=28861.

———. "Front Range Corridor is Years Away: Obstacles to Linking Parks Studied," The View from Here. *Colorado Springs Gazette Telegraph,* January 26, 1991. B:1.

———. "Garden to be Closed to Off-Road Bikes: Officials Want to Protect Park Trails," The View from Here. *Colorado Springs Gazette Telegraph,* June 5, 1993. B:2.

———. "Garden of the Gods Work Gets a Lofty Boost from Trust Fund," The View from Here. *Colorado Springs Gazette Telegraph,* March 22, 1995. B:6.

———. "Mountain Biking Ban to Be Enforced: Scarring of the Garden of the Gods Prompts Regulation," The View from Here. *Colorado Springs Gazette Telegraph,* July 3, 1993. B:1.

———. "Park Advisors OK Garden of the Gods Master Plan: Renovation may Cost about $1.2 Million," The View from Here. *Colorado Springs Gazette Telegraph,* May 20, 1994. B:2.

———. "Private Visitors Center OK'd for Garden of the Gods: Council's Vote Unanimous," The View from Here. December 15, 1993. B:4.

———. "Task Force Forming to Revise Master Plan for City Trail Network," The View from Here. *Colorado Springs Gazette Telegraph,* November 13, 1987. B:1.

———. The View from Here. *Colorado Springs Gazette Telegraph,* http://barrysblog.freedomblogging.com.

———. "Visitors Center Deal Still Lacks OK from Judge: Plaintiff Says Lawyer Didn't have Consent." The View from Here. *Colorado Springs Gazette Telegraph,* September 21, 1994. B:2.

———. "Visitors Center Foes Rebuffed: Construction to Proceed," The View from Here. *Colorado Springs Gazette Telegraph,* March 5, 1994. B:3.

Obee, Ruth. "Red Rock Canyon, the Secret Garden of the Gods." *The Colorado Springs Independent.* June 21, 2001. http://ww.csindy.com/red-rock-canyon-the-secret-garden-of-the-gods/Content?oid=1111903.

Oiler, Lou. "Trail Fixers on the Job at Park: Group to Continue Project Today." *Colorado Springs Gazette Telegraph,* June 4, 1995. B:2.

Owen-Cooper, Teresa. "Lottery Cash to Extend Trail: Greenway Receives $2 Million Grant." *Colorado Springs Gazette Telegraph,* October 24, 1996. A:8.

Payne, Stanley L. "Beautification and Recreation Keynotes of Park Development." *Colorado Springs Sunday Gazette & Telegraph,* March 25, 1945. 2:5:1.

Petersen, Pete. "City Parks Growing." *Colorado Springs Gazette Telegraph,* February 23, 1986. FF1–FF6.

Philipps, Dave. "A Century of Preservation." *Colorado Springs Gazette Telegraph,* February 8, 2009. A:1.

———. "Grant will Allow Completion of Path from Downtown to Manitou." *Colorado Springs Gazette,* October 7, 2008. METRO:13.

———. "Grants Ensure Wide Open Spaces." *Colorado Springs Gazette,* December 4, 2007. A:1.

———. "Issue 1C: Bid to Move Open Space Money to Parks is Failing." *Colorado Springs Gazette,* April 8, 2009. A:1.

———. "1C Would Alter Tops Tax to Pay for Existing Parks, Too." *Colorado Springs Gazette,* March 4, 2009. http://www.gazette.com/common/printer/view.php?db=colgazette&id=49367.

———. "No Brakes, No Reason to Worry." *Colorado Springs Gazette,* August 14, 2008. OUT THERE:35.

Ragan, Tom. "Wide Open Spaces: Region Cashes in on Lottery Proceeds." *Colorado Springs Gazette,* February 16, 2001. METRO:6.

Randall, Gail. "Man Honored for Long Service to Civic Beauty." *Colorado Springs Gazette Telegraph,* December 4, 1989. B:1.

Routon, Ralph. "It's Papa's Rink." *Colorado Springs Gazette Telegraph,* November 1, 1986. D:1.

Rutledge, Raquel. "Grant will Help City Link Parks: $702,000 will Buy Former Houck Land." *Colorado Springs Gazette Telegraph,* June 24, 1999. CITY/STATE:7.

———. "Plans for Confluence Park have Drawn Passionate Feelings—For and Against." *Colorado Springs Gazette,* March 28, 1999. CITY/STATE:7.

———. "Pool Going Swimmingly." *Colorado Springs Gazette,* July 24, 2000. METRO:2.

———. "Residents Urged to Bring along Their Wish Lists to Town Meeting: up to $145 Million on Tap for Construction Projects." *Colorado Springs Gazette Telegraph,* February 26, 1998. CITY/STATE:2.

———. "Voters Approve Plowing Back Revenue Surplus into Projects." *Colorado Springs Gazette,* November 4, 1998. A:3.

———. "Voters will Decide on Capital Projects: $88 Million Bond Proposed." *Colorado Springs Gazette Telegraph,* August 26, 1998. A:7.

———. "Voters OK $88 Million Bond Issue in Close Race: Election Caps Effort by SCIP Workers." *Colorado Springs Gazette,* April 7, 1999. A:6.

Sampson, Ovetta. "Keeping Parks Safe, Clean a Labor of Love for Gieck," *Colorado Springs Gazette,* April 29, 2002. LIFE:6.

Sealover, Ed. "A Boost for Parks, Open Space: Ruling Allows TOPS Tax to Continue Through 2025." *Colorado Springs Gazette,* February 28, 2006. A:1.

———. "A Part of History Won't Run Dry." *Colorado Springs Gazette,* April 10, 2004. http://www.gazette.com/common/printer/view.php?db=colgazette&id=16984.

———. "Away from it All, but Not Far: 650-Acre Open Space in Colorado Springs Offers Views of the Past." *Colorado Springs Gazette,* December 2, 2002. METRO:2.

———. "Board OKs Plans for Park in Briargate." *Colorado Springs Gazette,* May 12, 2006. METRO:2:1.

———. "Budget Limiting Plans for Area Parks." *Colorado Springs Gazette,* June 13, 2005. http://www.gazette.com/common/prnter/view.php?db=colgazette&id=8006.

———. "City Council Spending Trails, Open Space and Parks Money." *Colorado Springs Gazette,* March 14, 2006. METRO:9.

———. "City Council Tries Again: Voters to Decide SCIP-Like Ballot Issue Nov. 6." *Colorado Springs Gazette,* August 29, 2001. A:1.

———. "City will Cut Back on Water: Springs Plans to Reduce Usage by 10 Percent." *Colorado Springs Gazette,* April 12, 2002. METRO:6.

———. "Community Centers Saved: City Council Unwilling to go along with Proposed Cuts." *Colorado Springs Gazette,* October 16, 2003. A:1.

———. "Council Looking to Public to Plant City Gardens." *Colorado Springs Gazette,* April 20, 2004. http:www.gazette.com/common/printer/view.php?db=colgazette&id=15941.

———. "Council OKs what could be Land Buys under TOPS." *Colorado Springs Gazette,* February 28, 2001. A:1.

———. "Council Rides to City Parks' Rescue." *Colorado Springs Gazette,* November 3, 2004. METRO:23.

———. "For 1st Time, County, City will Join to Build Park." *Colorado Springs Gazette,* February 20, 2006. METRO:24.

———. "Fund Plans Aims to Build Parks." *Colorado Springs Gazette,* July 15, 2005. http://www.gazette.com/articles/parks-8197-parklottery.html.

———. "Help Tougher to Find in Parks' Hour of Need." *Colorado Springs Gazette,* April 24, 2005. METRO:29.

———. "More Parks Stretching Staff Too Thin, Department Says." *Colorado Springs Gazette,* April 15, 2002. A:1.

———. "Odds Against New Parks." *Colorado Springs Gazette,* December 19, 2004. A:1.

———. "Open Land Proximity Debated: Some Want Space Saved in Inner City." *Colorado Springs Gazette,* November 18, 2001. METRO:2.

———. "Opening a City Space." *Colorado Springs Gazette,* May 8, 2004. METRO:17.

———. "Parks Tax Won't Go as Far as Thought." *Colorado Springs Gazette,* June 13, 2006. METRO:11.

———. "Resources Stretched Thin for Embattled Parks Staff." *Colorado Springs Gazette,* October 5, 2003. METRO:22.

———. "Revived TOPS Looks for Land." *Colorado Springs Gazette,* July 25, 2001. METRO:2.

———. "SCIP it, Voters Tell City: Sales Tax Increase Suffers a Big Defeat." *Colorado Springs Gazette,* April 4, 2001. A:1.

———. "Some Suspect City Had Role in Lake Leak." *Colorado Springs Gazette,* February 12, 2004. http://www.gazette.com/common/printer/view.php?db=colgazette$id=16449.

———. "Sports could be Dried Out: without Rain, City May Halt Youth League." *Colorado Springs Gazette,* August 21, 2002. A:1.

———. "Springs Lands Outdoors Grant." *Colorado Springs Gazette,* December 9, 2003. METRO:11.

———. "Springs Parks Join Water Cutback." *Colorado Springs Gazette,* June 14, 2002. METRO:6.

———. "Tending Garden of the Gods." *Colorado Springs Gazette,* June 19, 2005. http://www.gazette.com/common/printer/view.php?db-colgazette&id=17214.

———. "Tight Budgets Prompt Park Partnerships." *Colorado Springs Gazette,* March 1, 2004. METRO:16.

———. "Union Meadows might be Next Open-Space Goal." *Colorado Springs Gazette,* June 2, 2003. METRO:13.

———. "Volunteer Flower Beds Criticized by Parks Board." *Colorado Springs Gazette,* July 9, 2004. METRO:19.

———. "Volunteer Gardeners Don't Dig Their Jobs." *Colorado Springs Gazette,* September 10, 2004. METRO:19.

———. "Volunteers Take over All Flower Beds Offered by City." *Colorado Springs Gazette,* May 17, 2005. METRO:11.

———. "Vote Shifts Projects' Pace: Springs Timetable Ranges from Slowly to Not at All." *Colorado Springs Gazette,* November 8, 2001. METRO:7.

———. "$1.6 Million Paves Way for Trails in the Springs: Money Dedicated to Construction." *Colorado Springs Gazette,* July 29, 2002. METRO:5.

Short, Christopher. "Budget Cuts Mean More Park Adopters Needed." *Colorado Springs Gazette,* May 8, 2009. http://www.gazette.com/common/printer/view.php?db=colgazette&id=53469.

Skodack, Debra. "Marathon Dedications will Open 21 City Parks." *Colorado Springs Gazette Telegraph,* September 28, 1980. B:7.

———. "Parks, Trails Suggested at Springs Public Hearing." *Colorado Springs Gazette Telegraph,* March 11, 1981. B:2:4.

———. "Public's Help Sought on Plans for City Parks." *Colorado Springs Gazette Telegraph,* March 10, 1981. 4:C.

Sosbe, Kathryn. "Rules of the Trail for Mountain Bikers Aim to Cut Clashes: Policy's Headed for Likely Approval by Springs Board." *Colorado Springs Gazette Telegraph,* November 10, 1995. B:1.

Stanley, J. Adrian. "A Place for All Kids at Memorial Park." *Colorado Springs Independent.* March 12, 2010. http://www.csindy.com/IndyBlog/archives/2010/03/12/a-place-for-all-kids-at-memorial-park.

———. "Tabor Tyranny: or Why our City will Never Really Recover from an Economic Downturn." *Colorado Springs Independent.* April 9, 2009. http://www.csindy.com/gyrobase/tabor-tyranny/Content?oid=1347928&mode.

———. "What We'll Lose: if Colorado Springs Community Centers Close, the Fallout could be Immeasurable." *Colorado Springs Independent.* February 18, 2010. http://www.csindy.com/gyrobase/what-well-lose/Content?oid=1626685&mode=print.

Stewart, Clarence. "City's Far-Flung Park System Ready for Summer Season." *Colorado Springs Gazette Telegraph,* May 2, 1937. 2-1.

———. "City's Magnificent Park System Almost Entirely Given by Region Benefactors." *Colorado Springs Gazette,* August 8, 1937. 8.

Stout, Hilary. "Effort to Restore Children's Play Gains Momentum." *The New York Times.* January 6, 2011. D:1.

Strong, Elaine. "Parks Department Earns National Honors Again." *Colorado Springs Gazette Telegraph,* February 22, 1987. FF:10.

Sunday Gazette and Telegraph. "CCC Workers Battle Erosion in City's Parks." Tourist edition. May 10, 1936. 4:1, 27-1.

———. "Two Camps Ready for Erosion Control and Park Improvement Projects Northeast of Colorado Springs." September 16, 1934. 2:8:1.

Sundvor, John. "City Heirs Agreement is Topic of Heated Debate." *Colorado Springs Gazette Telegraph,* August 25, 1970. B:1.

Swanson, Perry. "County Votes Cash for Prospect Lake." *Colorado Springs Gazette,* October 23, 2004. http://www.gazette.com/common/printer/view.php?db=colgazette&id=16516.

———. "Red Rock Funding Approved." *Colorado Springs Gazette,* October 29, 2003. METRO:1.

Swanson, Perry and Daniel Chacon. "Salaries Chew up Millions for Colorado Springs." *Colorado Springs Gazette,* October 10, 2010. http://www.gazette.com/common/printer/view.php?db=colgazette&id=63595.

Thomas, Jeff. "Open Space '90s Battle Cry" Preservation Efforts Galvanize over Section 16." *Colorado Springs Gazette Telegraph,* July 31, 1995. B:4.

Thomas, Katie. "Revival of a River Alters a City's Course in Sports." *The New York Times.* April 22, 2008. www.nytimes.com/2008/04/22/sports/othersports/22oklahoma.html.

Thomsen, Scott. "Hidden Inn Faces the End of the Road: Parks Board Votes to Tear Down Building." *Colorado Springs Gazette Telegraph,* July 12, 1997. B:2.

———. "Rec Center Idea Advances: Complaints of Northwest Springs Residents are Alleviated in Wide-Ranging Dispute over Recreation." *Colorado Springs Gazette,* July 21, 1999. CITY/STATE:4.

Vogrin, Bill. "An Investment in the City's Future." *Colorado Springs Gazette,* January 1, 2008.

———. "Board OKs Recreation Area, Putting Plan on Fast Track." *Colorado Springs Gazette,* June 18, 2004. METRO:19.

———. "Divine Intervention." *Colorado Springs Gazette,* March 11, 2007. http://www.gazette.com/common/printer/view.php?db=colgazette&id=20050.

———. "Side Streets: Money for Parks, Rec Centers Seems Like a Fairy Tale." *Colorado Springs Gazette,* May 26, 2010. http://www:gazette.com/common/printer/view.php?db=colgazette&id=99398.

———. "Visitors Center Is a Godsend." *Colorado Springs Gazette Telegraph,* May 14, 1995. E:1.

———. "Visitors Center Wins Rave Reviews." *Colorado Springs Gazette Telegraph,* May 16, 1995. A:6.

Vonderlage, Janie. "No New Parks Likely in '81, Says Director." *Colorado Springs Gazette Telegraph,* October 17, 1980. B:4.

Wadman, Bruce. "At Home in the Garden." *Colorado Springs Gazette,* June 11, 2007. Sports:19.

Warhole, Debbie. "Tree Program under Review by the City." *Colorado Springs Gazette Telegraph,* August 9, 1992. G:16.

Warren, Edward. "The Birds of Monument Valley Park." *Colorado Springs Gazette Telegraph,* May 28, 1915. 6-2, 3, 4.

Weiss, John and Steven Pope. "Yes on 2C, No on 300." *Colorado Springs Independent.* September 10, 2009. http://www.csindy.com/gyrobase/message-to-our-readers/Contemy?oid=1425860&mode=print.

Wilson, Dru. "Advisory Board Urges Expansion of Sertich Ice Center: $1.4 Million Plan Added to Wish List." *Colorado Springs Gazette Telegraph,* April 14, 1989. B:1.

———. "Alternate Funding Sought for Development of Parks: Master Plan Sees Little Budget Growth." *Colorado Springs Gazette Telegraph,* January 23, 1989. B:1.

———. "City Budgets $500,000 to Renovate Grounds of Museums: Development of Neighborhood Parks Stalled." *Colorado Springs Gazette Telegraph,* October 17, 1988. A:2.

———. "City Board OK's Park Master Plan." *Colorado Springs Gazette Telegraph,* November 24, 1981. D:1.

———. "GreenSprings Seeks Volunteers to Plant Trees." *Colorado Springs Gazette Telegraph,* April 6, 1989. B:1.

———. "Trail of History: Monument Valley Park's Historic Gems Reveal Clues about the People who Helped Shape Colorado Springs." *Colorado Springs Gazette,* June 25, 1998. OUT 1:1

Wohlgenant, Tim. "Investing in Parks Pays Off." *The Denver Post,* August 12, 2010. www.denverpost.com/opinion/ci_15746193.

Wolz, John. "City Parks Budget Shows Gain of 8 Percent over 1981 Figures." *Colorado Springs Gazette Telegraph,* October 14, 1981. A:4:4.

Zubeck, Pam. "Citizens' List of Priorities for Springs Is Surprising: Committees Rank Improvements." *Colorado Springs Gazette,* June 1, 1998. A:2.

———. "City Invites Masses to the Decision Table." *Colorado Springs Gazette,* September 21, 1997. A:9.

———. "Council Gives Green Light to Greenway, Open Space: $3.65 Million OK'd for Trails, Parks." *Colorado Springs Gazette,* April 28, 1999. A:6.

———. "Developers Dominate Panels: Council Defends Appointments." *Colorado Springs Gazette,* January 25, 1998. CITY/STATE:5.

———. "New Sales-Tax Money to Connect Park Trails: $410,000-Project Joins City, Nature." *Colorado Springs Gazette,* September 15, 1997. CITY/STATE:2.

———. "Rethink Land Offer, Panel Urges Council: 74-Acre Parcel Turned Down." *Colorado Springs Gazette,* May 28, 1998. CITY/STATE:3.

———. "Sales Tax Hike up to Voters: SCIP-Related Increase would be Biggest in 30 Years." *Colorado Springs Gazette,* March 17, 2001. A:4.

———. "Sertich Reopens after $1 Million Project." *Colorado Springs Gazette,* January 8, 2001. METRO:3.

———. "Springs Says Goodbye to 12-Year Fund Source: Recreation, Parking Costs to Rise in '97." *Colorado Springs Gazette Telegraph,* December 31, 1996. A:2.

———. "Springs Takes Possession of Open Space: 300 Acres Purchased from Stratton Trust." *Colorado Springs Gazette,* July 9, 1998. CITY/STATE:8.

———. "The Broadmoor Gives $100,000 toward Buying Stratton Land." *Colorado Springs Gazette,* February 18, 1998. CITY/STATE:2.

———. "Tireless Efforts Pay Off; Longer Route is Planned." *Colorado Springs Gazette,* March 5, 2007. http://www.gazette.com/common/printer/view.php?db=colgazette&id=19798.

———. "$1.1M will go into Greenway." *Colorado Springs Gazette,* June 14, 2008. METRO:20.

———. "$250 Million for Projects: Citizens Panel may Recommend Half-Cent Sales Tax Hike." *Colorado Springs Gazette,* October 4, 2000. A:1.

———. "Wanted: Full-Timer for TOPS Program: Open-Space Group Differs with City." *Colorado Springs Gazette,* April 29, 1997. CITY/STATE:3.

Other Media:

City of Colorado Springs. http://www.springsgov.com/index.aspx.

CityParks Blog: News and Updates from TPL's Center for City Park Excellence and the City Parks Alliance. http://cityparksblog.org/

"Colorado Springs Parks Advisory Board Meeting Minutes." (January–September 2010). http://www.springsgov.com/Agendas.aspx?CCBID=37

Donahue, Ryan. "Moving Traffic to the Trail: Boulder's Multipurpose Greenway." *City Parks Blog.* Last modified December 8, 2010. http://cityparks blog.org/2010/12/08/moving-traffic-to-the-trail-boulders-multipurpose-greenway/.

Gentles, Coleen, ed. *CityParks Blog: News and Updates from TPL's Center for City Park Excellence and the City Parks Alliance.* http://cityparksblog.org/.

"History." *Trails and Open Space Coalition.* Accessed July 22, 2010. www.trailsandopenspaces.org/history.html.

Palmer Land Trust. http://palmerlandtrust.org/

"Palmer Land Trust Adds to the Garden of the Gods Park." *Palmer Land Trust Website.* Last modified July 14, 2010. http://www.palmerlandtrust.org/node/179.

Peirce, Neal. "City Parks' Grand Rebirth." *Stateline.* Last modified September 6, 2009. http://www.stateline.org/live/details/story?contentId=423643.

Reynolds, Dean. "Welcome to Thin City." *CBS News.* Last modified October 25, 2009. http://www.cbsnews.com/video/watch/?id=5419712n&tag=api.

Vaughan, Jessie and Joe Morgan, interview by Ryan Warner. "When Segregation Ruled Baseball: Interview with Jessie Vaughan and Joe Morgan." *Colorado Matters,* KCFR Radio. July 21, 2009.

Periodicals, Pamphlets, Articles and Letters

Arden, Patrick. "The High Cost of Free Parks: Do Public-Private Partnerships Save Parks or Exploit Them?" *Next American City Magazine.* Summer 2010. http://americancity.org/magazine/article/the-high-cost-of-free-parks.

The Cañon Companion: A Guide to North Cheyenne Cañon City Park. Obtained from Starsmore Discovery Center at North Cheyenne Cañon, Colorado Springs, CO. 2009.

Cranz, Galen and Michael Boland. "The Ecological Park as an Emerging Type. [Research and Debate]." Places. 15, no. 3. July 1, 2003. http://escholarship.org/uc/item/68v5m7k2.

Ensign, Edgar. "Report to the Public Parks and Parkways in Colorado Springs, Colorado." *In The Century Chest Letters of 1901: A Colorado Springs Legacy.* Edited by Judith Reid Finley. Colorado Springs, CO: Colorado College, 2001.

Face The State. http://facethestate.com/articles/16746-q-how-many-local-elections-will-be-held-year-nobody-knows.

Imlay, Robert. "The Gardens of Charles M. Schwab, Esq., Loretto, PA, Charles Wellford Leavitt, Landscape Engineer." *The Architectural Record.* 47, no. 5, (May 1920): 387–407.

Leavitt, Charles Wellford, quoted in Robert Imlay, "The Gardens of Charles M. Schwab, Esq., Loretto, PA, Charles Wellford Leavitt, Landscape Engineer." *The Architectural Record.* Volume 47, Number 5. May 1920. Pp. 387-407.

Patton, Zach. "Colorado Springs' Do-It-Yourself Government." *Governing Magazine.* (September 2010). http://www.governing.com/topics/mgmt/Colorado-Springs-DIY-government.html.

Sawyer, Edwin A. "The Present Water Supply of Colorado Springs." In *The Century Chest Letters of 1901: A Colorado Springs Legacy.* Edited by Judith Reid Finley. Colorado Springs, CO: Colorado College, 2001.

Take A Walk on the Wild Side: A Visitors Guide to the Garden of the Gods Park. Colorado Springs, CO: Friends of the Garden of the Gods, 2000.

Warren, Edward. "The Birds of Monument Valley Park, Colorado Springs, Colorado." *Bird-Lore:. A Bi-Monthly Magazine Devoted to the Study & Protection of Birds* 18, no. 4 (July-August 1916).

Woodard, Bruce. *The Garden of the Gods Story.* Boulder, CO: Pruett Press, Inc., 1955.

LIST AND CREDITS OF ILLUSTRATIONS AND PHOTOGRAPHS

Cover:

Garden of the Gods. Photo courtesy of the Garden of the Gods Visitor and Nature Center.

Monument Valley Park. Photo courtesy of Special Collections, Pikes Peak Library District. Image 102-2249.

End Pages:

Park Systems Map. From *The Report of the Park Commission, 1908.*

Preface:

Nancy Lewis and Nancy Lewis Park photographs by Wendy Pearce Nelson, © 2010, Blue Fox Photography.

Chapter One: A City of Jewels

Page x:

Monument Valley Park. Photo courtesy of Special Collections, Pikes Peak Library District. Image 001-2250.

Page 2:

Glen Eyrie. Photo courtesy of Special Collections, Pikes Peak Library District. Image 001-409.

Page 3:

Surveyors on Plain. Photo courtesy of Special Collections, Pikes Peak Library District. Image 175-3855.

Palmer Hall. Photo courtesy of Special Collections, Pikes Peak Library District. Image 001-113.

Young General Palmer. Photo courtesy of Special Collections, Pikes Peak Library District. Image 001-376.

Page 4:

Huerfano Street Bridge. Photo courtesy of Special Collections, Pikes Peak Library District. Image 001-622.

Page 5:

Acacia Park. Photo courtesy of Special Collections, Pikes Peak Library District. Image 001-320.

Page 6:

Prospect Lake Skaters. Photo courtesy of Special Collections, Pikes Peak Library District. Image 001-5428.

Page 7:

Cascade Avenue. Photo courtesy of Special Collections, Pikes Peak Library District. Image 001-555.

Page 8:

View of the Paseo. From *The Report of the Park Commission, 1908.*

Page 9:

North Cheyenne Cañon. From *The Report of the Park Commission, 1908.*

Helen Hunt Falls. From *The Report of the Park Commission, 1908.*

Page 10:

Monument Valley Park. Photo courtesy of Special Collections, Pikes Peak Library District. Image 102-2249.

Page 11:

Monument Valley Park Map. From *The Report of the Park Commission, 1908.*

Monument Valley Park. From *The Report of the Park Commission, 1908.*

Page 12:

Stratton Park Swing. Photo courtesy of Special Collections, Pikes Peak Library District. Image 102-2240.

Stratton Park Swimming. Photograph by G. W. Murray from the collection of D. R. Kallaus.

Page 13:

Jewett Residence. Photo courtesy of Special Collections, Pikes Peak Library District. Image 001-9003.

Garden of the Gods Plaque. Photo courtesy of Special Collections, Pikes Peak Library District. Image 013-10227.

Page 14:

Garden of the Gods. Photograph by George Beam, courtesy of Denver Public Library, Western History Collection. Image GB-5162.

Page 15:

Acacia Park. Photo courtesy of Special Collections, Pikes Peak Library District. Image 001-5475.

Page 16:

Park Systems Map. From *The Report of the Park Commission, 1908.*

Page 17:

General Palmer. Photo courtesy of Special Collections, Pikes Peak Library District. Image 001-374.

Page 18:

Patty Jewett Golf Club Entrance. Photo courtesy of Special Collections, Pikes Peak Library District. Image 002-1312.

Chapter Two: Sending Down Roots

Page 20:

North Cheyenne Cañon. Photo courtesy of Special Collections, Pikes Peak Library District. Image 217-6713.

Acacia Park. Photo courtesy of Special Collections, Pikes Peak Library District. Image 102-2259.

Page 21:

Monument Valley Park. Photo courtesy of Special Collections, Pikes Peak Library District. Image 001-4535.

Page 22:

Shan Kive Celebration in Garden of the Gods. Photo courtesy of Special Collections, Pikes Peak Library District. Image 001-4147.

Page 23:

Monument Valley Park Skaters. Photo courtesy of Special Collections, Pikes Peak Library District. Image 001-2352.

Monument Valley Park Children. Photo courtesy of Special Collections, Pikes Peak Library District. Image 001-2253.

Page 24:
Palmer Park. Photo courtesy of Special Collections, Pikes Peak Library District. Image 001-5478.

Page 25:
Patty Jewett Golf Course. Photo courtesy of Special Collections, Pikes Peak Library District. Image 102-2394.

Page 26:
Prospect Lake Campers. Photo courtesy of Special Collections, Pikes Peak Library District. Image 001-5316.

Page 27:
Palmer Park Trail. Photo courtesy of Special Collections, Pikes Peak Library District. Image 102-2246.

Monument Valley Park Pool. Photo courtesy of Special Collections, Pikes Peak Library District. Image 001-2252.

Page 28:
Peter Pan Wading Pool in Monument Valley Park. Photograph by G. W. Murray from the collection of D. R. Kallaus.

Page 29:
Cascade Avenue. Photo courtesy of Special Collections, Pikes Peak Library District. Image 001-5019.

Page 30:
Monument Valley Park Formal Garden. Photograph by G. W. Murray from the collection of D. R. Kallaus.

Page 32:
Monument Valley Park Rock Garden. Photo courtesy of The Colorado Springs Pioneers Museum, Starsmore Center for Local History.

Page 33:
Easter Sunrise Service. Photo courtesy of Special Collections, Pikes Peak Library District. Image 013-1007.

Page 34:
Prospect Lake. Photograph by G. W. Murray from the collection of D. R. Kallaus.

Private Fence Surrounding Balanced Rock. Photo courtesy of Special Collections, Pikes Peak Library District. Image 013-10181.

Page 35:
Monument Valley Park Wall. Photograph by G. W. Murray from the collection of D. R. Kallaus.

Tahama Spring. Photograph by G. W. Murray from the collection of D. R. Kallaus.

Monument Valley Park Lake. Photo courtesy of Special Collections, Pikes Peak Library District. Image 013-1081.

Page 36:
Bijou Street Bridge. Photo courtesy of Special Collections, Pikes Peak Library District. Image 013-992.

Page 37:
Park Superintendent's House. Photo courtesy of Special Collections, Pikes Peak Library District. Image 013-991.

Page 38:
Tahama Spring in Monument Valley Park. Photo courtesy of Special Collections, Pikes Peak Library District. Image 013-7672.

Civilian Conservation Corps. Photo courtesy of Special Collections, Pikes Peak Library District. Image 001-673.

Page 39:
Monument Creek Restoration. Photograph by G. W. Murray from the collection of D. R. Kallaus.

Page 40:
Prospect Lake Bathhouse. Photo courtesy of Special Collections, Pikes Peak Library District.

Bancroft Park. Photo courtesy of the Colorado Springs Parks, Recreation and Cultural Services Department.

Page 41:
North Cheyenne Cañon High Drive. Photo courtesy of Special Collections, Pikes Peak Library District. Image 001-2412.

Bruin Inn in North Cheyenne Cañon. Photo courtesy of Special Collections, Pikes Peak Library District. Image 001-2574.

Page 42:
Community Gardens. Photo courtesy of Special Collections, Tutt Library, Colorado College, Colorado Springs, Colorado.

Page 43:
Horseshoe Players in Monument Valley Park. Photo courtesy of The Colorado Springs Pioneers Museum, Starsmore Center for Local History.

Page 44:
Brown Bombers. Photo courtesy of The Colorado Springs Pioneers Museum, Starsmore Center for Local History.

Page 46:
Prospect Lake Boaters. Photograph by G. W. Murray from the collection of D. R. Kallaus.

Page 47:
Colorado Springs Courthouse. Photograph by G. W. Murray from the collection of D. R. Kallaus.

Page 48:
Memorial Park Ball Field. Photograph by G. W. Murray from the collection of D. R. Kallaus.

Page 49:
Memorial Park Construction. Photograph by G. W. Murray from the collection of D. R. Kallaus.

Page 51:
Conejos Park Play Sculpture. Photo courtesy of Special Collections, Pikes Peak Library District. Image 002-5481.

Page 52:
Boulder Crescent Park Playground. Photo courtesy of Special Collections, Pikes Peak Library District. Image 002-3273.

Page 53:
Kissing Camels in the Garden of the Gods. Photograph by G. W. Murray from the collection of D. R. Kallaus.

Page 55:
Monument Valley Freeway Clearing. Photo courtesy of Special Collections, Pikes Peak Library District. Image 002-1364

Page 56:
Monument Valley Park Fishing Sign. Photo by Myron Wood, © Pikes Peak Library District. Image 002-1291

Chapter Three: Growing Pains

Chapter Four: The System Blossoms

Page 91:
Y.A.L. Players. Photo courtesy of the Colorado Springs Parks, Recreation and Cultural Services Department.

Page 93:
Girls SOCSY Team. Photo courtesy of Deborah Odell.

Ski Broadmoor. Photo courtesy of Special Collections, Pikes Peak Library District. Image 002-1540.

Page 94:
Patty Jewett Golf Course. Photo courtesy of the Colorado Springs Parks, Recreation and Cultural Services Department.

Palmer Park Hoodoos. Photo courtesy of the Colorado Springs Parks, Recreation and Cultural Services Department.

Page 95:
Playing Field. Photo courtesy of the Colorado Springs Parks, Recreation and Cultural Services Department.

Prospect Lake. Photo courtesy of the Colorado Springs Parks, Recreation and Cultural Services Department.

Page 97:
Pioneers Museum. Photo courtesy of the Colorado Springs Parks, Recreation and Cultural Services Department.

Page 98:
Adult League plays baseball. Photo courtesy of the Colorado Springs Parks, Recreation and Cultural Services Department.

Monument Valley Park Joggers. Photo courtesy of the Colorado Springs Parks, Recreation and Cultural Services Department.

Page 99:
Y.A.L. Football Players. Photo courtesy of the Colorado Springs Parks, Recreation and Cultural Services Department.

Page 100:
Cottonwood Creek Basketball Players. Photos by Tom Kimmell. © 2010.

Park Playground. Photos by Tom Kimmell. © 2010.

Page 101:
Hot Air Balloon Festival. Photo by Myron Wood, © Pikes Peak Library District. Image 002-769.

Page 102:
Garden of the Gods Run. Photo courtesy of the Colorado Springs Parks, Recreation and Cultural Services Department.

Chapter Five: Something For Everyone

Page 105:
Yucca Flats in Palmer Park. Photo courtesy of the Colorado Springs Parks, Recreation and Cultural Services Department.

Page 106:
Mid Shooks Run Trail. Photo by Tom Kimmell. © 2010.

Page 107:
"Goose" Gossage Youth Sports Center. Photo by Tom Kimmell. © 2010.

Page 108:
Starsmore Center Move and Opening. Photos courtesy of the Colorado Springs Parks, Recreation and Cultural Services Department.

Information not available at time of publication.

Page 109:
Starsmore Center in North Cheyenne Cañon, 2010. Photo by Deborah Odell.

Page 110:
Evergreen Cemetery Chapel. Photo courtesy of the Colorado Springs Parks, Recreation and Cultural Services Department

Page 111:
Shooks Run Creek. Photo courtesy of the Colorado Springs Parks, Recreation and Cultural Services Department.

GreenSprings T-shirt. Photo by Lyda Hill. Courtesy of Lyda Hill.

Page 112:
Section 16 Open Space and Pine Cone. Photos by Tom Kimmell. © 2010.

Page 113:
Ute Valley Park. Photo courtesy of the Colorado Springs Parks, Recreation and Cultural Services Department.

Page 115:
Garden of the Gods. Photo courtesy of the Garden of the Gods Visitor and Nature Center.

Page 116:
Visiting Garden of the Gods. Photo by Lyda Hill. Courtesy of Lyda Hill.

Ute Elder Austin Box. Photo courtesy of the Garden of the Gods Visitor and Nature Center.

Page 117:
Garden of the Gods Visitors Center. Photo courtesy of the Garden of the Gods Visitor and Nature Center.

Page 118:
Native American Dancers. Photo courtesy of the Garden of the Gods Visitor and Nature Center.

Palmer Park. Photo courtesy of the Colorado Springs Parks, Recreation and Cultural Services Department.

Page 119:
Four Diamonds Sports Complex. Photo by Tom Kimmell. © 2010.

Page 120:
Leon Young Sports Complex. Photo courtesy of the Colorado Springs Parks, Recreation and Cultural Services Department.

Page 121:
Ball Field. Photo courtesy of the Colorado Springs Parks, Recreation and Cultural Services Department.

Page 122:
Urban Trail Jogger. Photo by Tom Kimmell. © 2010.

Page 123:
Map of proposed open space properties, 1970. Open Space Plan. Courtesy of Colorado Springs Parks, Recreation and Cultural Services Department and courtesy of the Colorado Springs Utilities.

Proposed Open Space. Map courtesy of the Colorado Springs Parks, Recreation and Cultural Services Department.

Page 124:
Stratton Open Space. Photo courtesy of the Colorado Springs Parks, Recreation and Cultural Services Department.

Chapter Six: From Bloom to Bust

Chapter Seven: A Future of Possibilities

Bluestem Prairie Birdwatcher. Photo by Carey Harrington. Courtesy of Carey Harrington.

Memorial Park Skatepark. Photo by Tom Kimmell. © 2010.

Garden of the Gods Rock Climber. Photo courtesy of the Garden of the Gods Visitor and Nature Center.

Children Swinging in Monument Valley Park. Photo courtesy of Deborah Odell.

Swimming at Prospect Lake. Photo courtesy of Colorado Springs Parks, Recreation and Cultural Services Department.

Page 167:
Orchard House. Photo by Ron Wright. Courtesy of the Rock Ledge Ranch Historic Site.

Page 168:
Acacia Park. From *The Report of the Park Commission, 1908.*

Page 169:
Monument Valley Park Bridge. Photo by Deborah Odell.

Page 171:
Monument Valley Park Dog Walkers. Photo by Deborah Odell.

Page 172:
Monument Creek in downtown Colorado Springs. Photo by Deborah Odell.

Page 173:
Union Meadows Open Space. Photo by Tom Kimmell. © 2010.

Page 174:
Red Rock Canyon Open Space. Photo by Tom Kimmell. © 2010.

Page 175:
Forum Participants. Photo by Lyda Hill. Courtesy of Lyda Hill.

Paul Butcher. Photo courtesy of Paul Butcher.

Page 177:
Colorado Springs Flower Garden. Photo courtesy of Colorado Springs Parks, Recreation and Cultural Services Department.

Page 178:
Xeriscape Garden. Photo by Carey Harrington. Courtesy of Carey Harrington.

Page 179:
Judith Rice-Jones. Photo by Lyda Hill. Courtesy of Lyda Hill.

Page 180:
Nancy Lewis. Photo by Lyda Hill. Courtesy of Lyda Hill.

Page 181:
Bill Ruskin. Photo by Lyda Hill. Courtesy of Lyda Hill.

Page 182:
Mike Anderson. Photo by Lyda Hill. Courtesy of Lyda Hill.

Page 183:
Downtown Action Plan Map of "Ring of Connected Parks."

Bill Ruskin and Mike Anderson. Photo by Lyda Hill. Courtesy of Lyda Hill.

Page 184:
Jim Colvin. Photo by Lyda Hill. Courtesy of Lyda Hill.

Page 185:
Monument Creek Approaching the Bijou Street Bridge, 2010. Photo by Deborah Odell.

Back Cover Photo:

America the Beautiful Park. Photo by Tom Kimmell. © 2010.

INDEX

Photographs are indicated by page numbers in *italics.*

A

B

C

N

O

P

Q

R

S

X

Y

Z